JUST CALL ME MINNIE

My Six Decades in Baseball

Minnie Minoso

with Herb Fagen

SAGAMORE PUBLISHING
Champaign, IL

Production Manager: Susan M. McKinney
Cover and photo insert design: Michelle R. Dressen
Editor: Susan M. McKinney
Proofreader: Phyllis L. Bannon

Library of Congress Catalog Card Number:94-65394
ISBN: 0-915611-90-2

Printed in the United States.

This book is dedicated to:

my Mother and Father
for their decency and honesty;

my wife, Sharon,
for her love and tenderness;

and all my fans, then and now,
for their support and inspiration.

—*Orestes "Minnie" Minoso*
"Just call me Minnie"

CONTENTS

ACKNOWLEDGMENTS

This past summer I was fortunate enough to have been cast in the Glenview Theater Guild's production of "Brigadoon." This lovely Lerner and Lowe musical is about a mythical Scottish village and its townspeople who come alive only one day each century for a bittersweet festival of neighborly fun. I mention this because our director reminded us that the underlying theme of the story centers around a five letter word called "faith."

Faith is precisely what brought this project together. The faith between a writer, a subject and a publisher that the true story of a remarkable human being named Orestes Minoso could reach a large and interested readership. It is a deserving story about a deserving man. The story of an incredible athlete, professional baseball's only six-decade player, who loves the game today with the same verve and passion he did as a young boy growing up in the sugar fields of his native Cuba nearly 70 years ago. But there is so much more. It is a story of love and hardship, of challenge and triumph. It is the complete story of a man, his life and his times. It is a story whose time has come to tell.

No list of acknowledgments would be complete without mentioning a debt of gratitude to John Wasylik, Minnie Minoso's agent. A chance meeting and introduction at our barbershop was the spark which got the process going. His faith and certainty that I was the best person to write the Minnie Minoso story—a story that others wanted to write— is an honor I'll never forget.

At all times we had the full cooperation and backing of the Chicago White Sox organization. Our deep appreciation to Jerry Reinsdorf, Chairman of the Chicago White Sox, who graciously agreed to write the Introduction to the book, and to Anita at the White Sox office who always made sure that the "boss" got our messages, and who promptly returned my each and every phone call. Our deepest thanks to Orlando Cepeda and Billy Pierce, two of baseball's all time greats, who agreed to write the book's Foreword and Prologue.

To former Major League stars Bob Feller, Ray Boone, Ferris Fain, Jim Landis, Jose Cardenal, Lou Boudreau, Chico Carrasquel, Bill Melton, and Cal McLish, and to Negro League Star Nap Gulley, our deep appreciation for your your lively tidbits and anecdotes. The same to managers Tommy Lasorda of the Los Angeles Dodgers, and Tony La Russa of the Oakland A's for their interesting comments.

To writers Marcos Breton of the *Sacramento Bee*, Fausto Miranda of the *Miami Herald*, and to Bill Gleason, long-time Chicago sportswriter, thanks for sharing your thoughts, comments, and expertise, all informative contributions to our story.

To Mary-Frances Veeck, Tennessee State Senator Steven Cohen, Carol and David Forbes, Marilyn Arrieta (Minnie Minoso's daughter), and Gerry Healey, president of The Minnie Minoso Fan Club, our thanks for your personal remembrances of the Minnie Minoso we know and love.

I want to thank Scott and Mike McKinstry, editor and publisher of *Oldtyme Baseball News*, who first made it possible for my baseball writings to reach a national market. Also a special thanks to Paul White of *USA Today/Baseball Weekly*, John Kuenster of *Baseball Digest*, and Doug McDaniel of *The Diamond* for publishing my more recent work. We writers are only as good as the people we reach. Kudos to our publisher, Sagamore Publishing, who believed from the start that our story would have a large readership, and have done all things possible facilitate our effort. A class outfit, to be sure.

A special note of appreciation to my parents: my dad, Myron Fagen, who forever has been the real "wind beneath my wings," many times when those winds were not blowing in a particularly favorable direction; and my mother, Gertrude Fagen, whose faith and belief in her son helped make my transition from high school history teacher to professional writer so much the easier.

Finally to the incomparable Saturnino Orestes Arrieta Armas Minoso, " Minnie" to his throngs of fans and admirers, for the privilege of helping him write the story of his life, and who throughout this long process has shown me the meaning of what true greatness really is, my heartfelt and deepest thanks.

—Herb Fagen
1994

INTRODUCTION

Of all the players who ever played for the Chicago White Sox, and there have been some great ones, Minnie Minoso is the closest thing to a Mr. White Sox as there has been. While he played for the Cleveland Indians, and for a brief time with the St. Louis Cardinals and the Washington Senators, he has always been thought of as a Chicago White Sox.

I saw Minnie Minoso play a lot in the 1950s when I was a kid growing up in Brooklyn. He was a ballplayer who always gave 100 percent. He always hustled. Even if he didn't get a hit, he'd find another way to beat you. He was a very fundamentally sound player. He was a star, and a player you had to respect, because Minnie Minoso played every game as if it were the seventh game of the World Series.

In June 1993, Minnie Minoso became the first player to play professional baseball in six decades. That was on the 30th of June when Minnie took a turn at bat for the St. Paul Saints, a team owned and operated by Mike Veeck, son of the late Bill Veeck. In September 1993, Ron Schueler and I decided that Minnie should have the opportunity to play that sixth decade in the Major Leagues. Some of our players were upset and made an issue of this. That stirred enough controversy for Minnie to decline from our offer.

Those players acted silly and childishly. I probably should have asked the players before the announcement, but we already had clinched the division championship, and nothing was going to be affected by Minnie playing. I don't know what these players were upset about. We are in the entertainment business, and the fans would have loved it and Minnie would not have embarrassed anybody.

Minnie has been a great ambassador for the Chicago White Sox and for the game of baseball in general. He retired officially in 1964; that was 30 years ago. Yet every time is ever introduced, he gets a tremendous ovation. So people who never saw him play love the guy. He always says the right thing; he's always up; he's never down; he has had his share of personal problems, but has never let them out to the world.

To my mind, Minnie Minoso is ever a part of the organization. He's the best goodwill ambassador the Chicago White Sox have ever had. Minnie has a place with the White Sox as long as I am here.

—Jerry Reinsdorf, Chairman
The Chicago White Sox

FOREWORD

Minnie Minoso is to Latin ballplayers what Jackie Robinson is to black ballplayers. He was the first Latin American baseball player to become what in today's language is a "superstar."

Minnie was like a god to me. I'm not sure if he knows this, but I first saw him play in Puerto Rico back in 1944, when I was a seven-year-old kid and he was a 19-year-old rookie from Cuba who played against my father. He was very special to me then, and he remains very special to me today.

Respect, admiration and love: this is what I feel toward Minnie Minoso. I admired and respected the way he played the game and how he has kept himself in such great shape all these years. But most of all he has been an inspiration. He has been through a lot in life. He encountered racism in Cuba, then in the early years in the United States he had the additional burden of not speaking the language. But through it all he never complained.

To complain was not Minnie's way. I think he learned quite early in life that complaints get you nowhere. Minnie made his point in two ways: by being Minnie Minoso, and by playing the game of baseball the way few have ever played it.

All Latin ballplayer should pay a special deference to him for what he did for us. If things are better today, if people are more opened minded and willing to help the Latin kids of today, it is because Minnie and others like him paved the way.

This is not meant to be a complaint, but the language barrier back then was so difficult. When we came here we had only one thing on our minds, and that was to play baseball. To play in the big leagues was the real thing. That is what we dreamt about.

Players today who come from Venezuela, Panama, and other Spanish-speaking countries don't seem to realize that. They have no idea. This is too bad, because it diminishes a part of what Minnie has meant to so many of us. Every kid who has ever played the game of baseball, everyone who has been fortunate enough to have been associated with this great sport on a professional level, should know the story of Minnie Minoso. This is as true for Latins and non-Latins alike. Because the real beauty of Minnie Minoso is that he has a special quality, which is quite universal in scope.

—Orlando Cepeda

PROLOGUE

The 1940s had been the worst decade in Chicago White Sox history. Things hit rock bottom in 1948, when the team lost 101 games to finish last in the American League. The future looked anything but bright. It was then that young Chuck Comiskey took over the front office chores for the family franchise. In a bold move he hired former sportswriter and Big Ten official Frank Lane as the team's new general manager. A frank and brazen baseball executive, Lane sounded an early warning. He attested that there were no "sacred cows" on this club. It was a clear message that there would be some big changes taking place on the south side of Chicago.

At the time I was a 21-year-old left hander with the Detroit Tigers. I was a homespun kid anticipating a long career in the Motor City. How wrong I was. In November I was informed that I had been traded to the Chicago White Sox for catcher Aaron Robinson and $10,000.

In 1949, the White Sox jumped to sixth place and improved their record to 63 - 91. At the end of the year, Lane traded catcher Joe Tipton to the Philadelphia Athletics for an untested 22-year-old second baseman with limited credentials. His name was Jacob Nelson Fox. By 1950, Lane realized that our great shortstop Luke Appling, who had carried the club for 20 years, had to be replaced. So he tapped the well-stocked Brooklyn Dodger organization, and for $25,000 came up with a young shortstop from Venezuela named Chico Carrasquel. Then in November 1950, everything changed when Frank Lane signed Paul Richards to replace Red Corriden as White Sox manager.

Immediately Richards saw that Comiskey Park was not for the slow of foot. What the Sox really needed, he insisted, was pitching, a strong solid defense and speed—lots and lots of speed. Of all the minor league players he had seen, he was dazzled most by an exciting and versatile Cuban player who was with the San Diego club in the Pacific Coast League. He told Lane to get that guy, no matter what the cost.

The player that so excited Richards was, of course, Minnie Minoso. On April 30, 1951, Lane was able to obtain him from the Cleveland Indians as part of a three-team deal that saw the Sox send slugger Gus Zernial and fellow outfielder Dave Philly to the Philadelphia Athletics.

Minnie joined our club in time to suit up for an afternoon game with the New York Yankees. All true White Sox fans know what happened next. In his very first at bat, he slugged Vic Raschi's second pitch 415 feet into the left side of the center field bullpen for a home run.

Without question, Minnie's presence was the main factor in solidifying our club. He was the real catalyst behind the "Go Go" Chicago White Sox. With Nellie Fox hitting second, we needed someone who could hit after him and move the runner along. Minnie would hit the ball all over, not just try to pull. He would hit behind the runner. It was more than just baseball talent. It was the way he played. He got every inch of talent out of his body. He was there to win.

That was true then. And it is the same way today. A few years ago we were playing an old-timers game against the Chicago Cubs. We were ahead when we ran out of pitching. Because the game was for fun we brought in another guy who was really an outfielder, not a pitcher. Minnie was screaming bloody murder, because the guy wasn't getting anyone out.

The "Go Go" years of the 1950s were wonderful years for all of us. Even with guys like Minnie, Nellie, and Chico, there were no stars on our club. We could have five or six guys on the All Star team, but nobody was treated like a star. I recall once a ballplayer being traded from another team. He told me this was the first team he played on where there was no separation between the best and the journeymen. He was right! We were a unit, a good unit. We stayed that way for a long time, too. When you get guys like Minnie and Nellie who were on the All Star team each year who don't act differently, then anyone would have been a fool if they tried to. If any rookie came here with an attitude problem let's just say he wouldn't have it for long.

Minnie is still deeply involved in the game and in all aspects of baseball. I don't think there is a ballplayer living who has kept himself in the condition that Minnie has. He is also what you would call a real gentleman. He uses religion in his speeches and has a deep belief in God. He is a great person to represent baseball. This is so important to younger people, especially today.

One night last summer we were in skyboxes together. Minnie's Number 9, along with the uniform numbers of Nellie Fox, Luke Appling, Ted Lyons, Luis Aparicio, Harold Baines and I were to be officially retired in the new Comiskey Park. I was very proud, and I know Minnie was too.

Baseball has been Minnie's life. It has been a rich and rewarding life. He deserves to tell it. I am fortunate to have been a part of that story, and so very happy to make a contribution to this book.

—Billy Pierce

"It's a game! But is that all it is? It's a "Big Train" and an "Iron Horse." It's the Babe and the Bums. It's DiMag and it's Jackie. It is courage. It is heartbreak. It's a dream. It is love. It's a pastime. It's a lifetime. It's all we've ever been. It's all that we'll always be. It's baseball. And it's America!

—The Authors

THE SIX-DECADE MAN

June 30, 1993

Certain days are just special. They are landmark days in the story of a life. June 30, 1993 was one of those days for me. With one turn at bat I would become the first ballplayer in history to play professional baseball in six consecutive decades. There was an added delight because my appearance with the Saint Paul Saints of the "Northern Baseball League" was arranged by Saints' president Mike Veeck, son of the great Bill Veeck, who signed me to my first Major League contract way back in 1949.

I am often amazed, and certainly flattered, by the amount of recognition I still receive. More so perhaps because many younger people who weren't even alive during my playing days seem to know me. That is how it was the morning of June 30, 1993, when I arrived at Chicago's O'Hare Airport with John Wasylik, my agent and close friend. We presented our tickets to Northwest Airlines confirming our flight, when the young lady behind the ticket counter said with some excitement, "Are you really Minnie Minoso the baseball player?"

John told her that I most certainly was, and that this was to be a big day for me. He said we were flying to the Twin Cities for my record-breaking sixth baseball decade. She paused and told us to wait a moment, and she reached for the phone. A few seconds later she placed the receiver down and with a warm smile informed us that our tickets had been upgraded to first class—compliments of Northwest Airlines.

During the 90-minute plane ride with John, so many things passed through my mind. Not the least of these was a fleeting thought of my being denied a sixth Major League decade back in 1990, when Fay Vincent and the Commissioner's Office vetoed a Chicago White Sox effort allowing me to make an appearance in the last game to be played in the old Comiskey Park.

Sure, I was aware of the "unofficial status" of the Northern League in the eyes of the Major League baseball establishment. Consequently I knew that this record might not be recognized as "legitimate" by some keepers of the baseball flame. More will be said about this later in my story. But in my own heart the true satisfaction was in knowing that I was still a ballplayer with the ability to swing a healthy bat. And this is what I intended to do later that evening. I also knew that whatever the outcome, I would remain the only baseball player in this century to have played in five Major League decades. This record was undisputed and authentic. I only hoped that my new record might one day be recognized in Cooperstown as well.

So I knew where I was headed and what I was about to do. I ruminated on those thoughts as I looked out the window at the flooding Mississippi River, which played havoc on so many folks, and did such enormous damage—the product of those violent summer rains of 1993.

I was in fine shape and good condition, this I knew. My present weight was only two-and-a-half pounds more than in the prime of my playing days. My eyesight was as good as ever; I have never needed to wear prescription glasses. But most important, I would have something special to tell my five-year-old son, Charlie Orestes Minoso. This was a dream come true, pure and simple. A long and winding journey that had taken me from the sugar fields of my Cuban boyhood, where my odyssey first began 68 years ago.

Those, of course, were my personal feelings. My professional instincts insisted on something else, something quite different. This had now become just another game—no more or less important than my first Major League game in 1949, or that wonderful May afternoon in Chicago in 1951, when with one turn at bat I became an instant celebrity. Another game, another contract, another team, another league, another pitcher, these thoughts were uppermost in my mind when the airplane landed in the Twin Cities early that afternoon.

At the airport we were met immediately by Annie Huidekuper, a warm and personable young lady in her mid-twenties. Annie is Mike Veeck's all-purpose goodwill ambassador and his right-hand person, a job she does quite well. She would handle every detail of our stay with total efficiency.

It took only fifteen minutes to reach the ballpark. Truly, it was just wonderful to see Mike Veeck again. It was a sentimental reunion. How well I remembered Mike Veeck as a young kid, roaming around the ballpark making friends with the players. I was proud to have been one of Mike's heroes back in the days when his dad owned the Chicago White Sox. Now these many years later, Mike Veeck was giving me the opportunity to make baseball history.

We talked about his father, and how unique this situation was considering that Bill Veeck began this quest by bringing me back to the game in 1976 to become a four-decade Major Leaguer. I responded with a single in one of my eight plate appearances to become the oldest player in baseball history to hit safely in a Major League game. Again, it was Bill Veeck who made me the 20th Century's only five-decade player, when he once again activated me for the final three games of the 1980 season. To my mind, Bill Veeck is a double-duty Hall of Famer: a deserving Hall of Famer in the game of baseball, and a true Hall of Famer in the game of life.

Mike suggested that we first get a bite to eat and Annie accompanied John and me to lunch. We were quite concerned by the misty air and the intermittent showers, and hoped that the inclement weather would neither delay nor postpone the game. Mainly, however, we directed the conversation toward what might be the best and most effective way of bringing me in and introducing me to everyone.

Things could not have gone smoother. When we arrived at the Stadium, a large crowd was anticipating my arrival. We stepped out of the van to a wonderful ovation. Lots of jubilation all over the place. Reporters and writers were everywhere to meet me. There was lots of talking and handshaking.

I brought whatever equipment I felt I would need. But when I went to the locker room to change, it was the uniform of the St. Paul Saints that I put on. I was escorted to Mike Veeck's office to sign a contract with the Saints, making my participation in the game official.

To allay all lingering doubts, let me say the Saints belong to the newly formed Northern Baseball League, which is fully professional and complemented with a large number of players who have recently seen action in the majors or the high minors. I might add as well that the League drew large and enthusiastic crowds in its inaugural year.

Ultimately what made the day so thrilling for me were the fans. They showered so much warmth and affection on me. The moment I walked from the dugout to the playing field to warm up, there was a standing ovation from the near-capacity 4,000 fans who bucked the rain and damp Minnesota weather to come and see me play. It was impossible to predict what would happen when I came to bat, of course; but I knew one thing. I could make good contact with the ball no matter who was pitching, or whether the pitcher was throwing 50, 80, or 90 miles per hour. Truly, my confidence was intact.

I must emphasize something else as well. And it is important that this be understood. I would never do anything to embarrass myself or the game of baseball, which I love so deeply. I may be sentimental, but never at the expense of my own dignity, or the dignity and integrity of my profession. True, I can't play 160 games any more. Yet give me a couple of practice swings to get my timing set, and I can still hit a baseball. What's more, I will hit whatever the pitcher throws.

These were my feelings as I stepped to the plate to face Yoshi Seo of the Thunder Bay Whiskey Jacks, who at 19 years old was the youngest pitcher in the Northern League. Yet what followed was just unbelievable. There was a spontaneous standing ovation which seemed to last more than ten minutes. What a great thrill and how very lucky I felt!

Yet, as I made clear earlier, now was the time for sentiment to stop. From this point on it was just another turn at bat. I may have been Yoshi Seo's senior by almost fifty years, but as soon as I dug in, he became my enemy. I was the hitter, and he was the pitcher; just as it was three decades earlier when I was a big league star. It was combat—no more, no less! The crowd was cheering for me the same way they did during my glory days.

Just as I knew I would, I made contact with my very first swing. The first two pitches were bad, high and inside. The next pitch was a pretty good slider. I hit a hard bouncer back to the mound. The pitcher grabbed it on the high hop and threw me out by a few steps. I hadn't missed by much. I hit the pitch straight away; I did not try to pull it. If the ball had bounced six inches higher, I would have been on first with a hit. As I trotted back to the dugout, I received another standing ovation.

I think too much has been made of my age. I really feel that age is irrelevant. Nothing is impossible if you take good care of yourself, which is what I have always tried to do. People always want to know how old I really am. The official sources have me listed as being born on November 29, 1922. That would make me 71 years old, and I would not make excuses or apologies. I am actually just 68 years old. I was 19 years old when I arrived in the United States in 1945, but my papers said I was 22. I told a white lie in order to obtain a visa, so I could qualify for service in the Cuban army. My true date of birth is the 29th of November, 1925.

If the night of June 30, 1993, was special to me, it was a sheer delight for Ms. Rosie Sieracki of Baldwin, Wisconsin. Mike Veeck happened to spot her in the stands wearing a Minnie Minoso #9 Jersey. When the time came to present me with a special bat commemorating my six decades, Mike had the public address announcer page "The woman wearing the Minnie Minoso # 9 jersey." Rosie Sieracki, a lifelong Chicago White Sox fan, was escorted to the field to make the special presentation to me. Later she told reporters that she almost fainted from the excitement, and that this was the most marvelous thing that had ever happened to her. It gave the evening a certain flare for the dramatic; an appropriate homage to the ordinary fan, which is vintage Bill Veeck and son.

Let me say as well that I am extremely proud of that commemorative bat. I am one of only six players featured in the first of three series of such baseball bats designed by the Hoosier Bat company of Valparaiso, Indiana.

After the game I changed out of my uniform. I had promised Mike that I would sign autographs for 21 young people who had asked to meet me personally. I was led from the clubhouse to an area under the bleachers, where I began signing autographs. Soon other fans saw what was happening and joined the gathering. It makes me quite happy to have people, especially kids, ask for my autograph. I look upon it as a real compliment.

The autograph session lasted more than an hour. When things settled down, John, Annie, and I went for dinner. Dinner was to be at a nearby restaurant, but we arrived so late that the kitchen was closing. I was able to order a steak sandwich and a beer, a local brew that Annie recommended. We reminisced about the day's events and how well things went. I still was astounded by the warmth, the gratitude, and all the respect that came my way. That evening John and I spent the night reminiscing in a rather unique hotel that was a converted railroad station.

The following morning we left for the airport. My picture and coverage of the day's events were in all the papers. The major networks, as well as CNN, had picked up the story. People were passing by shouting things like, "Hi Minnie," "Congratulations," and "Nice going!" Yet not until I got on the airplane and things settled down a bit, did I feel the full magnitude of the 30th of June, 1993 and the feat of becoming professional baseball's first six-decade player.

My life and my career began to unfold before my eyes. It had been a long journey—an odyssey that had taken me from the sugar fields and sandlots of my native Cuba, to the Cuban Professional Leagues, to those great Negro Leagues of yore, to the majors and big-league stardom. And now into baseball history. How fortunate I had been. With God's help, I had been able to achieve things I never would have dreamt possible as a young boy. How very lucky I was. I shut my eyes and began thinking about my place of birth and my boyhood, the little town of El Perico, exactly 175 kilometers from Havana. There was so much I wanted to say. And so much I haven't been able to say until now. It was finally time to open my heart and tell my story— the real story of my life.

2

EL PERICO

Sugar was king in Cuba. This was particularly true in the town of El Perico, where I was born and raised. For those workers who were fortunate enough to gain employment in the big factories where the raw sugar was processed from the cane, jobs were good, work was steady, and wages were rewarding. For others who toiled the sugar fields of the farms and ranches, sugar was sheer survival. It was our bread and butter. Every aspect of life revolved around the sugar industry. The actual sugar season was short; perhaps only about three-and-a-half months. These were the months which counted, the months when the money was good; there was no time for laziness. What a family made during the short sugar season had to last them for the entire year.

Carlos Arrieta was one of many blacks who labored in the Cuban sugar fields. Like all the workers who lived on the ranch of Mr. Carlos Lopez, he cut the sugar. But unlike the others, he also loaded the sugar cane onto the trucks and delivered it to the factory to be processed. These trucks were not driven by gasoline or any other fuel; they were pulled by a team of donkeys or bulls, and Carlos Arrieta was the driver.

Carlos was a good-looking man, rather quiet and respected by everyone. He was not a particularly strong man. There were no bulging muscles on his lean frame; nor was he a good athlete by his own admission. But he was a healthy man, a very good worker indeed, whose greatest satisfaction in life was a job well done.

In 1924, Carlos Arrieta married Cecilia Armas, a divorced woman with four children from a previous marriage. The following year, Carlos and Cecilia had a son of their own. Born on the 29th of November, 1925, they named their son Saturnino Orestes. Soon the Saturnino was dropped, and everyone simply called the lad Orestes.

Truly, God could not have blessed me with better parents. While my mother and father would separate and then divorce eight years later, they gave me so much. Much more than material things could ever buy. I never felt a bit cheated. I really enjoyed my early childhood in El Perico. Sure, we were poor, but so were all the other workers on the ranches. We didn't have electricity. We didn't even have the more commonplace pleasures, such as a radio. We used gas light and would make our own lamps. At times we had only candlelight. Yet we got on well as a family, because there was lots of love. Most important, we had a proper share of values; my parents always taught me good values.

There was much more to my father than just being a good worker. He was intelligent, a very bright man with lots of common sense. I remember him having the most beautiful handwriting. He was very good with figures and numbers. He could figure out anything that had to do with numbers. My father and Mr. Lopez got along particularly well. Mr. Lopez considered him an outstanding worker. More important the two men liked and respected each other. Mr. Lopez respected my father's work ethic, a work ethic that my father passed along to me. Similarly, my father liked Mr. Lopez's fairness and his genuine concern for his workers.

Americans may have difficulty fully understanding the nature of these ranches and farms. Men of European ancestry like Mr. Lopez owned the ranches. But Mr. Lopez did not run the ranch. The foreman, Mateo Rocher, lived on the premises and was in charge of the day-by-day operations of the ranch. Mr. Rocher was also white, but like Mr. Lopez, was very well liked by the black workers. Mr. Lopez was a good provider for his workers, giving each worker and his family a house of their own. On the *La Lonja* ranch, there were 15 houses —one for each worker and his family.

We were the kids of the ranch. In many ways we were not unlike kids anywhere. We laughed and cried, we were playful and were punished, we behaved and we misbehaved, we worked and we slept. Until the times became too difficult, and we could no longer make ends meet, we would go to school. For the boys on the ranch, a fifth or sixth grade education was all that was expected. Then it was full-time work in the fields with the adults. The girls often left school to attend to household chores.

My situation was a little different. I grew up with two brothers and two sisters from my mother's first marriage. My sister, Juanita, was almost 20 years older than me. Cirilo, my oldest brother, whom I greatly admired, was 15 years older. Francisco, was next, and was 12 years older. Flora, the youngest of my mother's four children, is about five years older than I am. Flora is the only one of the four who is still alive. She lives in Havana, and I haven't seen her in many years.

My mother's first husband was a man named Julian Minoso. He loved me as if I was his own. Often he would take care of me and helped teach me how to work on the trucks. Sadly, he died when I was still a rather young boy. He was a kind man, whom I still think of from time to time. So as you can see, my brothers and sisters went by the name Minoso, the name of my mother's first husband. But I was not a Minoso. My real name was Saturnino Orestes Arrieta Armas. "Arrieta" for my father and "Armas" for my mother. Because my brothers and sisters had a different father, they called my father 'uncle' instead of daddy. So I began doing the same thing. I called my father 'tio,' which was Spanish for uncle.

I didn't address my mother in the formal way, either. I called her Celia, short for Cecilia, which is what everyone called her. She couldn't read or write, but she expressed herself just beautifully. She spoke beautiful Spanish, which is one of the most difficult languages to speak correctly. My mother could speak it as well as anyone. She was one of the greatest ladies I have ever known.

We spent a lot of time together in those early years. Never could I have imagined how distant our family would become in later years. Much of that had to do with the change of government in Cuba in 1959. I had never liked the Communist party, and once Fidel Castro began showing his true colors and took freedom away from the Cuban people, I knew I could not live in Cuba any longer. I'll have more to say on that matter later. For now, I'll just say that when I left Cuba for good in 1961, my sisters,

Juanita and Flora; my brother, Francisco; and my father, Carlos Arrieta, chose to remain behind. My mother and my brother, Cirilo, had long since passed away.

Now is as good a time as any to tell how I came to be called Minoso. You see, my two brothers, Cirilo and Francisco, were very good baseball players. They played for the local factory team. I'd tag along whenever they practiced and played their games.

When people would see us they'd yell out, "Those are the Minoso brothers and that's little Minoso. He's one of the Minoso brothers. He's a good baseball player, too."

"Little Minoso!" That's what they called me back then. I just loved baseball from the start, and I truly believe that I was born with baseball in my blood. As a youngster, I organized a ballclub on the ranch. We would play teams from the other farms and ranches. Sometimes we'd play the kids from the factories.

Neither my mother or father were exactly thrilled; they didn't like baseball particularly. Yet they still bought me the best glove they could. I recall my mother saying once that while she didn't like baseball, but maybe God liked it. One of my biggest regrets is that my mother never lived to see me play professional baseball either in Cuba or in the United States. I like to think that maybe from heaven she has been watching and protecting me.

I was the big boss on the ranch. The other kids all listened to "little Minoso." and believe me I was tough. I'd fine the other kids 50 cents for each missed sign. I was a pitcher then, and I'll tell you I could really fire that ball. My arm was like a rifle; I was untouchable. In fact, the other farm teams were all afraid of me. Whenever there was a game they would ask who was pitching. If the answer was Minoso, they would sigh "Oh, no! He's too fast. He's too tough." My big hero in those days was Martin Dihigo, the great Latin ballplayer who distinguished himself in the United States with the Negro Leagues. Martin Dihigo is the only baseball player to receive Hall of Fame honors in four different countries: The United States, Cuba, Mexico, and Venezuela. I was disappointed in later years when Dihigo became Minister of Sports for Fidel Castro.

We would beat all the farm teams. The real challenge was the team from the factory. The kids playing for the factory had fancy uniforms, real nice uniforms. Basically, it was the rich kids playing the poor kids. Since I was the big boss, the kids would listen to me. "Look guys," I said. "We can make our own uniforms." We would buy empty sugar boxes and sell them for a dollar profit. Then we gave the money to a woman to make uniforms for us. We even had spikes. Our uniforms were made from cotton flour sacks, but we were simply thrilled to have these uniforms. I don't think there is a kid around who ever played baseball who doesn't remember his first baseball uniform and how it felt to put it on.

Our team was called *La Lonja*; this was the name of the ranch. I recall how proud both the owner, Carlos Lopez, and the foreman, Mateo Rocher, were of all of us. Many years later in 1955, when I was an established Major League star, I brought a Minnie Minoso All Star Team back to El Perico. What a thrill it was to play baseball in the town of my birth, in front of people who knew and remembered me as a little boy. I have never forgotten. In fact, I am very proud of anything I may have done to have furthered and bettered the cause of Latin ballplayers everywhere.

There was sadness in my young life as well. After eight years of marriage, my parents parted. My father moved to the province of Camaguey where there was more work. My sister, Juanita, had moved to Havana. She worked for people of comfortable means as a cook. Juanita was a wonderful cook. She rented an apartment in Havana and my mother took Flora and myself to live with her. We were living in Havana when my mother suddenly took sick and died.

I was a boy of ten and went back to El Perico to live on the ranch with my oldest brother, Cirilo, who was a hero to me. Not only was he my brother, he was one of the very best baseball players I ever saw. People who later saw me play would insist that as good as I was, Cirilo may have been even better. He just never had the opportunities in life that I had.

I lived with Cirilo and his wife for a year. One day when I was doing my chores I heard there had been an accident on the ranch. I ran back to see who was hurt. It was then I heard the news that just shot through me. Cirilo had died while trying to lift up a tree that had fallen. The strain of lifting it had caused an artery to burst in his head. I was devastated; I just couldn't believe what people were telling me. Not my brother, Cirilo. To me he was bigger than life. I went to the funeral, but never looked at the body. I had such good feelings for him. A part of him has always remained with me.

My brother, Francisco, was a different story. He never took much interest in the family. He was an independent kind of guy who was rarely around. While the rest of us worked together to keep ourselves above water financially, he never did his share. He was more interested in horses and trained horses for an American businessman in the village of Central Espana. He did pretty well for himself. The family lost contact with him quite early. I ran into someone from Cuba about five years ago who told me that Francisco had died. I felt badly, but had not had any contact with my brother for many years, even before I left Cuba.

After Cirilo passed away, his wife Ebilia couldn't keep the house by herself. She moved in with her own father and mother and I went to live again with my sister, Juanita, in Havana. She was married with two kids by then. Juanita was later divorced and lived out her entire life in Havana. We never had much contact after I left Cuba. Her sympathies, I believe, were with the Communist government. When I left Cuba in 1961, I took her 16-year-old son, Damaso, and her 12-year-old daughter, Marian, with me to America. My nephew, Damaso, has worked with the ground crew at Comiskey Park now for thirty years. My niece, Marian, whom I raised as my own daughter died tragically in Mexico in 1971. My sister, Juanita, lived to an old age and died in Havana in the early 1980s.

I started to move around a lot. I did not like Havana, so I went back to El Perico to live with my Auntie Juaquina, who was my father's sister. Her son, Pepe, was a big guy, long, lean, and about eight years older than me. We got along real well. Pepe loved baseball; he was a walking baseball encyclopedia, in fact. He had wanted to be a pitcher, but with his height, I suggested that he play first base.

Pepe protected me like a little brother. Together we went to Camaguey, where my father was working. There was more work there for us, and Pepe and myself made some money by loading the sugar cane on the trucks. My father loved Pepe, his nephew, the son of his sister. But he didn't exactly want me hanging around him, and for good reason I imagine.

At times, Pepe would take me to a little club a few miles from the work compound. We would go there to dance. I was too young to drink, but Pepe certainly wasn't. One night we decided to "go out on the town," so to speak. I knew my father would not like this idea, so I thought up a plan to fool him. He was sleeping at the time Pepe and I were going to the club. Cleverly, I put a bundle of things together, wrapped them up, and placed them in the hammock right next to where my father was sleeping. Now if I was out late and my father woke up, he would think I was sleeping too. I would fool him, or so I thought.

As luck would have it, Pepe had a beer or two too many and fell asleep. There was no way for me to get back on my own, so I, too, slept at the club. To make matters worse, I had met a pretty young lady. The moment she saw me, she liked me. I was a young boy, and still quite naive and innocent. In other words, I was not privy yet to certain ways of the world. She gave me a medallion and told me to keep it for her. She said she wanted me to be her man.

My father awoke in the morning and was angry as a wounded bull when he saw I wasn't there. He tracked me down, and when he caught up with us he lowered the boom: "Pepe," he said angrily, "You're not going to corrupt Orestes. He's just a young kid. If you do that again, Pepe, I'll whip you. I promise." He wasn't exactly tender with me either; in fact he was even less tender when he saw the remembrance the young lady had given me. He instructed me to give it back to her immediately. I was not that kind of guy he said. I would not live that type of life.

The message was clear: If I ever messed up like this again, I would pay a heavy price. My father always tried to keep me a clean- cut guy. I am glad he was this way; I had the greatest respect for my father. More than any person in my life, he taught me to know good from bad.

With Pepe now deemed a bad influence, I went back to Havana again to live with my sisters, Juanita and Flora. Flora had moved to the city and shared an apartment with Juanita. Juanita earned money working as a cook for a wealthy family. Flora helped out by cleaning homes. Together, they rented a larger apartment; but I still was uncomfortable in Havana. I found more fun and satisfaction on the ranch. Havana was a big city; it was too big. I couldn't get used to it. There was just one thing holding me back. I had met a beautiful young woman whom I liked a lot. It would be tough, I thought, but I believed I could forget her once I got back to El Perico.

I returned to El Perico to live on the ranch once more. This time I stayed with a friend of my father's and his family. Because I was a guest in his house, I was always on my best behavior. This was one more lesson my parents taught me well.

One thing I particularly recall was an old man who became a very good friend. He was a fascinating old gentleman, the grandfather and patriarch of the family. He had been a slave in Cuba many years before and told such interesting stories of what things had been like. I loved to hear him talk about all of the people he had known and the places he had seen.

Despite his advanced age, he was a very good worker. His grandchildren were only a year or two younger than me, but he thought they were lazy. They couldn't keep up with him, he would say. "You're going to be a good man, Orestes," he told me. "You know how to cut and clean the sugar. You are not lazy like my grandsons. I want you working next to me." I considered that a great compliment, especially coming from him.

The entire family was very good to me. I never took any pay from them, and would help out by bringing water every day. I worked for my room and board. However, I was starting to get restless. True, I hadn't liked Havana before, but somehow now I wanted to get back. I hadn't been able to get the young lady off my mind as I thought I would. Even more important, I wanted to play baseball, the best caliber of baseball, and there was lots of baseball in Havana. Yes, I wanted to get back there; I just didn't know how.

Then I had an idea—a ruse you might call it. A fellow named Umberto who had played baseball with me was also a mailman. I asked him to do me a favor. Would he write a letter saying that there was a job for me in Havana playing baseball?

I asked him to address the letter to me, 'Orestes Minoso,' and to sign the letter with the owner's name. Umberto did a good job. He wrote the letter for me, stamped it with the appropriate postage, and mailed it from Havana.

We were cleaning a big cornfield a few days later. There was lots and lots of tall green grass. Suddenly someone came shouting. "Orestes! Orestes! There's a letter here for you from Havana." Of course I played dumb. I pretended to be surprised. I opened the letter and read it. I looked shocked. "They're crazy!" I said. "They're really crazy." "What is it Orestes? What is it?," the guys asked. "They want me to play baseball in Havana. I can't do that. There's too much work to do here." My father's friend took the letter from me and read it. "What do you mean? What are you waiting for, Orestes?" he said.   "You better go right now. Get your clothes and get ready. Here, I'll give you a little money for bus fare."

I knew I had been less than truthful. Yet I was young and in love, so I thought. There was baseball and more baseball in Havana. So I stretched the truth and made excuses for myself. But in my heart, I knew that everyone wished me well, regardless. I was a baseball player, and a darn good one. Havana was the place to be.

I said goodbye to my friends on the ranch. I thanked my father's friend and his family for their hospitality and their kindness. Quickly I packed my bag. I caught the first bus that came my way, and headed to Havana. I headed for Havana with thoughts of baseball and a beautiful young lady weighing heavily on my mind.

Minnie Minoso used to tell me that he played every game like a rookie. A rookie, he said, played each game as if he were trying to make the team. That was the secret to his success. I remember Minoso playing baseball with the Cuban Miners. He was a good bunter; he was a good runner, and a man who could steal second base. He was a tremendous player in the clutch. He was only the second Latin American player to play in an All Star game in the big leagues. He said many times he liked to play before a full house, but when the stadium was empty, he played the same way. He did that to convince the people to come and see baseball.

Minoso was great in the big leagues, and Minoso was great in Cuba. He respected everyone, especially the children. He used to sign balls; he would even buy many baseballs and sign them for the kids. He is a tremendous man in all ways. In Chicago, he is remembered as a man who could change a possible loss in a game into a win.

Before the first game in a very important Series in New York, Casey Stengel was called to a press conference. They were playing for first place, and one of the writers asked Casey what he thought about the three-game series with Chicago. Casey answered, "If we can stop Minnie Minoso, we can win this series." The White Sox won two games, and the Yankees only won one. He was tremendous.

In the history of the Chicago White Sox, you have some very good ballplayers such as Luke Appling and Nellie Fox. But Minoso was one of the most important ballplayers, and he was a very good man for the sport. He was a good Cuban; a good Latin. He'd visit anyplace he was called to help the people, like hospitals and schools. He deserves everything great you can write about him, because he *was* baseball. Sportswriters liked him because he'd speak to everyone, and he had class. He always said "If I buy a car, I buy a Cadillac." He loved his Cadillacs. He was a first-class man, believe me. I think today it's good to remember the life of Minnie Minoso, because it would do so much for the youngsters today.

Fausto Miranda, Sportswriter
The Miami Herald

3

HAVANA

I get very annoyed when I hear tales of how Cuba was a sort of racial paradise, a country free from the segregation and discrimination practiced in the United States. This is complete nonsense. Discrimination and segregation were very much alive and flourishing in the Cuba of my birth. There was one distinct difference, however. In the United States, there were laws sanctioning these practices. In Cuba conditions were more subtle, but just as real.

Nothing illustrates these practices better than baseball. Amateur baseball in Cuba was very popular. In Cuba, the amateur teams were always associated with certain social clubs. In reality, the word "club" simply meant "whites only." Therefore, any chance of playing amateur ball was nonexistent. The "Havana Federation of Amateur Baseball" consisted of a number of teams, but none had any black players. Neither did the baseball team at the University of Havana. Black students could attend the university, it is true, but no blacks were allowed to play baseball.

If you were black, the only chance you had was on the semi-professional level. Then if you were good enough, there was professional baseball. But your chances were very small, considering there were so few professional teams in the country.

So when I came to the United States, at least I knew what I was facing. Sure, there were lots of problems along the way, but I got the chance to play professional ball in the U.S., both in the

Negro Leagues and the Major Leagues. Who could ask for more? It was the dream of every young boy. I enjoyed myself immensely and have never forgotten the debt of gratitude that I owe this wonderful country.

I arrived in Havana in 1941 with very little in my pocket. Cirilo and my mother were gone. My brother, Francisco, had little to do with the family. So I stayed in the apartment with my sisters, Juanita and Flora. We paid seven dollars a month for a one-room flat.

In Havana, I began working for a lady who had a small home in the Vedado. The Vedado was a high-class area of the city. I made six dollars a month for delivering canteens to various homes. Then I started working for a man named Jose Santa Cruz. Everyone called him "TiTi." He had a little shoe shine business, and truly I wasn't very good at shining shoes. But TiTi would give me half of everything I made to help pay the rent. The two of us became the closest of friends; for the next 20 years he would be my best and most loyal friend.

I had not forgotten that certain young lady, either. Soon she became my "official" girlfriend. I use the word "official," because courting back then was very different than it is today, especially here in the United States. In Cuba, we ascribed to the old-fashioned standards and values. No proper young lady could be seen without the presence of a chaperone. I asked her mother for permission to see her daughter. She granted me two hours, three times a week to visit with her daughter; I still recall the exact days: Wednesday, Friday, and Sunday. Of course, her mother was always present. This type of setting, I'm sure, seems totally foreign to the youngsters today. But back then we operated by a different set of rules. One thing I did learn, however, was the proper way to treat a lady. I have always tried to be a gentleman, and never treated any woman in a way that I would not want another man to treat either my mother or my sisters.

I was playing baseball then, too. A little bit at first, and then much more later. First, I played semi-professional ball for the Partagas Cigar Factory team, and worked part time at the factory making cigars. Then I decided to try out for the Ambrosia Candy Factory team. Ambrosia was one of the best semi-pro teams in Havana.

A cousin of mine, Jose Divino, had arranged a meeting between me and the Ambrosia manager. I showed up at the tryout with an old uniform that I had worn in El Perico. I was waiting for Jose Divino to meet me and introduce me to Rene Midenstein, the manager, when someone spotted me. He asked me what I was doing. I told him that my cousin was supposed to meet me here and introduce me to Mr. Midenstein.

"Hey, Rene," he called to the Ambrosia manager. "This young fellow says his name is Minoso. His cousin said we would take a look at him."

Rene was a big, tall guy, a real strong man. "What position do you play?" he asked. I wasn't sure what to tell him. I had played all the positions, including catcher at one time or another. I looked around; everyone seemed so good. Everyone except the third baseman, who was having some trouble; he didn't measure up to the others. "I play third base," I answered. In truth, I had played *some* third base, but certainly not very much.

My response was the right one. I suited up and took over third base. The regular third baseman did not seem to like the idea much. I knew that I didn't have a great glove, but what I did have was a rifle for an arm. I could really pop the ball to first. My throw was like trajectory—straight, low, hard, and on the mark. Back home I had even broken the first baseman's glove a couple of times.

Well, that day I grabbed everything that was hit my way. I went to my left; then to my right. When the ball was hit directly at me, I blocked it off my chest. "Wow, this kid is something," I heard them shouting. Everyone was looking around, bewildered; they wanted to see more. "Come back tomorrow," the manager said.

The next day may well have changed the course of my baseball career. I reported to the park, and this time I received a uniform. I started the game in the dugout, with the regular third baseman at the hot corner. We were playing a team with lots of ex-professional ballplayers. It was the top of the ninth; the bases were loaded and there were two outs.

The manager looked my way. "Hey chicito," he pointed at me. "Go hit for Nazario." Nazario was a pretty good left fielder but had struck out three times already. Here I was now: the kid nobody knew, the kid from the ranch. This was my big chance.

The manager took me aside. He pointed at the pitcher. "This guy's been around a long time," Rene warned me. "He knows how to pitch." He also gave me a bit of advice I have never forgotten. "Whatever you do, don't go down with your bat on your shoulder. If the pitch looks hitable, just swing!" That's exactly what I did. I swung at the first pitch and lined it over first base. It landed fair, clearing the bases. When the dust settled, I was on third base with a triple. We won the game, 4-2. Suddenly everyone was talking about that kid, Minoso.

I was sixteen years old, and I had come to play ball. There were a couple of bruised egos on the team, I imagine. After the game, Nazario, whom I pinch hit for, wanted to talk with me. He tried to be friendly and to convince me that everything was all right; but I knew he was a little hurt. The next day the regular third baseman was on the bench. He was madder than hell; I wasn't too popular with him, either.

I hit more than .400 the remainder of the year. The other third baseman never played again. The next year I led the league in batting with a .367 average. I won the batting title by making a great play at third and throwing out Kid Gavilan, (no relation to the boxing champ), who had won the batting title the year before.

In 1943, I left the Ambrosia team and Havana and went to Oriente Province to play for the Cuban Miners, one of the best semi-pro teams in the country. How well I remember my debut with the Miners. We were involved in a double header. In the first game, we were losing 1 - 0. We had the bases loaded and nobody out against Lino Donoso. Lino, who later would pitch for the Pittsburgh Pirates, was a tough pitcher. I hit safely twice earlier in the game against another pitcher, but Lino was especially tough. He promptly struck me out and sent the next two hitters down on strikes to strike out the side and preserve the win.

The second game was an all-together different story. Lino started this game. The first time up I tripled with a man on base. The next time I homered with a man on base. My third time at bat, I singled to go 3 for 3 on the game. I drove in three runs as the Miners beat Lino in the second game, 5 - 2.

After the game, the crowd kept yelling, "Minoso! Minoso!" I was an instant hero in my new town. I started kidding some of the guys. I said that I was lonely here in Oriente and I wanted to go back to Havana. The manager was scared to death. "Minoso, are you crazy? They'll kill me if you go back. They'll kill me here, Orestes!" On the one hand I said this all "tongue in cheek." On the other hand, however, I just wanted them to know that I couldn't be taken for granted.

I had a great year with the Miners. I became the idol of the town. Mr. Sand, the owner of the club, was an American. He wanted me to stay here very badly. So much so that he paid me $100 a month plus expenses. This was nice money at the semi-pro level. He said that I always had a home with the team and I could stay as long as I wanted.

My second season with the Miners was lined with great expectations. It was November 29, 1944, and I was celebrating my 19th birthday with my girlfriend at the LaPlaza Marte. We were about to go dancing when the manager of the club, Juan Solis, ran up to me waving a telegram. "Orestes, look! They want you in Havana. Marianao wants you to play professional baseball."

Truly I was taken aback and was reeling on my heels. "The Cuban Professional League," I remember thinking. So few ever got there. I really wondered if I could make the pros. My problem at the moment was what to tell Mr. Sand, the owner of the Cuban Miners, who had treated me so well. I certainly wanted to give it a shot; but I also wanted to make sure I'd still have a job in Oriente if I didn't make the team. So I told Mr. Sand that I had to go to Havana for a week to care for my sister. I was worried he'd find out the truth, but it was needless worry on my part. Shortly he would read in the papers that I had been signed by Marianao. Instead of being angry, he was very understanding and encouraging.

When I reported to the Marianao Tigers, I didn't even have a full uniform. They gave me a pair of pants that were too big. My shirt belonged to someone else. And the rest of the gear didn't fit either. The next day we had a game. I hadn't signed a contract yet, so I was a bit nervous. We were playing Cienfuego. On the Cienfuego roster was one of the all-time great Cuban baseball players: Cristobal Torriente. He was a great old timer; something like Babe Ruth in this country. In his heyday, in fact, he was called the Cuban Babe Ruth. Later he went on to play in the American Negro League. Torriente was a legend, and although his skills had diminished, he was still a big attraction. How well I remember Torriente calling me over that day. "Hey little kid, Minoso!" I said, "Yes, Mr. Torriente, what is it?" He said he was going to give me a tip. He said I was wearing my baseball shoes wrong. I had always put a ring on the shoelace of my spike and then tied it. "That's not the proper way to wear your baseball shoes," he reminded me. Actually it was more of a reprimand than a reminder. The uniform is to be respected. Needless to say, I never tied my baseball shoes like that again.

The next day things started to happen. We were playing against the Almendares club. They were loaded with great ballplayers including a young second baseman from Mexico named Roberto Avila. Bobby, incidentally, would go on to a fine big-league career with the Cleveland Indians, capturing the American League batting title in 1954. That same year, I finished second to him for batting honors. Two outstanding outfielders, Roberto Ortiz and Santo Amero, played right and left field respectively. Their catcher was Mike Guerra who later caught in the big leagues with the Washington Senators. One of my team-mates with Marianao that year was Charo (Charolito) Orta, whose son Jorge would have a good career with the Chicago White Sox. Jorge (George) Orta was the Sox second baseman during the mid and late 1970s when I was the White Sox first base coach.

Our third baseman at Marianao was a fellow named Tony Costano. He bruised his knee chasing a pop fly, yet continued to play. By the 7th inning it was hurting pretty badly. Suddenly, the manager looked over at me. "Hey kid, you take over!"

I could see my dream coming true. I was ready. I grabbed my glove and ran to third base. We were ahead 1 - 0 and they had a runner on third. The hitter was Bobby Ortiz. Bobby was a big guy, around 6-6. Our pitcher was a smart left hander with lots of guts and savvy named Daniel Perra. He got Ortiz to bounce to him, but Perra slipped on the wet grass and the ball dribbled out of his glove. That scored the tying run. Daniel Perra then retired the next two hitters. We came to bat in the top of the ninth, with the score tied 1 - 1.

The first batter lined a single, and the next hitter bunted him to second. Now it was my turn. I hit a shot between first and second for a line drive base hit. This put us ahead 2 - 1. We took that lead into the last of the ninth. We were on the field now. The first batter singled for a base hit. The next guy bunted. I picked it up and threw to first base. One out! The second batter slammed a ground ball between short and third. I speared it and threw; two outs! The next hitter lifted a fly ball to right field. The right fielder caught it for the third out. We won!

Everyone by that time was talking about me; the new kid. The kid no one knew; the kid that didn't even have a number on the back of his uniform, a uniform that didn't even match. He got a base hit that won the game. He made a couple of sparkling plays in the field. Who is he? Overnight, the name Minoso was in all the papers. They were talking about me on the radio. People were starting to say what a great star I was going to be.

Try to imagine how I felt. I couldn't believe this was really me. Orestes Minoso from El Perico. Orestes Minoso from the ranch of Mr. Carlos Lopez. I never dreamt that this could happen. Here I was playing against the best. The best Cuban ballplayers in the world. American players who had played in the Major Leagues and the high minors. Outstanding minor league stars like Bobby Avila. This was Cuba's best, and I got a base hit to win the game.

Life had been good to me. I was young—just 19 years old. I was carefree; I was alive. I was playing a game I loved more than anything in the world. And more than that, I was getting paid for it. I thought that perhaps someday, just maybe someday, I would get a chance to reach my ultimate dream; to play baseball in the United States with the Negro Leagues. That was where the best black ballplayers in the world played. Major League baseball never crossed my mind at that time. Jackie Robinson had yet to arrive on the Major League scene, and the color line in the United States still seemed an impregnable fortress.

After the game, I got on the streetcar and headed back to the Vadado where I was staying. When I arrived, there was near pandemonium. People were yelling, "Hey Minoso, is that you? We didn't know you played baseball. Why didn't you say anything? You are Orestes Minoso. You got a base hit to win the game."

One reason I said nothing was because I never wanted glory and fame to change me, and after all these years, I don't believe it has. I was still the same Orestes Minoso. This is something I have never forgotten. I knew who I was and where I came from.

I never looked at other people as being any better than me. Likewise, being a celebrity never made me better than others. I like the recognition and attention, to that I readily admit. But I have never let that dominate my thinking. This was the attitude I carried through my entire Major League career. It is the same attitude I have today.

Amidst all the celebrating, a thought suddenly hit me. What about Mr. Sand, the owner of the Cuban Miners? I told him I was visiting my sick sister. He would read all this in the papers, and probably think badly of me; I felt terrible. The very next day, a telegram addressed to me arrived at my sister's address:

"Orestes! I know you can make it. You are great. How come you never told me? I would have put you on a special plane to Havana myself." —Senor Sand

I was on a roll. The next day we had to complete a suspended game against the Almendares club. They were ahead 4 - 0. We scored one run, then another. The two teams went back and forth until the last of the ninth, when the score was tied 7 - 7. The bases were loaded and I came to bat. Pitching for Almendares was Raymond Brown, one of the most famous black ballplayers to play professional baseball. There were two outs and Brown had a 3 and 0 count on me. I looked around to the third base coach who gave me a take sign. Brown delivered a fast ball. I took it. "Strike One!" the umpire yelled out. This time I looked over and the third base coach gave me the hit sign. However, I decided to take it again. Brown delivered. "Strike Two!" Now I was on my own. I couldn't take a chance on a walk.

I'll never forget what happened next, not if I live to be 100. With the count now 3 and 2, Brown threw me a knuckleball that fluttered up to the plate. I swung too hard and hit a big bouncer to Bobby Avila at second. Bobby never knew how quick I was; he picked up the ball as if it was a routine grounder and made the routine peg to first. I was already past the bag. "Safe!" the umpire screamed. We won the game 8 - 7.

Bobby Avila was really angry, and he looked at me and yelled some caustic remarks about my background on the ranch. I yelled back that he should just keep quiet and play the game. We didn't know each other then. There are some ironies in this game of baseball; Bobby and I would both come up with the Cleveland Indians. He would stay and I would be traded away.

Years later, as I have mentioned, we would finish first and second in the American League batting race.

I went back to the dugout and everyone was patting me on the back and shaking my hand. The crowd was yelling, "Minoso! Minoso!" Two straight days I had broken up the game. Then to my surprise, I saw someone in the dugout. I recognized him; his name was Jose Pasquel. He and his smooth-talking brother, Bernardo, had attracted disgruntled Major League ballplayers to jump to the Mexican League. Their prime inducement was a bundle of money. Fred Martin, Max Lanier, Danny Gardella, Luis Olmo, Mickey Owen, and Sal Maglie were some of the Major League ballplayers who succumbed to their offers. In turn, Commissioner Happy Chandler proclaimed the Mexican League an "outlaw league," and announced that anyone who played there would be banned from Major League baseball for five years.

Mr. Pasquel grabbed my hand immediately and shook it. "Mr. Minoso," he said. "I want to talk with you. " He asked me to meet with him later that day at the Rio Hotel located in the Prado. I agreed, knowing that most likely I was in for the biggest sell of my life. Since I was almost broke at the time, I asked our general manager Emilio Armas to please lend me $50 and to take it out of my salary.

When I arrived at the Rio Hotel, Pasquel was waiting for me. We went up to his room and he promptly opened a big black bag, like the kind used in the army. What I saw stunned me; I had never seen so much money in my life. Thousands and thousands of American dollars in assorted bills. Then he made his offer— he would give me $10,000 to play one season in Mexico. I never knew that kind of money existed; that was big money in those days. For me particularly—big, big money. He enticed me even further by saying that Armando Marson, the team manager, would look after me and take good care of me.

"No!" I said immediately. "No!" I told him my hopes were to play baseball in the United States. That had been my dream from day one, and I made it very clear.

"I'll give you $30,000 to play for two years," he shot back instantly. "I'll put this money in the bank under your name."

I remember well what happened next. I put my hand in my pocket and showed him the $50 that I had just borrowed. "Mr.

Pasquel," I said. "Compare what you have in your bag with what I have in my hand. My $50 is like two pennies compared with what you just showed me, But money isn't everything to me. I'm going to America some day."

Then he pulled the racial card on me. He said because I was black I'd be treated like a dog in the United States. I replied that there were a lot of great black athletes playing baseball in the United States, and that I hadn't heard of many lately who were being killed or whipped like dogs.

Still he wouldn't quit. "Are you sure, Mr. Minoso? I am offering you a lot of money." Again I made it clear that the United States was my dream, and that one day I'd be playing for one of the great teams in the Negro Leagues. When that happened, I would have the pleasure of representing my native Cuba in the U.S., and that was a pleasing thought to me. I told him he was wasting his time. I excused myself and walked out the door, away from Mr. Pasquel, his black bag, all his big money, and whatever else he thought he had to offer. I never regretted this for even a second.

I hit .301 for the Marianao club that year, and was chosen "Rookie of the Year." The United States and the Negro Leagues were even closer than I had hoped when I turned down Mr. Pasquel's offer. One of the coaches at Marianao, Jose Fernandez, was the manager of the New York Cubans in the Negro Leagues. He had told Alex Pompez, the owner of the New York Cubans about me. Pompez was interested. How would I like to play baseball in New York, he asked? Did I want to play for the New York Cubans?

You bet I did! This was the dream of every black baseball player anywhere. I was thrilled and scared at the same time. I had never been out of Cuba. I had never even been on a plane. I was scared, all right. But I was also about to live out a dream. I was going to the United States to play baseball; the land where the best baseball in the world was being played.

When I met Minnie, I was with the Cleveland Buckeyes. Minnie came to the New York Cubans in 1945. I was in the western division.He was in the eastern division. I played against Minnie from 1945 through 1947. Then I made the transaction to the eastern division, when I went over to the Newark Eagles.

Minnie was an aggressive ballplayer and difficult to get out. He was not a big out for anybody. Minnie was just good at everything he did and played more than just one position, and he was a good base runner. He came to win anyway he could. He could catch anybody's signs as good as anyone in baseball. He was a student of the game, and his head was always on the field, it wasn't in the stands.

He ran his life in baseball like a business. He wanted to be successful; you knew that when you watched him play. He always had the attitude that if he wasn't the best ballplayer in a certain capacity, he wanted to be among the very best.

He gained respect as a hitter, as a fielder, and as a man on the base paths. He never ran around talking about what he could do or couldn't do, he would just do it when he got out there. In the end result, his desire was to win. I have never seen a man who was as hard a loser.

When we talked about Minnie, we talked about what a fashion plate he was. Minnie must have had more than 40 or 50 suits. Immaculately dresesd, correctly dressed, he never wore the wrong colors. He should have been a model, too. He could have worked for Esquire in those days.

He moved around a lot and enjoyed himself in those days. He didn't drink a lot like some of the guys. He always loved this game of baseball right from the beginning. It shows, it's in his heart; it's not just something he did for a living. Most of all, Minnie loved life.

People don't respect the fact that his abilities haven't ended yet. He can play now. He could play right now, and not just be out there as a figurehead. In our time, you didn't get too old to play. As long as you could perform, you could play. Fay Vincent could have made something happen in 1990 when the White Sox wanted to play Minnie, and he didn't do a damn thing. That was too bad.

Nap Gulley Negro League Star
Cleveland Buckeyes and Newark Eagles

4

THE NEW YORK CUBANS

The Negro League was an experience all its own, and one that I would not trade for the world. For starters, it gave me the opportunity to play alongside and against the best black baseball players in the world. Secondly, it gave me the chance to be seen by thousands of American baseball fans.

Finally I was able to see the United States of America, the land I had heard so much about as a child.

It was always my dream to come to America. My journey began with a plane flight from Havana to Miami. In Miami, I caught a train to New Orleans, where I joined the New York Cubans for spring training. Owned by Alex Pompez, the New York Cubans had both Cuban blacks and American blacks on its roster. We spent one month training in New Orleans before boarding the team bus for the long bus ride to New York.

It was a tiring ride. We slept a lot and usually ate our meals on the bus. Racial segregation was rampant in the South, so there were only certain places where we were allowed to get off the bus and buy things. Occasionally we would stop for something to eat at night, but we had no other sleeping accommodations other than the seats on our bus.

Yet, I enjoyed the long ride. I gazed out the window constantly, taking in sights I never dreamt I would see. I enjoyed talking and exchanging stories with my new teammates. I knew things weren't perfect here, but this was the United States of

America, and for me a dream come true. When we finally reached New York, I couldn't believe how big it really was. So many people and so many different shades and skin colors. Never in my life had I seen so many people.

There were lots of Latin people in New York as well. There certainly were many Cubans. What wonderful places to visit! What an exciting night life! Most of the time I lived on 116th Street near 7th Avenue. I learned a lot from my fellow Cuban teammate Silvio Garcia. An outstanding baseball player, he was a little too fiery for Branch Rickey's integration plans. Silvio showed me how to live, how to play, and how to relax in New York.

Buying clothes became a special fancy for me. I had so little in the way of clothes as a boy that now I wanted to compensate. My ambition had always been to dress well and to be a gentleman both on and off the field. I bought only the sharpest and most stylish outfits. Some people like to drink, others play golf. I liked buying sharp clothes. Sometimes I'd change outfits two or three times a day. I looked like a man about town, and in certain ways I guess I was.

Whenever we returned from a road trip, we'd go back to the team office on 11th Avenue to unload our gear. I'd change into one of my most spiffy outfits then take a taxi to wherever I wanted to go. I liked to dance, and New York had so many fine clubs. A particular favorite of mine was a club called *Casino Espanol*. Every conceivable nationality could be found there. A thousand people might be dancing, but never were there any arguments or fights. People just wanted to have a good time and to get along. Another favorite spot was the Paladium on 142nd St. All the great Latin bands played there, including the band of Tito Fuentes, which was one of the best around.

I loved music as well, and would spend time hearing some of the best vocalists in the world. Many became personal friends. Sarah Vaughan was one of my favorites. As a singer, she was my idol. How fortunate I was to have known Sarah well. She was a great lady, and I fell in love with her voice. Others who became good friends were Nat 'King' Cole, Billy Eckstein, and June Christy. In fact, Nat Cole once dedicated a show to me when he was performing in one of the big clubs in Havana during the winter.

Getting back to Sarah Vaughan for a moment, there is a favorite story I like to tell. It concerns Sarah, the great Heavyweight Champion Joe Louis, and myself. The three of us became close friends when I played for the White Sox and lived in Chicago. Joe and I would kid a lot, always sparring for Sarah's affection.

"Hey Minoso!" Joe would say. "Leave Sarah alone. She's my girl."

"Joe, you have so many girls. She's my sweetheart," I'd shoot back.

Joe Louis would start jabbing away. "Sarah Vaughan," he'd say. "You don't like Minnie, he can't even speak good English."

Sarah would look at Joe and smile. "Sure I do, Champ. He's my boy." Whenever I went to hear Sarah sing, she would always sing one song just for me, "Over the Rainbow."

Joe Louis was a very decent man. We were close friends at one time. When we would play in Detroit, he would let me use his apartment if I didn't want to go back to my downtown hotel. Joe's big problem was that he just wore out. He was a great champion and a classy man. He wore his Heavyweight title with dignity and pride. There was none of that vaudeville-type, "I'm the Greatest" stuff later champions seemed to thrive on. When I knew Joe Louis, he had already retired from the ring. But he was a champ outside the ring as well; a true gentleman.

New York is the first city in the United States that I got to know. I barely saw Miami. We spent most of the time training in New Orleans. To me, New York epitomized all I thought America was. I was amazed by those tunnels, especially the Lincoln Tunnel. I recall driving one day and wondering if it would ever end. I learned a lot about life living in New York. All the different people. So many different faces. I had read about these things in books and seen them in movies. Seeing the Empire State Building for the first time was just unbelievable. There are bigger skyscrapers today, but then it was by far the tallest building in the world. There was nothing to resemble it in Cuba.

When I first started playing with the New York Cubans, I was paid $300 a month. I originally signed in Cuba for $150 a month plus five dollars a day for food. Most players were given only two dollars a day for eating expenses, but because of the language handicap, the Cuban players were given a little more with the condition that we did not tell the other players.

We had some great ballplayers on the New York Cuban squad. Silvio Garcia, as I mentioned, was my roommate and was an outstanding athlete. In fact, back in 1945, Leo Durocher commented that if black ballplayers were allowed to play in the Major Leagues, he'd pay $50,000 for Silvio. He was a great shortstop with a good glove and a tremendous arm. He was a big man, weighing about 190 pounds; yet he was fast enough to beat me in a 100-yard dash.

I really wasn't a base stealer in the Negro League. I could steal bases, but my job was to run carefully and to score runs. We played our games in Yankee Stadium and the Polo Grounds; we used the same facilities and the same dressing rooms as the Yankees and the Giants. What a wonderful feeling using the Yankee locker room where the retired numbers 3 and 4 of Babe Ruth and Lou Gehrig were displayed in front of their lockers. Their uniforms, their gloves, their bats, their caps, they were all there.

When we played at the Polo Grounds, we had exactly the same uniforms and lettering as the New York Giants, except we had "Cubans" instead of "Giants" on our shirts. The same for our caps. When we played on the road, we had our own gray traveling uniforms, but they too were beautiful. We used to look better than all the other teams. We dressed well so people would know we were New Yorkers.

Most important of all, we had a good bunch of guys. Those of us who were from Cuba always tried to show our best side, because we knew we represented Cuba and the Cuban people here in the United States. We had pretty good crowds, too. We played at the Polo Grounds when the Yankees were at home. Most of the crowd was black, but white fans would watch us as well. We regularly drew about 15,000 fans, and against a team like the Kansas City Monarchs, we could draw as many as 18,000 to 20,000 fans.

Still, I had no idea that I would ever play in the Major Leagues. None of us did, until the Brooklyn Dodgers signed Jackie Robinson in 1947. If there was bitterness among the Negro League ballplayers, I never heard much of it. Most players accepted the fact that this was as far as we could go and gave their best efforts, regardless. Maybe some thought differently, but I heard little to indicate such feelings. This was our League, and we were proud of it. Many of our ballplayers felt that they could play in the majors and rightfully so. But anger and bitterness was not the order of the day. We had great respect for the Major Leagues and their players. The important thing was that their league was theirs, and our league was ours. We were very proud of what we had.

The three years I played with the New York Cubans gave me the chance to play against and alongside many of the best black ballplayers, ever. One whom I have never forgotten was the great Josh Gibson. Josh was a big, baby-faced guy. He was very strong, although not as aggressive as he might have been. He was a quiet, easygoing man. He smiled a lot and liked to kid around. Josh had a nice easy way about him. But he could hit; boy could he hit.

Once we were playing in Pittsburgh in the old Forbes Field. There was a man on first and nobody out. I was playing third, and the manager started waving me back. "Minoso, back," he yelled. "Move back!" So I moved back and positioned myself. Because we were leading by just one run, I still believed that Josh would bunt. Was I surprised! He hit one so hard that it bounced off my glove and into the box seats for an automatic double. I couldn't believe how hard he had hit it. As he ran to second base, he looked over to our pitcher Pat Scateberry and laughed.

"Hey Pat, keep pitching me there, and I'll move the right field bleachers back. Keep pitching me outside, and I'll kill somebody in the bleachers."

Comparisons are always hard to make. I feel that Josh Gibson could have played with the best the Majors had to offer. Many others as well could have competed, but were denied entry because of the color barrier. Others eventually became great Major League stars. The Negro Leagues have been reinvented today, and that is good. There is a renewed interest in them. There is even a tendency among some to put the Negro Leagues on a par with Major League Baseball. This is difficult to assess. We had some of the best ballplayers I have ever seen anywhere. We also had others who could never have made it past Double A ball. In this respect, it was not unlike Cuba. What I do know is that I have been privileged to have been associated with the two greatest baseball leagues anywhere in the world. The Negro Leagues carry a rich and proud tradition. I am just so happy to have been a part of it.

And I certainly did play with many greats who could light up any baseball diamond. One was Monte Irvin who would have some fine years with the New York Giants. Monte led the National League in runs batted in 1951 and helped to lead the Giants to the National League flag that year. Monte was one of the unfortunate ones. He came up to the big leagues about ten years too late.

I remember playing against him in Cuba when he was with the Newark Eagles, and I have a scar on my lip to prove it. It was 1948, and we were involved in an extra-inning game. One of the great pitchers, April Bonyhill, was on the mound for us. He was a short little guy with lots of stuff. The game was scoreless in the 12th inning. Monte Irvin was at bat and hit a sharp ground ball to third. It bounced up and hit me in the mouth. I had six stitches as a result. Later, I heard we lost the game 1 to 0.

Another great player with the Newark Eagles who would later become a good friend and teammate was Larry Doby. He was well ahead of everybody; that's how good he was. Of course, Larry was the first black in the American League, and was instrumental in leading the Cleveland Indians to the World Championship in 1948. He played the game so aggressively. Larry was originally a second baseman; a lot of folks don't know that. Larry also had lots of style. Good looking, well dressed, he seemed to tower over everyone. When you looked at him, you'd say to yourself that this is a guy who belongs on a poster board. No one ever looked better in a baseball uniform.

A lot of players didn't like Doby because of these characteristics. On the bases he was such an aggressive slider. He was a rough, tough guy who wouldn't let anyone push him around. If you didn't mess with Larry, he was just a quiet, elegant man who could play baseball well. If you overstepped your bounds with him, he could let you have it.

I knew Satchel Page and played against him when he pitched for the Kansas City Monarchs. One thing I'll never forget is a game in the Polo Grounds when we were losing by about four or five runs. There were two men on base and two outs. I was the batter. Satchel gave me an intentional pass to get at the next hitter, Fernando Pedroso. Than zap! He quickly fanned Pedroso to win the game.

Fernando Pedroso was a lot like me. He laughed and talked a lot and liked to have a good time. Now it seemed that the owner of the ballclub, Alejandro Pompez, had promised Pedroso two expensive hats if he got two hits off of Satchel Page. Somehow Satchel found out about it. After he fanned Pedroso, he started laughing up a storm and said, "So, you thought you could get a couple of hits off me, did you, Pedroso!" I couldn't stop laughing myself. It was just as well, because I would have had a hard time hitting him. I'm just as happy he walked me and saved me some likely embarrassment. I probably would have struck out too.

Satchel was not only fast, he knew how to pitch. Exactly how fast he was is hard to say, because they didn't have the gun in those days. But he was right up there with Bob Feller and Nolan Ryan. I faced lots of great ones in my time and I can say in all certainty that Satchel Page was one of the greatest pitchers who ever lived.

One time I really got Satchel mad. Many people don't know that we were both with the Cleveland Indians in 1949. Satchel was an ageless sophomore with the club, and I was a rookie for a short time before I was sent down to San Diego.

Satchel and I shared a berth on the train while we were traveling. Well, I parked myself in the lower berth, which was not good protocol for a young rookie. When Satchel went to retire for the night, he was forced to take the upper berth, much to his dismay. He sure was a little peeved at this young rookie. I learned quickly not to break rank. Baseball had a definite seniority system.

Another guy who could throw steam was Sad Sam Jones. Old "Toothpick Sam" hit me in the head once in a game we played at the Polo Grounds. Being hit was nothing new to me, but getting hit like that was something you never forget. Sam could throw fast all right, but he was wild. He was the kind of guy who would either walk you or strike you out. I think it was in 1955, when Sam was pitching for the Chicago Cubs, he pitched one of the strangest no-hitters ever. In the top of the ninth he walked with the bases loaded. Then he bore down and proceeded to strike out the next three hitters—one, two, three. In spite of his faulty control, Sam Jones put together some pretty good years with the Cubs, the Cardinals, and the Giants, including two 20-game seasons.

Of all the Major League teams, the old Brooklyn Dodgers were ahead of the pack in signing black ballplayers. I regret not having played against Jackie Robinson in the Negro League. That was because we were each in different leagues. But I did play against Jackie in an All Star Game. I never had the pleasure of meeting him until I was a Major League ballplayer myself. We never became close friends or talked a lot, but he was always very cordial to me.

I had the greatest respect for Jackie. Only through him were so many other black ballplayers able to make the big leagues. He had such raw courage. Too many people today do not know all that he did and what he went through—the taunts and insults he had to endure without being allowed the luxury of fighting back. That was true courage. Jackie Robinson was a great role model for young people; a four-letter athlete at UCLA who served his country with great distinction as an officer during World War II.

There were some other Dodger ballplayers I got to know better. A real good one was Don Newcombe. Newk gave me lots of trouble; I couldn't follow the rotation on his pitches. When a hitter cannot follow the rotation, he is in trouble. Newcombe's big problem when he pitched in Cuba was that he was wild. Because of that, few people thought he would ever be the dominant pitcher he later became with the Dodgers.

Two future greats I never played against were Hank Aaron and Willie Mays. I met Willie briefly when he was in Cuba; he didn't remain there long, only about one month. I was never sure why.

I played three-and-a-half seasons with the New York Cubans, 1945, 1946, 1947, and part of 1948. I can't say for sure what I hit the first three years. I only know that each year I was getting better. By 1948, I was batting way over .300 and getting a lot of attention. By then, of course, Jackie had already established himself, having been selected Rookie of the Year in 1947. In 1948, Roy Campanella was behind the plate for the Dodgers. Larry Doby had already come up with the Cleveland Indians and was in the starting line-up when the 1948 season unfolded.

With the integration of Major League baseball a reality, my ambition only increased. For the first time, I realized I had a chance to be a big-league ballplayer. I think that was true of others as well. It doesn't mean that we weren't trying like hell before, only now we knew we had to be better. Before we could say, "That's it. That's as far as I can go." Now enough was never enough. It was, so to speak, an entirely new ballgame.

I was not a home run hitter with the Cubans. I hit lots of doubles and triples, and I always tried to stretch the extra base. I had good speed and ran the bases well. I hustled and had a great throwing arm. I hit 22 home runs at San Diego in 1949 and 20 in 1950. I would not hit that many again until I hit 21 home runs with the Chicago White Sox in 1956.

1948 was a big year for me. I was having my best season with the New York Cubans and was selected to the All Star team. We played two All Star Games that year, the first in Chicago, and the second in New York. My teammate Jose Santiago, a young right hander with lots of stuff, and myself were both named to the All Star squad. Jose was a small guy from Puerto Rico with a good fastball and a good curve. Being from Puerto Rico, he also spoke fluent English.

Before the game, Jose told me that there was a scout from the Cleveland Indians who was interested in me. Jose said that the scout had spoken to him because he could speak better English. He said that Cleveland might sign both of us, but that I was the one they really wanted. It was a big chance for me and I knew it.

At my first time at bat in the lead-off position, I hit a little pop fly blooper over the shortstop's head. I just turned on the steam and kept running. By the time the fielders could make up their minds, I was on second with a double. My next time up, I hit a line-drive single to win the game. I went two-for-three and fielded like a champ at third base that day.

After the game the scout approached me. It was August 22, 1948; how well I remember. He told me he had purchased my contract from Mr. Pompez, the owner of the New York Cubans. The Indians also purchased the contract of right hander Jose Santiago.

We never found out how much money our contracts were purchased for. However, we did tell Mr. Pompez that we felt we were entitled to some money to hold us over. He gave us perhaps eleven or twelve hundred dollars. I'm not sure of the exact amount, but it wasn't very much. There was a month to go in the season, and the Negro Leagues were behind us. Our new destination was Dayton, Ohio, the Class A affiliate of the Cleveland Indians.

Minnie joined us in Tucson for spring trainng in 1949 after Bill Veeck purchased the club. He was outstanding in speed, throwing, and playing his position. He was a foreigner to some of the traditions we had; he had to learn to put his valuables in the valuable trunk. He didn't realize what the trunk was for.

We had been World Champions in 1948. There were a lot of sportswriters there in spring training, and Minnie took to everything very well. He was very sociable, and a very congenial young man. I knew he had the ability to run, throw, and to hit. What worried me was how he would handle the type of play we had in the Major Leagues, and how it compared with his play in Cuba and in the Negro Leagues. His fundamentals were great, and he learned to take different signs, catching on very fast. He was a very friendly individual and had friends all over the place.

He was sent down to San Diego in 1949; it takes a little while to grasp the Major League style. He was a raw star in the beginning, but in only two years he was a seasoned ballplayer.

One story about Minnie that I remember concerns that valuable trunk that he didn't trust. He put all his money and his change and whatever else he had in his jock strap. Well I didn't know that, and one particular day he attempted to steal second. He took a diving slide and knocked himself out, and all his valuables spilled out on the field.

He came up as a third baseman, and I told him we had Al Rosen coming up. I couldn't see him beating out Rosen, so I suggested he work in the outfield. He had good speed and his knowledge of the game defensively was very good. He knew how to hit the grass with his throw and where it would skip. Minnie became an excellent outfielder.

Lou Boudreau, Hall of Fame, 1970

Minnie was a very fine ballplayer. He really bloomed in Chicago, where he became a very good hitter. He could hit the inside pitch to right field like Luke Appling. And as an outfielder he was good. He had an exceptionally good arm, and he was a very good base runner. He had that great personality, which was a great help to him and still is. I see him at Oldtimers' games and social functions. He looks great. Minnie is a real personality, and he's a great athlete who is good for the game of baseball. He's always promoting the game of baseball, like Mudcat Grant. There's nothing wrong with that; we all do it, because we love this game.

Bob Feller, Hall of Fame, 1962

5

ALMOST THERE

To Cleveland and Back

There I was. Just a step from the Major Leagues. It had all happened so quickly. I did very well at Dayton, hitting about .525 for the month of September. The manager later told me that the Indians had flirted with bringing me up in September instead of sending me to Dayton, but he had suggested otherwise. If I went to Cleveland, he argued, I would only sit on the bench. In 1948, the Cleveland Indians were locked in an extremely tight pennant race with the Yankees and the Red Sox, a pennant that they took by beating the Boston Red Sox in a one-game postseason play-off.

As it was, things worked out well. I had a great month of September at Dayton. I was also able to play winter ball in Cuba with the Marianao club. The Indians had a team policy that if you were involved in a World Series, you were not allowed to play winter ball in the off months.

But I did have to deal with something new. For the first time in my career, I was the only black player on my team. In fact, there were only about four or five black ballplayers in the entire Central League. My good friend, Jose Santiago, helped me with my English, and that made things much easier. But Jose was more brown skinned than black and could stay with the whites. I stayed at a black hotel and with black families when we were on the road.

I have no way of knowing how the Dayton folks felt about having a black ball player around. If there were feelings of hostility, I never heard them expressed openly. A few guys slid into me hard on the ballfield, but that was it. On one occasion, my teammates backed me up completely. We were playing somewhere in Indiana when one of their guys came into me unnecessarily hard. He directed some nasty names my way. When he came to bat, he learned a lesson. Our pitcher sent him to the ground with a couple of high, inside pitches under the chin. The guy got the message and never bothered me again.

There is another incident that I'll always remember because it taught me a valuable lesson. One afternoon I was at bat with two runners on base; the count was 3 and 0. The manager wanted me to take the next pitch, but I wasn't quite sure about the signs. I was confused, so I looked over at Jose Santiago in the dugout. Jose indicated that I should swing, and swing I did. The ball went over the fence in right center for a three-run homer. The crowd was roaring.

We won the game, but the manager was far from happy. He came down on me pretty hard. "Minoso," he said, "'take it' means look, not swing." Jose took the blame. The manager came down even harder on him. "Look!" he told my compadre, "This guy is already supposed to be in the big leagues. Instead of helping him, you will confuse him and make him a worse player."

I wanted to make sure that would never happen again. It was my responsibility to learn the signals, language problem or not. When I returned to my hotel room, I got an idea. I drew sketches of little ballplayers on my wall. I had each one doing something else. If he was touching his cap, for example, then I knew it was a take sign. I made similar diagrams for bunt, hit and run, steal, and other signs. The chest would mean bunt. The left foot would be hit and run. The right foot would be steal. The top of the belt would be squeeze. Whenever I came back from a game, I would sit down on the bed and give the signals to myself. That was the last time I would ever get in trouble for missing a sign.

Jose "Pantalones" Santiago would spend some brief time with the Cleveland Indians and the Kansas City Athletics in the mid-50s. He had promise as a pitcher, but he was more dedicated to horse racing, his real passion. Unlike most of the Latin ballplayers, Jose did not need baseball for financial security. His father was a doctor in Puerto Rico, so Jose was never forced to take the kind of flack many other Latin ballplayers had to take. Jose was a nice guy, but because of his financial condition, he could tell you what he really thought and he often did. Jose Santiago has done very well as a boxing promoter in Puerto Rico. About three years ago, the White Sox were playing an exhibition game in Puerto Rico, and I saw him after so many years. Now in his mid sixties, he's made lots of money. We had a wonderful reunion together.

Dayton was in the Central League, where a good brand of baseball was played. We finished fourth that year. I recall that one time on the road, the bus unloaded at the hotel; I believe it was in Waukegan, Illinois. The bellhop saw me sitting in the bus and mentioned to someone how nice it was that the team had a black batboy. One of my teammates set him straight and said I was not the bat boy. Rather, I was the best player on the club, and that he should go to the ballpark and see for himself. He attended the game, and I obliged him by going four for four.

I had enough money now to provide myself with something I desired all my life; my first car. Flashy cars and sporty clothes came to be associated with Minnie Minoso for many years to come. And like a first love, a young man rarely forgets his first car. This one wasn't particularly flashy, but it was nice car, and it was mine. It was a 1947 four-door brown Plymouth Sedan. Since I didn't drive, I had someone else drive with me to Miami. I put the car on a ferry boat and brought it back to Cuba with me. Soon my cars became the talk of the Cuban people.

The Cuban people knew then that I had a real shot at the Major Leagues. Jackie Robinson and Larry Doby had cleared the way for others like myself. Marianao paid me $600 a month, which was a lot of money at the time. That winter, I received a contract from the Cleveland Indians. I was told to report to Tucson, Arizona, in March for spring training.

The Cleveland Indians were the reigning World Champions of baseball in the spring of 1949. What a team they were! Player/manager Lou Boudreau had been an inspiration both in and out of the dugout. In guiding the Indians to their first American League pennant and World Series title since 1920, Lou hit .355 with 18 homers and 106 runs batted in.

Bob Feller was the biggest name on the team. He was still very fast. In addition to Lou Boudreau and Bob Feller, the Indians were packed solid with guys like second baseman, Joe Gordon, and third baseman, Kenny Keltner. Gordon and Keltner provided lots of power in 1948, hitting 32 and 31 home runs, respectively, and driving in more than 100 runs each. Larry Doby had a great rookie year, hitting a solid .301. Left fielder Dale Mitchell hit a hefty .336, third in the American League behind Ted Williams and Lou Boudreau.

Talk about pitching. The Indians were just loaded. Bob Lemon posted the first of his seven 20-game seasons with the Indians in 1948. Bob Feller was still Bob Feller. Gene Beardon went 20 and 7, including that final playoff win against the Red Sox, and led the American League with a 2.43 ERA in 1948. He never came close again. The hitters waited on him in 1949, and Gene's record plummeted to 8 and 8, with an over-5.00 ERA. But the staff was bolstered greatly in 1949 with the addition of right hander Mike Garcia and tough Early Wynn who came to Cleveland in a trade with the Washington Senators. Bob Lemon, Mike Garcia, and Early Wynn would give the Cleveland Indians the Majors' best trio of starters for many years. To make things even nicer, Jim Hegan was the best defensive catcher in the American League and would remain so for years to come.

As with the Dodgers, the Cleveland Indians were far ahead of their time in signing black ballplayers. I was not the only black player in camp that spring. Larry Doby and Satchel Paige were there. Old Satch had shown them all after joining the Indians in 1948. He won six and lost just once during the year. Harry 'Suitcase' Simpson, Al Smith, Toothpick Sam Jones, and Luke Easter were also in the Indians Organization.

The player who helped me the most that spring was Bob Kennedy. Bob taught me a lot about playing the outfield. Remember, I had been a third baseman with the New York Cubans. He really showed me how to throw from the outfield. Bob Kennedy had one of the finest arms from right field I have ever seen. The only other American League right field arm to compare with his belonged to Rocky Colavito. Rocky Colavito and I were teammates with the Cleveland Indians in 1958 and 1959. Then in the National League, you had Roberto Clemente and Carl Furillo of the Brooklyn Dodgers.

I had a good, strong arm, but my outfield throws seemed to sink off just before they got to the base. What Bob showed me was how to hold the ball close. I used to throw the ball just as I picked it up. Bob taught me to quickly get the right feel on the ball before I uncorked my throw. The throw would stay true longer and not tail off. If I would have learned that earlier, I could have avoided a lot of errors.

Most of my time that spring was spent at third base. I was still an outfielder in training. We had some promising infielders in spring camp as well. Bobby Avila was just a couple of years away from replacing Joe Gordon as the Indians' regular second baseman. Ray Boone, a converted catcher, was waiting in the shadows to replace Boudreau at short. And Al Rosen was my main rival to take over the third base chores from Ken Keltner.

He didn't make it easy for me, either. When we'd be working out together at third, Al had a habit of shooting right in front of me to take Bob Kennedy's throw from right field. He did the same thing when we worked out together in right field.

I had a strong arm and the other guys liked to see me throw, but Al would cut the ball off in front of me and make the throw himself.

One day Boudreau asked me why I wasn't throwing more from the field. I told him the truth. That everywhere I went Rosen was cutting me off. Lou told Rosen to stay at third and to let me throw from right field. In spite of our competition with one another, Ken Keltner was still the slated third baseman. Al and I would both be sent down for more seasoning. But the next year Rosen replaced Keltner at the hot corner. All he did was to lead the American League in home runs with 37 and drive in 116 runs in his rookie year of 1950.

I would play seven games in the outfield for Cleveland in 1949 before being sent down to San Diego. I was up 16 times and got three hits including my first Major League home run against the Boston Red Sox. It was at San Diego that I really learned to become an outfielder. It was the right move; my career would not have been nearly as good as a third baseman.

There is one story I love to tell about spring training with Cleveland in 1949. A bunch of the players were involved in a little pepper game. I was the guy who was hitting the ball. Bobby Avila threw the ball, and I peppered it back to this guy who missed it. The ball rolled to the fence. Half kidding I yelled to the guy, "Hey boy, get the ball!" "Sure Orestes," the guy answered. "I'll get it!" He kind of limped over to the fence to get the ball. Later I saw the guy in the clubhouse. I turned to Bobby Avila. "Hey Bobby," I said, pointing at him, "Who's this guy anyhow?" Bobby starts laughing. "You know what Minoso, the guy you called 'boy' before, just happens to be the boss. He's the guy who pays us. That's Mr. Bill Veeck!"

The manager of the San Diego Padres was Bucky Harris. Bucky, who had managed the New York Yankees to a World Championship in 1947, was fired by the team when the Yankees fell to third place in 1948. Bucky was a good baseball man. So was coach Jimmy Reese who coached all those years with the Dodgers. We had a real good hitter in Max West. Max was an outfielder who never could hit big league pitching like he hit on the Coast. He owned the pitchers in the Pacific Coast League. Harry Simpson, Al Smith, Al Rosen, and Luke Easter were teammates of mine at San Diego in 1949.

Luke Easter was a good friend of mine in those days. I was shocked and saddened when I read that Luke had been killed in the streets a few years ago. Luke Easter was a big and powerful man, about 6'5" tall and almost 250 pounds. He had a great body; strong as a rock. Yet he had a baby face that gave him an aura of innocence. He even played like a kid.

Luke was my roommate at San Diego. We'd travel around a lot after hours, and he really knew the streets. But management didn't approve of our association. Luke had a passion for women, and the owners felt he was a bad influence on me. I told Luke that the club didn't want me hanging around him, and that I didn't know quite why. I think he was hurt, but said he understood.

Big Luke replaced Mickey Vernon as the Indians' regular first baseman in 1950, after Vernon was traded to the Washington Senators. All he did that year was to hit 28 homers and drive in 108 runs. Luke averaged 30 homers and more than a hundred RBIs from 1950 through 1952 when he was the Indians' starting first baseman. Then his legs went out, and the combination of bad legs and heavy living ended his promising career prematurely. He played in only six games in 1954, and by 1955 Luke Easter was out of baseball.

The Pacific Coast League was interesting and certainly worth the mention. Lots of folks don't realize that we would play more than 180 games a year. In some respects, it was an entity unto itself, because in those days St. Louis was the westernmost city in the Major Leagues. We would play each club for a seven-game series. For example if we were playing the Los Angeles Angels or the Hollywood Stars—or for that matter any of the seven other teams—we would play our first game on Tuesday. Then we would play single games Wednesday, Thursday, Friday, and Saturday, and wind up with a doubleheader on Sunday.

There were fine stadiums as well. The best, I think, were Wrigley Field in Los Angeles and Seals Stadium in San Francisco. We had a pretty good park in San Diego, too. But it could not compare with Los Angeles, San Francisco, Hollywood, or Seattle. The Seattle park was like a Major League stadium itself. I liked San Diego very much then, and I still do now. The people were friendly and the weather just ideal. My daughter, Marilyn, lives there today so I get to visit regularly. There's a big hotel now where the stadium once was. Like cities everywhere, so much has changed.

Certain Coast League ballplayers actually made more money than some Major Leaguers. At times, they even had to take salary cuts once they reached the Major Leagues. Again, Max West comes to mind. Max played a number of years in the Major Leagues, never hitting more than 19 home runs in a single season. When he began playing in the Coast League, he always batted around .300 and hit 30 homers each year. He never made the money in the Majors that he did in the Coast League.

I made $500 or $600 less at San Diego than I made when I signed with Cleveland. There were two reasons for this. First I didn't come here with a big name like some ex-Major Leaguers. Secondly, my language problem didn't exactly help me with my contract. There were no agents like today. When the contract came through the mail, I'd discuss it with my cousin and if it looked pretty good to us we would sign it.

I was with San Diego in 1949 and 1950. Many of us, including Al Smith, Harry Simpson, Luke Easter, Al Rosen, and I went on to productive big-league careers. I hit .297 with 22 home runs and 75 RBI's at San Diego in 1949. Then in 1950 I hit .339 with 203 base hits, the only time in my entire baseball career that I topped the 200 hit mark in a season. I drove in 115 runs, and my .339 average was second to Frankie Baumholtz who led the Coast League in hitting with a mark of .345.

But things did not always go smoothly between myself and Hank Greenberg, who was Bill Veeck's second in command at Cleveland. After I hit .297 in 1949, Greenberg told me that it was the policy of the ballclub not to let anyone who would be up the following year tire themselves by playing winter ball. I believed him and sat the winter out at great financial hardship. I went to spring training with the Indians in 1950, and I played a few games before getting hurt. I worked my way into shape and joined the club in San Diego for an exhibition game. Then, instead of keeping me, the Indians left me there for more minor league seasoning. When I finally spoke to Greenberg about that issue, I made my position clear. In straight money talk, his ruling cost me about $2,000. I reminded him that I had made my mother a promise before she died that I would take care of my sisters. What little money I had went toward helping my sisters and paying rent myself. The money from winter ball would have helped out a lot. In a sense it was like stealing money from my pocket.

Hank Greenberg told me that he had nothing to do with the decision to keep me at San Diego. The idea probably originated somewhere else in the organization, he assured me. After this little exchange, our relationship improved. The next year, after the season ended, I was allowed to play winter ball in Cuba. But truly, I could see myself again spending the 1951 season at San Diego for the third straight year.

But something had been going on of which I had been totally unaware. It seems there was someone out there looking attentively at my every move on the ballfield. He was an ex-Major League catcher by the name of Paul Richards, who was now managing the Seattle club in the Pacific Coast League. I guess he was quite impressed by my play, because he made himself a promise. If he were to ever manage a Major League team, he would do everything in his power to obtain my services. Of course I never knew this, so I didn't pay any particular attention when I read that Paul Richards had been signed to manage the Chicago White Sox in November 1950. How could I know that a change of managers on the south side of Chicago would also change the entire course of my life? So much for destiny.

I went to Tucson again for spring training in 1951. Much had changed in the Cleveland camp in two years. Al Lopez, himself a big league catcher for 19 years, was now the Cleveland manager. Bill Veeck was gone too, having taken ownership of the St. Louis Browns. The Indians had dropped to third place in 1949, then one notch to fourth place in 1950 behind the Yankees, Tigers, and Red Sox. Al Lopez spoke some Spanish, which made things a little easier and a bit more comfortable for me. Yet I did not speak to Lopez in Spanish. I was in America and my job was to speak English. I never wanted any special favors, no matter what the problem might be.

Even though they finished in fourth place, the Indians won 92 ball games in 1950 and had quite a team. Their pitching staff was clearly baseball's best. Bob Lemon had led the League with 23 wins in 1950. Early Wynn won 18 games and led the American League in earned run average. Feller, though no longer overpowering, could still pitch, and would have a great comeback season in 1951. And Mike Garcia was about to become a 20-game winner.

With Luke Easter and Al Rosen at first and third, there was power to spare on the corners. Bobby Avila and Ray Boone had replaced Gordon and Boudreau at second and short. Jim Hegan was the classiest catcher in baseball. A superb defensive catcher, he handled himself like a movie star around the plate. As good a catcher as Yogi Berra was, Hegan was better defensively. Outfielders Dale Mitchell and Larry Doby both hit better than .290, and Bob Kennedy was still a fine right fielder with an arm second to none.

Perhaps the adrenaline was especially active that spring. My confidence began to soar, and my bat was hotter than the Tucson sun. I was having a great spring, yet I never took anything for granted. Each day was a new day. Each time at bat was a new time at bat.

When the season opened in April, I wasn't in the starting line-up. I was getting my share of playing time, however, as a replacement for Luke Easter at first base. I remember well a game in Detroit. I had replaced Luke at first base. There was a man on third and two outs. Bob Lemon was on the mound. The batter hit a ground ball to Lemon. It looked easy enough. But in his effort to make a simple peg to first, his throw somehow hit the ground.

If I had missed it, the game would have been tied. But I scooped it out of the dirt for the final out. Lemon looked so relieved. "Don't worry about it, Bob," I yelled. "I'm Lou Gehrig in Technicolor!"

I had friends in Cleveland. A feeling of belonging that I thought I could never find elsewhere. I was able to pal around again with Luke Easter, and Larry Doby and I had become good friends although Larry was married and living with his family in Cleveland.

Everything about Cleveland's Municipal Stadium looked good to me: the infield, the design, the lakefront, and the capacity to hold so many fans. Other guys would get out of the clubhouse fast. I was an independent guy. I liked to dress my best, so I would be one of the last guys to leave the clubhouse. There would be kids outside wanting autographs. I never refused; baseball was my life, and it had been so since I was a boy. So I never forgot how important we were to these kids. They would follow me from the ballpark to downtown Cleveland. Sometimes I'd sit with them and talk.

So I never expected what was about to happen. I had played both ends of a doubleheader against the Browns in late April. Luke Easter's knee was acting up, so I was in the line-up for both games. I went four for four the first game, and three for four the second game. We lost both games, but my average had soared to .429.

After the second game, I was getting myself together in the clubhouse. I was by my locker when Al Lopez called me over from the other side of the locker room. I felt he was going to congratulate me on going 7 for 8 on the day, or maybe mention an error that I had made. Instead he simply said, "Minoso, you have just been traded to the Chicago White Sox." That was it. There were no soothing words, no warmth, no show of appreciation. Just, "Minoso, you've been traded to Chicago." That was it. Just like that, they let me go.

I had never expected that. Not in my wildest dreams. Cleveland had become my surrogate family. I was starting to play more regularly and was hitting well. I was hurt, very hurt and disappointed. We hadn't even reached the month of May, and I thought my life had ended. Little did I know that a new and wonderful life was just about to begin.

The first time I saw Minnie play was in Puerto Rico in 1948 when we went to play one of the Cuban clubs. Then in 1950, when I came to the White Sox, he was in the Cleveland organization. He played in San Diego that year and had a very good season, and in 1951 he was traded to Chicago. I remember well, because Paul Richards was our manager and we had a meeting before the game. Richards told us that Minnie was coming to Chicago and he would be the first black player in the city. Paul told us how he was going to help the ballclub; that he was a very nice guy and an outstanding baseball player. He asked if there were any objections, but there were none. When Minnie heard about the meeting some time later, he asked me, "Chico, how come you didn't raise your hand?" I told him, "Minnie, if I had objected, Paul Richards would have shipped me back to Venezuela."

I was very happy about the news. I had heard of Minnie and had watched him play, but I had never met him. Then the first time he came to the plate he hit a 415-foot homer off Vic Raschi into the centerfield bullpen. Everybody was happy, but most especially the Latin players.

We then started winning almost immediately. We had more fans in the stands then we had ever had. To me, Minnie was one of the best baseball players I ever saw in the big leagues. He'd give you 100 percent every day. He could run, he could field, he had a good arm, and he could steal the bases. He could do everything. A lot of people talk of Roberto Clemente and Willie Mays in the National League. I think in the American League, Minnie was one of the best outfielders I ever saw.

Minnie and I were good friends off the field. Let me tell you, there were places where he couldn't get off the bus with the rest of the team, but we had lots of fun traveling on the train. We'd sit up and talk until 1:00 or 2:00 in the morning about his growing up in Cuba and how he worked with the sugar cane in Cuba.

Playing the outfield in those days, there was no protection on the outfield walls as there is today. Once I remember we were playing the Yankees in Comiskey Park one Sunday, and someone hit a fly ball close to the fence. I saw Minnie go after the ball and hit the fence with his face. He didn't feel the pain, he just kept on playing.

I think he has a good chance to get into the Hall of Fame. I'm not just being a sentimental friend. He had some great years; he hit over .300, he was a good RBI man, and a good outfielder. He stole bases. He was a complete baseball player, as complete as anyone I have seen. I believe completely that Minnie could have played in that sixth decade game last year. He's a remarkable athlete and he can still swing the bat. It's too bad he couldn't have done it.

Chico Carrasquel, first Latin baseball player
to start in an All-Star game, 1951.

6

1951 AND THE "GO GO" WHITE SOX

It was a long and lonely train ride from St. Louis back to Cleveland, maybe the loneliest of my life. What would I do in Chicago? I would be the first black to play Major League ball in the city. How would the city react? What about my teammates? I was not afraid. I was uncertain. And with uncertainty, you begin to question your confidence.

I went to my room and locked the door. I didn't talk to anyone. I didn't put on music. I just laid in bed and stared at the ceiling. There were more than a few tears. I felt like I was lost, and I didn't know what to do.

Then there was a knock on my door. It was Ray Boone, who had recently replaced Lou Boudreau as the Cleveland shortstop. I'll never forget his words. "Minoso," he said calmly. "This is good for you. I hoped if someone would be traded it would be me. You are going to have a chance to play in Chicago and the people are going to like you right away. You are a very good ballplayer and this is going to help your career."

Ray was a class act. While we respected each other and got along fine on the field, we hadn't known each other long enough to have become good friends. Yet Ray was the only one on the squad to offer this kind of solace. Ray Boone would get his wish two years later. He was traded to the Detroit Tigers where he immediately became an All Star third baseman and one of the

American League's better run producers. Ray drove in 114 runs after being traded to the Tigers in 1953, and in 1955, Ray led the American League with 116 runs batted in.

When we returned to Cleveland, I got word that Hank Greenberg wanted to see me. With Bill Veeck gone, Greenberg was in charge of the Indians' front office. I was still quite angry when I went to the club house to clear out my gear. But I swallowed my pride and went to see him. There was another factor involved as well. I began to think how lucky I was; even if things would go no further, at least I was here. I was a kid from Cuba who grew up picking sugar cane, who had made it to America and the Big Leagues. Never in all my dreams did I think it would even go this far.

Hank Greenberg was waiting for me in his office. He knew that I had been avoiding him and asked me why. Frankly, I told him that I thought I had done real well with Cleveland and could not understand why they wanted to trade me. What more could I have possibly done to make the club!

Greenberg replied that I had certainly made the ballclub. There was no doubt about that. But the White Sox wanted me very badly, and Cleveland needed some left-handed pitching to help take on the New York Yankees, and had a chance to pick up Lou Brissie from the Philadelphia Athletics. Brissie had won 37 games in three seasons with the Athletics in spite of the great handicap of a leg badly shriveled by a war injury. The White Sox would not be a part of any deal unless they could get me. They wouldn't settle for anyone else. I still didn't buy the entire explanation. I said that maybe the Indians just had too many black ballplayers and didn't want to play so many Negros. That was why I was expendable. And if so, why did it have to be me?

I accepted my fate with difficulty. I did make one request, however. I asked Greenberg if he would talk with Frank Lane and ask the White Sox general manager if he would buy me a car and deduct the amount from my paycheck in some reasonable way. At Cleveland I could live in the downtown area and walk to the ballpark. Now I was going to a strange city with little money, and would need a car to get around. Greenberg assured me he would do all he could. He would talk with Frank Lane.

There were no tearful farewells. I simply said goodbye to the guys I was most friendly with and boarded the train for

Chicago. I was met at Union Station in Chicago by some people who knew me from the Negro Leagues, Mr. and Mrs Lewis. They rented me a room in their house at 6409 S. Maryland. I lived with the Lewis' the whole year. I ate there and sometimes cooked for them. The following year I turned the room over to Hector Rodriguez, a fellow Cuban who was slated to be the new White Sox third baseman.

It was Mr. Lewis who took me to Comiskey Park on the streetcar the morning of May 1, 1951. He was in the stands when I hit my historic first inning home run off Vic Raschi of the New York Yankees. After the game, Mr. Lewis came to the clubhouse to take me home, once again on the streetcar.

People say that my debut with the Chicago White Sox is the stuff from which legends are made. Perhaps so! I sure remember that day. My debut was at third base, not in the outfield. Paul Richards batted me third in the order. Paul Lehner, who came to the White Sox from the Philadelphia Athletics in the same three-way trade, singled, putting a runner on first. I was up, and Eddie Robinson, our big first baseman was on deck. Eddie had been around for a while and was a darn good hitter. He called me over. "Minoso, do you know Vic Raschi?," he asked. I said "No!" I had never faced him, nor had ever seen him pitch for that matter.

"Be careful," Eddie warned, "he throws fast, real fast. He also throws a good slider and a good sinker. Be careful!" I told Eddie that I was going to swing hard at the first good pitch. If I struck out, it might have been all over. But if I made contact, I would have a chance. I'm glad Eddie Robinson talked to me. That's why I was so ready when I came to bat.

Funny, but I don't remember taking Raschi's first pitch for a ball. I remember only hitting the ball hard and hitting it far. I watched the center fielder run and run, back to the wall. At first I could have sworn he caught it. But then I realized that it had cleared the fence into the bullpen for a home run.

I think the pitch I hit was a fast slider, but I'm just not sure. When a hitter gets real good wood on the ball, it's hard to tell exactly where the pitch is. Maybe Yogi Berra remembers; he was behind the plate for the Yankees that day. The only guy I knew who could tell exactly where he hit a baseball was Ted Williams. Ted was without question the very best hitter I have seen anywhere. A hitter like him comes around once every fifty years, and that may be stretching things a bit.

It was only when I heard stories or read accounts of the game that I came to realize that I actually took one pitch for a ball before I hit his second pitch into the bullpen. I might also add that same May 1st afternoon, an 18-year-old crew cut kid in Yankee pinstripes named Mickey Mantle hit the first of his 536 career home runs for the New York Yankees.

Before proceeding with the 1951 baseball season, permit me to talk about my new team, the Chicago White Sox, the players and the management. And what better place to start than with the skipper himself, Mr. Paul Richards.

Without qualification or reservation, leaving no room for hesitation or ambiguity, I can say that Paul Richards was the best manager I have ever played for. Paul was the most knowledgeable baseball man I have ever known, and I have known many in my time. I wish I could have played my entire career with Richards. He knew every aspect of the game and was responsible for pushing my career wide open. Only Casey Stengel was in his league as a manager.

Paul treated everyone the same. The rules applied to everyone, whether you were a big star, a journeyman ballplayer, or an untested rookie. Pitching, defense, and speed were the ingredients he employed to build a team best suited for a ballfield like Comiskey Park. He felt strongly enough to trade away Gus Zernial, the team's top slugger and home run threat to get me. Big Gus set a White Sox record for home runs in 1950, and went on to lead the American League in homers and RBI's once the Sox traded him to the Philadelphia Athletics.

An excellent defensive catcher in his playing days, Paul was a "Miracle Man" with pitchers. He would show his pitchers things that no other manager could. Pitchers who didn't win anyplace else became winners with Richards. He did wonders with Billy Pierce in 1951, teaching Billy to throw that remarkable slider, and to tone his control. He made a winner out of Saul Rogovin, whom he had managed in the minor leagues at Buffalo. Saul came from nowhere to lead the American League in earned run average in 1951, once he was traded from the Tigers to the White Sox in late April for pitcher Bob Cain.

Paul Richards knew every aspect of the game: infield play, hit and run, bunting, outfield; he knew them all. And you didn't take him for granted— Paul could be as tough as tough can be. If a player didn't give everything he had, or would fool around and not take care of himself, he'd be in deep trouble. An avid golfer himself, Paul would not let his players play golf during the season; he believed it would hinder their swing. He wasn't keen on swimming either, believing that swimming was not good for your baseball coordination. Did the players listen to him? You bet they did! In those days you listened to your manager.

We had great coaches too. Doc Cramer was one of the very best and really helped me along. Doc was our first base coach and was my buddy from the start. Later he was like my right arm. We used to hang out and talk a lot. Knowing my language problem, he'd try to take the blame if I messed up on a signal. Then we would argue over who should be blamed. That's when Paul Richards would intercede and tell us that we argued like we were married to each other. Paul and Doc were good friends.

Jimmy Adair was another excellent coach. Like Paul Richards, he was born in the town of Waxahachie, Texas. Jimmy worked with the infielders and more than anyone else was responsible for teaching Nellie Fox how to turn a double play.

Chuck Comiskey, the owner of the Chicago White Sox, was a very decent sort of guy. He was a stylish man who looked like a movie star and dressed beautifully. I liked him a lot. He was caught in the middle when bad feelings developed between Richards and Frank Lane later on.

I'm not certain what happened between Lane and Richards. Both men had strong egos and liked to do things their own way. Lane was a human dynamo, and Paul wouldn't take much guff from anyone. No one could push Paul around. After turning things around for the White Sox, Richards took over the entire show at Baltimore in 1955. He started and built the system that eventually made the Baltimore Orioles into a winning organization.

Of course there was Mr. Frank Lane, the man who engineered the trade that brought me to Chicago. Lane came down to the dugout to meet me that first day. My initial impression was correct. He was totally dynamic, a human dynamo. He was very friendly, but also very direct. What he had to say he would tell you. If he didn't like you, he would let you know. There was nothing "wishy washy" about Frank Lane. He'd never stab you in the back. Frank had been a sportswriter and a Big Ten Official in his earlier days. He was hired as Sox general manager by Chuck Comiskey following the Sox's dismal 1948 season, when they lost 101 games and finished in the American League cellar. His job was to turn the White Sox around. That he did with a series of brilliant trades that earned him the title "Trader" Lane.

Frank Lane liked me, and I liked him. In spite of our much-discussed contract disputes, we had a wonderful association together during our years with the Chicago White Sox and later with the Cleveland Indians. Other ballplayers may have had difficulty with him, but to me, Frank Lane was a surrogate father. Through our long association, he always called me 'son,' and he really meant it. In turn, Frank was always my "Daddy Number Two." That's what I called him. These names resulted in some interesting yarns and anecdotes along the way, which I shall relate later.

Then there were my teammates, the original "Go Go" Chicago White Sox. What a wonderful group of guys! What a talented bunch of athletes. A more amiable and unique group of ballplayers you will never find anywhere.

At age 24, Billy Pierce was our elder statesman in years of service. He came to the White Sox from the Detroit Tigers in 1949 and was just about to emerge as one of the game's great left handed pitchers. Billy was a quiet guy who had married Gloria, his high school sweetheart. He was a real gentleman both on and off the field. Billy never cussed at a teammate for making an error like some other pitchers have been known to do.

I knew from the start that he had the makings of a great pitcher. Billy was not a big man, but had a strong arm and a lively fastball that moved. It was obvious he was going to throw the ball by a lot of hitters. In addition to that great slider that Paul Richards taught him, Billy had one of the smoothest deliveries I have ever seen. Billy would win 15 games for the Chicago White Sox in 1951, and was among the League leaders in earned run average and complete games. American League batters were just getting a taste of what they would have to contend with in later years. Billy and Nellie Fox were like brothers, the closest of friends. They were roommates for the eleven years that the two of them played together with the Chicago White Sox.

Nellie Fox was something else. If Billy was quiet, Nellie always had something to say. He would hustle all the time. He was always moving, pure energy and perpetual motion around second base. Nellie was an aggressive player. No ballplayer ever got more out of his God-given talent. Nellie was an instigator on the field. He'd cuss and say what he wanted, but he never threw a punch. Yet for his first four years under Paul Richards he always addressed Paul as "Mr. Richards." Then only cautiously did he start calling him "skipper."

Nellie drove Casey Stengel crazy. "Casey, you bow-legged son of a gun," he would yell. But Casey seemed to enjoy it. He had only the greatest respect for Nellie and the many ways that Nellie could beat you. "That little feller, he ain't so big, but he's all fire," Casey once said. "He's in your hair all the time. He can beat you with his glove or his bat."

I first saw Nellie Fox in 1951. I hadn't known much about him before I came to the White Sox. But I knew he hadn't done much previously. But I am told he never stopped working or trying to improve his game. He worked and worked on the double play and the pivot, which was his weakest point. Then Doc Cramer got into the act. He thought Nellie could use a wider bat and choke up some more. He showed Nellie how to hit off his back foot as well.

Nellie got tough in 1951. He raised his batting average over 60 points and became the American League All Star second baseman. More amazing, Nellie struck out only 11 times in more than 600 at bats in 1951. Confidence and courage, grit and determination. That is what Nellie Fox was all about.

It angers me that so many of the old ballplayers are not remembered as they should be. The writers don't mention the very guys who gave so much to the game that they now write about. Somehow they are not kept in the public eye. This is why it was so nice to see former White Sox teammate Saul Rogovin inducted into The Chicago Jewish Sports Hall of Fame recently. Billy Pierce and myself were at the Westin Hotel to help honor Saul, whom we had not seen in years. And what a nice reunion we had on that Sunday afternoon.

Saul may have taken some teasing in his day, but he was one tough guy; make no mistake about that. Saul was a competitor. He'd be the first guy to jump right into a fight to defend you.

Nellie and "Jungle Jim" Rivera teased him a lot, but Saul would give it right back. They'd kid him in a good-natured way about his Jewish background. When they'd go shopping, Nellie would say something like, "Hey Saul, you're rich. Why don't you buy me this?" Saul would gaze down on him. "Nellie, you little punk," he'd answer, "I'll break your pint-sized neck."

Saul was a good guy to have around. He'd give 100 percent to the club, and 100 percent to a teammate who would get in trouble. Sure, he'd catch a few winks of sleep in the dugout, and he took lots of kidding, but on the mound he was all business. He challenged the hitters as well as anyone. Against the Red Sox in July, Saul toiled the entire 17 innings of a night game, only to lose by the score of 5 - 4. I never saw anyone tougher than Saul Rogovin that night in 1951. He pitched brilliantly for the White Sox in 1951 and came back with another nice season in 1952. Saul earned a graduate degree after leaving the game and worked as a high school English teacher in New York for more than 20 years until he retired.

Many people think I was responsible for the famous "Go Go" chant associated with our club. But truly, the crowd was shouting "Go Go" even before I came to town. The reason was our speedy center fielder Jim Busby. Story has it that Jim so dazzled the fans with his exciting running early in the year that the shout "Go Go" would ring out spontaneously from the stands whenever he was on base.

Jim Busby could fly. He was really fast. If you would let him loose on the bases today, with his speed he'd be right up there with the top base stealers. He finished right behind me in stolen bases in 1951; I had 31 and Jim had 26. I think I was the better base runner, but in a straight race I believe Jim Busby could have beaten me.

We hear so many stories about great shortstops, and there have been many outstanding ones. But let me assure you that for the few years he was at the top of his game, Chico Carrasquel was the best shortstop I have ever seen. And I do mean ever! Chico was just that good.

Chico Carrasquel was the first Latin player selected to start an All Star Game. When I first came to Chicago, it was Chico's second year. I had seen so many good shortstops, but he played like no one I had ever seen before. I looked in amazement. I said to myself, "Gee whiz, this guy never misses the ball! What a glove. What hands. Perfect throw to first base all the time."

He had the best range on both sides—to the left, to the right. The best range I have ever seen. Chico and I became good friends, and we still are. Today, he does color commentary on Spanish-language broadcasts for the Chicago White Sox. Part of the bond was that we were both Latin ballplayers—Chico was from Venezuela. But we genuinely liked each other as well.

In the old days with the White Sox we would go to Chinatown together. On the road we'd spend a lot of time together going to cowboy movies and playing Cuban dominoes on the train.

Chico and I would also play against each other in Puerto Rico after the regular season was over. He was with an All Star team from Venezuela and I played with a team of Cuban All Stars.

Nobody could beat us. Not Venezuela, not any other Latin country. They couldn't even touch us. In frustration they even brought in the fences and introduced dead ball to make it more competitive. That didn't work either. We handled all the All Star teams from the other countries.

I have many good memories of Chico and myself. We were playing the Chicago Cubs in the City Series. The temperature was in the 20s or 30s. Man was it cold! We were kidding around a bit on the field. I must have thrown the ball when his back was turned, because I hit him in the ankle. We had to pack his leg in ice, and Chico was madder than hell. "What are you trying to do, Minnie? Ruin my career!" But he wouldn't tell Paul Richards. He knew if he did, Paul would come down on me.

Then there was the time in a regular season game when we got our signals crossed. A pop fly was hit between shortstop and left field. Chico ran back. I ran in. Chico yelled "I got it. I got it." Well he didn't get it. Neither did I. The ball dropped between us.

Paul Richards had seen enough. He ran out of the dugout and was not particularly gentle with his words. "What's the matter with you two?" Richards yelled. Chico and I both tried to cover for the other. "That's O.K, Paul," I said. "It's my mistake." Then Chico started yelling, 'No, Paul. It was my fault, not Minnie's." Richards looked at us bewildered. Then shaking his head, he shrugged his shoulders and started to laugh. "I'm going to send the two of you back to school to learn Spanish." He walked away, but not before adding one more thing. "Next time, Chico, let Minnie take it!"

A combination of injuries and an increasing weight problem would cut his career short. Each year Chico would come to camp about ten pounds over his playing weight. He had to work harder than anyone else to get that weight off. I think it took a toll on him. A player pays a price for not keeping the same weight all year around. Many people don't realize that. Each year he put on eight or ten pounds, and in the effort to take it off he lost a lot of speed and energy. He was also a guy who played every day. He didn't get a lot of rest like the ballplayers today. You could not let a key man go for long in those days, because it broke up the momentum and the teamwork. We needed both Nellie and Chico around second base. Nellie wasn't the same without Chico, and Chico wasn't the same without Nellie.

Another factor was that Chico hurt his knees, and eventually that would affect his throw. A shortstop has to plant that right foot firm in order to make a strong throw when he goes to his right. Otherwise you throw with just your arm and don't get anything on the ball. You need your whole body for the mechanics of a good throw. It's like with a car; everything must be in gear.

In 1951, Chico Carrasquel set an American League record (since broken) by handling 297 consecutive chances without an error. When I was in the Negro Leagues, I would watch Marty Marion of the St. Louis Cardinals get everything hit his way. He was the best, I thought. Then I saw Chico Carrasquel, and I've never seen anyone better. Remember too, I played behind him in left field so I watched him play day by day. Like I said earlier, he was that good!

So here you have the original "Go Go" Chicago White Sox: Billy Pierce and Nellie Fox. Jim Busby and Saul Rogovin. Eddie Robinson, outfielder Al Zarilla and catcher Phil Masi. Pitchers Lou Kretlow, Harry Dorish, Randy Gumpert, and Marv Rotblatt. Two future White Sox greats, Sherman Lollar and "Jungle" Jim Rivera were one year away, waiting in the wings. And of course a guy they just called Minnie.

And don't ever forget the skipper. The man who molded and developed this unique group of baseball players, who made them winners and paved the way for a new and exciting baseball era here in Chicago, Mr. Paul Richards, The "Wizard of Waxahachie, Texas."

Two great sports columnists covered the Sox during the glory days of Minoso; John Carmichael of the *Daily News* and Warren Brown of the *Chicago American* were Minnie's dedicated publicists. Brown was the originator of colorful nicknames. Because of Minoso's nocturnal ramblings, Brown called him "O Restless Minoso."

On a Sunday morning in Cleveland, Brown and Al Lopez, manager of the Sox, were in a hotel lobby waiting for a cab to take them to early Mass. At about 7:05 a.m., Minnie whirled through the revolving door.

"Where the hell have you been?" Lopez asked. Plaintively Minnie replied, "Oh, Señor, I'm just coming back from 6:00 Mass."

Bill Gleason, longtime Chicago sportswriter
and sports personality

7

A VERY GOOD YEAR

When I speak to groups or talk with fans, I am often asked what was my best year in baseball. I had many good seasons, some might say a few great ones. But everything considered, I have to go back to my rookie season of 1951.

Many things were different back then. For starters there were only 16 Major League teams, eight in the American League and eight in the National League. There were no divisional playoffs, no artificial turf, no designated hitter, and the baseball season was 154 games. Translated to the absolute, this means that each team in the league played every other team a total of 22 times a year. Secondly, there was an enormous amount of talent around. This was the early post World War II era. Many great ballplayers like Joe DiMaggio, Ted Williams, and Bob Feller returned from service to resume outstanding careers. Many whose careers had been delayed because of the War were now established stars. Finally the color line had been broken, and there was a slow but steady infusion of black ballplayers into Major League baseball.

Yes, there were many great ballplayers in the game, but there were some truly outstanding baseball teams too. In the American League, the New York Yankees, the Boston Red Sox, and the Cleveland Indians could rank with the all-time great clubs in American League history. Moreover, in 1950 the Detroit

Tigers won 95 games and finished second, only three games behind the World Champion New York Yankees. Imagine at the start of the year, anyone suggesting that the Chicago White Sox would be a first division club in 1951. He would have been accused of flirting rather dangerously with reality. After all, the White Sox finished the 1950 season in sixth place with a 60-94 record. To even imply that the White Sox would occupy first place at All Star break, would be bordering on sheer lunacy. But all this really happened in 1951.

If a dramatic Chicago debut was my calling, then what better team to do it against than the New York Yankees. Don't ever underestimate how good they were. They were a complete, well rounded, and superbly managed ball club. Joe DiMaggio was still one of the game's reigning stars—the term "super star" had not yet made its way into our popular lingo. Phil Rizzuto was coming off his MVP season and hustled as much as any player in the game. Yogi Berra was a menace in the batter's box. He was the best bad ball hitter I ever saw. If you wanted to get Yogi out, you had to throw him strikes. Ex Marine Hank Bauer was tough and sturdy. He could beat you many different ways. Gene Wodling and Gerry Coleman were solid ballplayers, as was third baseman Bobby Brown, the current president of the American League. With three great starting pitchers like Allie Reynolds, Vic Raschi, and Eddie Lopat, the Yankees were worthy World Champions.

Of course my first inning homer against Raschi is what everyone tends to remember. But I remember something else. I messed up some in the field. I think we were losing 4 to 2 at the time. The bases were loaded and Phil Rizzuto was the batter. I was playing a little close to the bag at third and Richards moved me over. Rizzuto smacked a ground ball that hit the base. The ball careened off the bag and hit my shoe for an error.

I felt badly; I never liked making errors. I promised myself to show the club the next day that I wasn't a defensive liability. The following day I was in left field and made another error, this time on a low line drive. After the game, Paul Richards and Frank Lane took a look at my glove. It was the glove I used in the Negro Leagues. "You can't use that glove," Richards said. "The glove is too soft and the pocket is too thin." I told them I would fix the glove and make it tighter. But Frank Lane would have none of that. He would buy me a new glove, he insisted. I used that

McGregor glove Lane bought me for many years. Then I signed a contract with Rawlings for a glove that they endorsed with my own name.

The real fun was about to start. On May 15 we embarked on our first eastern road trip. We would stop at such places like New York, Cleveland, and Boston to battle the very best. When we returned home two weeks later, we had won 14 straight games, and had leaped amazingly from fifth place to the top of the American League standings. We began this terrific surge against the Red Sox. Nellie Fox got us going. He tied the score with a double in the ninth inning. Then in the eleventh inning, after twice missing an attempted bunt, he hit the first Major League home run of his life to win the game.

The following day Nellie hit a 408-foot triple as we beat the Red Sox again, 9 - 5. In the game after that, Nellie hit another homer, to help beat the Yankees 7 - 1. In yet another game, he got a triple, as we edged the Senators 5 - 4. Then going hitless for one game, Nellie hit his third home run in a week to help turn back the Senators, 9 - 8. When we returned home Nellie was hitting a robust .370, prompting one Chicago writer to write that the great baseball name of Foxx, no longer had to be spelled only with a Double XX.

We were as hot as we could be. I was surging, too. When Nellie wasn't leading the league in hitting, I was at the top of the American League charts. In fact, Nellie and I alternated as the League's top two hitters for some time. Eddie Robinson, too, was swinging a big bat. All season Eddie would challenge Ted Williams and Gus Zernial for American League home run and RBI honors. Chico Carrasquel was being widely hailed as baseball's new "Mr. Shortstop." Some old liners were even saying that Chico might be the best since Honus Wagner.

What a wonderful feeling. Out of nowhere the Chicago White Sox were flush on the baseball map. When we arrived back in Chicago, lots of people were waiting at the airport to greet us. By June, the city was in a frenzy of excitement. Suddenly, Paul Richards' Chicago White Sox were the baseball darlings of the world. On June 2, Mayor Kenelley hosted a gala City Hall Reception to honor us. Lapel buttons and car stickers with the White Sox insignia and the "Go Go" logo were emblazoned everywhere.

There was another reception too. It was in the Mexican community, and Chico and I spent the whole day there. This truly marked the arrival of the Latin ballplayer on the Major League scene in Chicago. The festival would become a yearly occurrence, and as long as Chico and I both wore a Chicago White Sox uniform, we always managed to attend.

Yes, the Chicago White Sox had become the baseball darlings of the world. Magazines such as *Colliers, Life,* and *The Saturday Evening Post* started running features on the team, the manager, and the players. How happy I was. Happy to be playing major league baseball; happy to be in a city like Chicago; happy to learn how much Paul Richards admired my baseball ability. I don't feel I could have done as well had I not been made to feel so comfortable here. My main goal and my biggest responsibility was to help the ballclub. This team played together and respected each other so much that we would go on the field believing the whole world belonged to us.

It seemed that the city of Chicago had fallen in love with Minnie Minoso. I was just called "Minnie" now. The name "Orestes" seemed to fade away. Bob Elson, the White Sox announcer, always had nice things to say. "The Cuban Comet" was his special name for me. No group of fans could have been better. No city more ingratiating. Truly the people and the fans made Minnie Minoso. They opened the door and let me be me.

If I excited my share of the fans, it was because Paul Richards gave me the green light to run. What this meant was that I could go on my own, which is something I was never allowed to do before. It became a ritual. When I would get to first base the fans would shout "Go, Go! Go Minnie, Go Minnie!"

But I never ran just because of the fans. I ran only when I thought it could help the team. I may have had the green light, but I used it carefully.

To run intelligently you have to take the same lead, whether or not you are going to run. This way you keep the other team off balance. If you tip your move by taking a different lead, 99 percent of the time you are dead. The same thing goes for the hit and run. You take the same lead you normally do. After the pitcher delivers, you take off.

Who was the toughest pitcher to steal against? That's easy to answer. For me it was Bill Wight. Wight was a left hander who once pitched for the White Sox. Later he pitched for Boston, Detroit, and Cleveland. Our catcher Phil Masi was a real veteran, a pro who knew the ropes. In 1952 I believe Wight was on the mound for the Tigers and Masi was on first base. Paul Richards made a special point to tell Phil to be careful. Wight still picked him off. He didn't give you an inch. He had the best move I ever saw in my life and got me a couple of times.

Once I did the impossible, though. I scored on him from first base. Wight uncorked a wild pitch as I was attempting to steal second. I turned the base, unleashed some steam and headed for third base. I guess he was surprised because instead of backing up the catcher as he should have done, he just stood between the mound and the plate. It was a long distance between the catcher and the wall, so I rounded third and kept going. Wight finally caught on and started shooting for the plate. When Joe Ginsberg, the catcher, threw him the ball, Wight raced me to home plate. He tried to tag me but I slid on my stomach, under three men who had gathered around the plate, Wight, Ginsberg, and first baseman Walt Dropo, who had come in from first. "Safe!" The umpire yelled. I'll never forget that.

Paul Richards allowed me to make my own decisions on the bases. Two particular instances still stand out. Early in the '51 season we were playing the Red Sox at Fenway Park. There was one out, and I was perched on third base. Al Zarilla hit a pop fly to center field. Dominic DiMaggio, the Red Sox centerfielder started running in. He caught the ball about twelve or fifteen feet behind second base. Jimmy Adair was coaching third base. I tagged up. Jimmy tried to halt me. "Minnie!" he yelled, "No. No. No..." "Too late, I'm going," I shouted as I tore for the plate. Dom DiMaggio's throw was on the mark, but bounced a little high. When the catcher, Matt Batts, got it, he reached for the tag. But I slid into the plate safe. I beat the throw. Everyone looked amazed, especially the Boston players and the Fenway Park crowd. We won the game!

The next day we were in New York, and I had to contend with another center fielder named DiMaggio—a guy named Joe. Again I was on third base, and I'm sure Joe had heard about the Red Sox game. This time the batter lifted a fly ball about 320 feet to dead center. Normally I might have gone, but I had other thoughts, and rightfully so. I pretended I was going to tag up, although it wasn't my intention. Joe fired the ball so perfectly to home plate that I would have been out by a mile.

The infield then moved in to stop me from scoring. A pop fly was hit behind second base. Gil McDougald caught the ball on the run, his back to the infield. This time I did tag up. I shot for the plate. McDougald whirled and threw, but I beat the throw. I got a rousing hand from the fans at Yankee Stadium. It drove Casey Stengel crazy. Casey yelled, "Hey, Minoso! What are you doing to me?" "Casey!" I yelled back. "You know Minoso doesn't fool around."

I had the greatest respect for Casey Stengel. He was a comedian, but he knew baseball and he knew how to manage. If there was one manager I would have liked to play for besides Paul Richards, it would have been Casey. I think we would have done well together.

There was a feeling on the 1951 White Sox that I have never quite experienced again. We went out each day to win. We didn't care about tomorrow. The game we wanted to win was the game we played. If we played a doubleheader, we thought only about the first game and looked no further ahead. We knew the strength of the other teams, but we thought like we were a championship team— and we kept on winning.

Who would ever have guessed that on July 4th the Chicago White Sox would be atop the American League standings? Or that six members of the team would be on the American League All Star squad. Chico and Nellie were selected by the fans to start at second and short. Casey Stengel also chose Jim Busby, Eddie Robinson, pitcher Randy Gumpert, and me in rounding out the team. I was especially proud to have finished behind the great Ted Williams in the All Star voting in this my rookie year. It was the first of seven All Star Games for me.

But bubbles burst, and so do first-place clubs. We were still tied for first place on July 20, when the Washington Senators arrived in town for a four-game series. It looked easy enough; we had done quite well against Washington till then. In Game One, we took a 1-0 lead into the ninth inning.

Suddenly things fell apart. With two outs, the Senators rallied and scored. They took the lead, then the game. Washington went on to win the next three games to sweep the series. We were swept from first place and we wouldn't be back. For 44 straight days we had occupied first place in a very tough American League. And we had a lot of fun doing it.

The Chicago White Sox finished in fourth place in 1951 with an 81-73 record. Given our lack of experience, and the overall strength of the Yankees, Indians, and Red Sox, it was quite a feat. More important, by melding pitching with defense and speed, Paul Richards had established a winning formula that would carry the Chicago White Sox for years to come. We would remain a first-division club for another 16 years until 1968. Seventeen straight winning seasons, 17 straight first-division finishes. No Chicago sports franchise in the entire post-World War II era can make a similar boast. In all of Major League history, only the New York Yankees (1926-1964), and the Baltimore Orioles (1968-1985) have had more consecutive winning seasons.

It would be a terrible shame if this wonderful era and the exciting "Go Go" years in Chicago should ever recede too far into the pages of time. In 1951, the Chicago White Sox came alive. We led the American League in base hits, triples, stolen bases, and in team hitting with a .270 average. Even more impressive was our pitching. Our unheralded and uncertain pitching staff, under Richards' expert tutelage, posted a 3.50 earned run average, second only to the strong Cleveland Indians pitching staff. Saul Rogovan led all American League pitchers with a 2.78 ERA, and Billy Pierce was fourth at 3.03. Pierce with 18 complete games, and Rogovin with 17 complete games were also among the League's top five in that category. Moreover, our pitchers issued less walks than any pitching staff in the American League.

We placed among the League leaders in many other categories. Chico led all American League shortstops in assists and fielding percentage. Eddie Robinson tied a club home run record by hitting 29 homers to match Gus Zernial's mark set the previous year, and his 117 runs batted in were the most for any White Sox hitter since 1939. In both home runs and RBI's, Eddie trailed only Gus Zernial and Ted Williams.

Nineteen fifty-one was the start of many great seasons for Nellie Fox, and a career complete with Hall of Fame credentials. Nellie hit .313, fifth best in the American League. He was second in base hits with 189, and tied for second in triples with 12. It was the first of six .300 seasons Nellie would have with the White Sox.

For me, it was a very good year. I finished among the American League's top five in six separate offensive categories in

1951. My .326 average was second to Ferris Fain's .344, and I had almost 100 more at bats. I led the American League with 14 triples and 31 stolen bases, and was second with 112 runs scored—just one short of Dom DiMaggio's league-leading total of 113. My 500 slugging average was fifth best in the League.

Having said all this, I must now say something else; I have rarely been accused of complaining. I feel my whole career and life speaks for that. *The Sporting News* named me the top rookie in the American League for 1951. The entire baseball world agreed. But somehow I was denied that honor by the Baseball Writers of America, who passed me over for Rookie of the Year honors in favor of Gil McDougald.

Please don't get me wrong; Gil was a very fine baseball player. He was versatile and did many things well. His numbers may have been deserving in some other years, but not in 1951. Some slights linger, and after 40 years, it is time to close the book on this one. I hit for a higher average, stole more bases, had more doubles and triples, scored more runs, and batted in more runs. Gil hit 14 home runs to my 10 and a home run in the World Series. The rest of the numbers weren't even close. When it came to naming the Most Valuable Player in 1951, the same writers who named Gil McDougald Rookie of the Year, placed me fourth behind Yogi Berra, Ned Garver, and Allie Reynolds. Gil finished ninth in the MVP voting. It never made sense.

Mine isn't the only example. Over the course of my career, I have seen similar cases of bias on the part of the Eastern writers, particularly the New York baseball writers. I am not alone in this view. I know many other ballplayers who feel this way; some have said so publicly. The politics of favoritism has reached deep into MVP and Hall of Fame selection as well, robbing many deserving, but lesser profile ballplayers of their rightful due. I will have more to say about these matters later. But having made my case, I will close the book on an episode that has bothered me for more years perhaps than it should have.

I learned an important lesson rather early in life. If you let what people say get inside of you, then you are through. Sure, I always smiled a lot, even when there was lots of hurt and pain inside. I, too, experienced discrimination and bias.

That was part of the territory so to speak. I heard the names and insults. Being Latin compounded the problem because I didn't speak the language well. Yes there were hoots and howls from the stands at times. I wasn't deaf or blind. But you must shut it out and concentrate 100 percent on your game.

On the other hand, I honestly feel that overall I was treated well by the baseball establishment. I realize other minority athletes may disagree. But I call things as I see them. I think most people respected me, because I always gave my best. When you show respect for yourself and give it to others, the chances are great that you will get respect in return, no matter what your color or your origin. This has been my philosophy from day one. Too many people look for discrimination around every corner. That way they will always find it; often, perhaps, when it really isn't there. I have always loved and respected my profession. My profession has been baseball all my life, and baseball has been very good to me.

Yet there were people who gave me a particularly hard time. One was Jimmy Dykes, a long-time favorite in Chicago as a player, a coach, and a manager. When I came to the White Sox in 1951, Dykes was managing the Philadelphia Athletics. There was not one game against the Athletics that he didn't hurl every kind of name to me. He would always do it from the dugout., never from the field where others could see and hear him. "Black Dog" was one of his favorite expressions.

Dykes used to tell his pitchers to throw at me. Once when we were playing the Athletics, one of his relief pitchers hit me hard. Someone had yelled earlier that he should "hit that nigger." I was laying on the ground all black and blue. Paul Richards was very upset; he said, "Minnie, let me take you out." He told me to take a rest and join the team in New York.

"Paul," I said. "You're the manager, but please don't take me out. It's my first year and if I go out everyone will think I'm scared." I told him if it was war and I was going to die, at least I wanted to do it in uniform. He said, "O.K. Minnie, go to first base." I got up and trotted to first.

Ferris Fain was the Athletics' first baseman. He was supposed to be one tough cookie; the kind of guy you didn't mess with. Stay clear of him, I had heard. Boy, did he surprise me; Fain wanted nothing to do with these kind of tactics. "To hell with Dykes," he yelled back at the pitcher. "Give the guy the best pitch you've got and try to get him out the right way. Watch, he'll go

to second on the next pitch. Then he'll find a way to score on us."
Ferris Fain played hard. He could be tough and ornery; but he
was always fair. I learned to respect him greatly. He was the kind
of guy who would stand by a friend to the end.

Once after a game I saw Jimmy Dykes in the hotel lobby. He
said, "Hello, Mr. Minoso!" I looked at him and said that that was
not what he called me on the field. "We're not on the field now,"
he replied. I asked him directly why he was being friendly now.
Why, I wondered, would he say hello to me now after those
names he called me on the field? It was damned two-faced of
him, I said. He had no answer. The next day he was the same way,
and he said the same things. I just did my best to stay away from
him after that.

Another incident bothered me even more. This was because it involved a player I had always admired and who had
been a hero of mine. I always liked Hal Newhouser and rooted for
him to win each time he took the mound for the Detroit Tigers.
Now I was in the big leagues batting against him.

We were playing in Detroit one day, and Newhouser was
pitching. I came to bat and hit one out of the park. The next time
I came up, he hit me. I had my sunglasses in my pocket. The pitch
cracked the glasses and cut me pretty badly. He cussed me.
Something like, "You nigger, you have no right to hit me." I was
shocked. I said to myself, "Holy Cow!" Then I looked at him and
said, "You might be Hal Newhouser, but I am Minnie. Who the
hell do you think you are? You don't own the whole world!" As
with Jimmy Dykes, I just ignored him after that. I wished him no
harm. I just ignored him. He was recently elected to the Hall of
Fame, perhaps rightfully so. I have no real measure to judge Hal
Newhouser as a pitcher. By the time I came up and faced him, his
better days were behind him.

I was a genuine celebrity now, especially in Chicago. People
knew me and recognized me. Recognition and accomplishment
make you feel good; don't let anyone tell you differently. I would
taste my share of heartache in later years, but at that time, things
were as fun filled and exciting as I could have imagined. I was
young. I was popular. I was a Major League ballplayer. I was in
love with Chicago, especially the southside neighborhood where
I lived. After the games, I would go back to the neighborhood
where there was so much to see and do: great nightclubs, music,

dancing, jazz. People were on the street all the time. Sometimes I would spend a month or more without even going to the downtown area. Everything was alive and vibrant. Today you look around, and it's all so different. All the drugs, the gangs, the shootings. You tell people today how the south side of Chicago used to be, and they don't want to believe you.

My black south side fans honored me at the end of the season. On September 23, 1951, I was given a Day at the park. They showered me with gifts such as a television set, a radio, a camera, and a new Packard automobile, which I took back to Cuba with me.

What a wonderful return to Cuba. I received a hero's welcome at the Jose Marti Airport. I was presented with a key to the city. The President of Cuba, the Army Chief of Staff, and the Mayor of Havana were all there. At another ceremony in Marianao, I was given many more gifts. I was not only rookie of the year in my native Cuba; I was man of the year.

For 26-year-old Orestes Minoso, 1951 was truly a very good year.

Minnie came to spring training with the Cleveland Indians in 1949. We were training at Tucson and from day one he was a pretty exciting little player. He was a great guy to be around. Even today when I see him at the old timers games, he still has those ripples in is stomach. I don't think he has put more than a pound or two on since those early days.

We had a nucleus of a lot of good rookies in camp. We had Minnie Minoso and Harry "Suitcase" Simpson, and they were both very exciting right from the beginning. In 1951 we needed a left handed pitcher, and Lou Brissie was available. It was down to who Cleveland was going to give up, Simpson or Minnie Minoso.

The way it worked out was that Chicago wanted Minnie only. The day he was traded we were in St. Louis playing the Browns. That particular night, Lopez played Minnie at first base and he went four for four that game. After the game they announced the trade. Minnie had tears in his eyes. I had a long talk with him knowing how much he wanted to stay. I said I knew he would be a sensational ballplayer in Chicago, and it was true. The Chicago White Sox were just waiting for a Minnie Minoso.

The nice thing about Minnie is that he is not an "I" guy, he's a "We" guy. On hot days in Chicago, if he was not hitting, he would lay right down in the runway where it was cool. He said to let him know when there were two outs. On the third out, he'd run out to left field like he was running to first base. If you spent as much energy as he did you'd need a little rest once in a while. He never put on any false pepper. It was real stuff from the first day he came to spring training.

My home town is San Diego. When I came back after the season, my buddies who were San Diego Padre fans just raved about Minnie Minoso. He was as popular at San Diego in 1949 and 1950 as he was in Chicago. We had a popular outfielder in San Diego, a fellow named Dane Clay. He played with Minnie and a ball was hit in left center. Minnie came running over saying, "Got it, Got it, Got it!" Then Minnie stopped and the ball fell between them. Minnie picked it up and threw it in. He pointed at Dane and said "Got it. Got it. Got it, Boy!" Dane thought when Minnie was yelling, it meant that Minnie would get it. But Minnie meant just the opposite. After that they got their language straight. Like I said, he was just great to be around.

Ray Boone, 13-year Major League career
with Cleveland, Detroit, and Chicago

8

THAT "SOPHOMORE JINX"

One of the biggest surprises I encountered during the winter months in Cuba was seeing Frank Lane waiting for me in the dugout between innings of a ballgame. Each year, of course, I would play winter ball with Marianao. I had written Lane telling him what I expected to make after such a fine rookie year. He sent me a contract through the mail that in no way matched my offer. I sent the contract back unsigned. That's when he decided to jaunt to Cuba to deal with me directly.

I was running in from left field when I saw Frank waving to me from the Marianao dugout. "Son! Hey son!" he yelled. I couldn't believe my eyes. "Daddy, is that you! How are you doing?" Then and there he laid the contract on top of the dugout. I opened it and looked. "No daddy. This won't do!"

"But son! Look!"

I stopped him there, and told him to see me after the game. He did just that. After the game, when I was in the clubhouse, he knocked on the door. The clubhouse man opened the door and asked Lane what he wanted. "I'm Minoso's daddy," he told the astonished clubhouse man. "Oh, no you're not!" he answered, shutting the door. "Oh yes, I am," Frank explained. "I'm his Papa Number Two." The man was even more puzzled. He came over to me and said, "Mr. Minoso. There's a guy out there who says he's your daddy." "Sure, sure," I answered. "Let him come in. He's my general manager. That's my Papa Number Two!"

Frank Lane came over. "Look, son," he pleaded. "I can't do any better. This is all I can offer you." I said, "No! No. I want $20,000, but I'll make a deal with you."

I told him if I signed for $20,000, I'd never ask for another raise as long as I was with the White Sox, not even if I had many more great years. I also promised that if I had a bad year he was entitled to cut me 25 percent. He told me he couldn't do that because it was against all club policy. The most he could offer me was a $10,000 raise. That was as much as they offered a Most Valuable Player, not a Rookie of the Year. He also said that what I had asked for really wasn't fair. I would have many more good years and later could ask and deserve far more. I trusted Frank Lane and signed the contract. I went from seven thousand to seventeen thousand my second year. Actually I made even more, because any time I won a game for the club or got a key homer, he would give me something. Today this would be called an incentive clause. Then we didn't sign anything to that effect. We just did it.

You would never really know where you would run into Frank Lane. He was the kind of general manager who was all over the place. He'd be in the dugout before the game. He'd be in the clubhouse after the game. He might even be at your favorite bar that evening. Once in 1951, I was at a night club in Detroit. I was a rookie and did not want anyone to see me drinking, so I would always order a glass of milk. Frank Lane spotted me there and came over with some friends. "This is my kid," he told them. "This is my son! Look what he is drinking. He's intelligent. He's O.K."

As I have already indicated, Frank Lane was controversial, and he could be difficult. I guess that's why he and Paul Richards had that falling out. Richards was as different from Lane as night is from day. While Lane was direct and vocal, Paul Richards was a serious, quiet man who measured his words carefully. But there was another side to Paul. Make no mistake, Paul had a temper, and when he'd get mad, you would think he was about to explode. Between the two, it had to be a case of the immovable object and the irresistible force. Something would have to give, and give it did. After directing the White Sox together for four years, Richards decided not to work under anyone's wing. He took the Baltimore offer, which for him I feel was the right thing to do.

Frank Lane could give me lots of trouble. He'd sit out there in the upper deck, and if I made a mistake he would yell down to the field so I would hear him. Once I dropped the ball and he began to yell, "Hey, Minoso! I'm going to send you back to Cuba to cut sugar."

I waved my glove at him and hollered back, "Here! You're so good, you come out here and play." Meanwhile, White Sox announcer Bob Elson just loved it. "Believe it or not. We have the 'Cuban Comet' Minnie Minoso and Frank Lane arguing on the field," he'd announce over the radio. Then we would win the game, and Lane would come to the dugout as if nothing had happened. "Nice going, son," he would say. I'd shoot back, "What do you mean you're going to send me to Cuba?"

Yet everything considered, he really did treat me like a son. He made me feel the ballclub was my home. Instinctively, I knew I could trust him. He never did anything to hurt me, and I really think I was special to him. Once I had a slight fracture in my toe, the result of being hit with a pitch. He knew I was hurt and told me not to play, but I wouldn't listen to him. We had a three-game series coming up with the Yankees. I cut my baseball shoe in various places and tied it with tape so I could move my toe without friction. It worked, and I was O.K. We went out and beat the Yankees all three games. After the series, Frank Lane bought me two pair of Featherweight spikes. They were the best around and quite expensive.

With a new and lucrative contract under my belt, it was off to Pasadena in March 1952, for my first spring training with the Chicago White Sox. There was lots of reason for optimism that spring, but in 1952 we fell short of expectations on many accounts, but especially with our bats. I was as much a part of that decline as anyone; my average dropped off 45 points to .281.

Frank Lane was constantly busy making deals. In an attempt to gain more power, early in the season he traded Jim Busby to the Washington Senators for outfielder Sam Mele. Mele led the American League in doubles in 1951 and drove in 94 runs. Lane hit a true jackpot with two other trades. Nineteen fifty-two was the year that Sherman Lollar and Jim Rivera joined the Chicago White Sox. Both Sherman and "Jungle Jim" became an integral part of the team for many years to come.

Many people don't know that the White Sox actually traded Jim Rivera, then a promising rookie, and five other players to the St. Louis Browns for Sherman Lollar. Then a few months later, Lane reaquired Jim Rivera in a trade that sent outfielders Ray Coleman and J.W Porter to the Browns.

Sherman Lollar was a very quiet man, a serious man. He was also an excellent catcher. During his years as a White Sox catcher, only the Indians' Jim Hegan had an edge on Sherm defensively. Sherman could hit also. He'd get that run in with the bat when needed. He was like the unofficial captain of the team, the guy who in many ways held us together. He worked extremely well with the pitchers, most of whom had the greatest confidence in him. He was a great addition to the team.

So was "Jungle Jim." Jim Rivera was one tough ballplayer. He hustled and talked all the time. Everybody liked him, because he always gave you 100 percent; he'd play hurt. His standard line was, "You can't hurt Jungle Jim." Pity the poor pitcher who threw at him. He'd just stare him down with disdain and bait him. "You can't hurt me with the garbage you're throwing." He tried like hell to lose that hitch in his swing. Without it, he would have been a much better hitter. Paul Richards worked and worked with him. But he just couldn't do it.

Jim, of course, put a 'patent' on that head-first slide. It drove Richards nuts, but he never tried to stop it. He just told Jim he'd get hurt someday. Jim was very likable. Each year, Chico, Jim, and myself would attend an annual event at a Mexican/ American Catholic church. Jim was liked very well by the priest and the parishioners. He'd joke with the kids who always loved being around him.

I have already mentioned that I lived with Mr. and Mrs. Lewis at 6409 S. Maryland in their south side home. They had three kids and treated me like one of their own. I always liked a family setting and spent most of my time living with families back then. In 1952, I moved into a south side hotel.

I moved because the White Sox had signed another Cuban ballplayer. His name was Hector Rodriguez, and Lane had signed him out of Montreal to take over the third base chores for the White Sox. Because he didn't know much English and certainly didn't know his way around, I gave him my room in the

Lewis house and went to live in a hotel that was managed by the great Jesse Owens. Living in the hotel would lead to an unpleasant and disturbing episode, which I will relate in some detail later.

But now let me say something about Hector. Hector Rodriguez was the best third baseman Cuba ever produced. He played in the minors at Montreal for five or six years. He had moved from third to shortstop. By the time he got here, he had some years on him; I think he was already 32 years old when Lane signed him to a contract. He had a terrific glove but was never really able to impress Frank Lane with his play.

Hector and I became very close. People used to say "Minoso and Charo," when they would see us. "Charo" means a person's reflection. We would do a lot of things together, so when you saw one of us the chances are you saw the other.

I really hoped that Hector would make it with the White Sox. He opened the season at third base for us, and for a while he hit the hell out of the ball. He would hit Allie Reynolds particularly well, when everybody—including me— seemed to have trouble with Allie. Hector got hurt one day and sat out a few games. He was prone to getting a "charlie horse" now and then; he'd stiffen up and it would affect his play.

When he wasn't feeling better, I went to the doctor with him. The doctor said he should get more rest, but Hector did not want to listen. I agreed with the doctor. "Hector!" I said. "Don't play. You won't be able to move the same way as if you were OK." He still wouldn't listen; he was a rookie and wanted to play. He felt he had to. "Minnie," he answered. 'I'm leading the league in hitting. I'll be all right."

He wasn't. We were playing at Philadelphia and Gus Zernial hit one hard. Gus was big and strong, one of the strongest guys in baseball. He hit a ground ball to third. Hector moved over and the ball hit him on the shoe, and shot into the outfield. When I picked the ball up in left field I saw the black from the shoe on the baseball. I began yelling at Hector. "These guys over here eat a lot of T Bone steaks. What's the matter with you? I told you that you shouldn't be out there today. These guys are strong. They don't hit the ball here like they do in the minor leagues."

When I came to the dugout at the end of the inning, I asked, "What happened?" "Damn!" Hector said pointing to his foot. "That hurts!" He could not move well again all year. Somehow Hector was unable to put things together in the field. He was never more than an ordinary hitter, and his inflated .360 average early in the season fell to .265 by the end of the year. The next year the Sox released him to Montreal. Hector played in the Majors only that one year. He eventually moved to Mexico where he has been now for many years. Even if he didn't live up to full expectations, giving up on Hector so quickly was a big mistake I thought. Third base was the one position that would continue to plague the Chicago White Sox.

When I wasn't on the ballfield, I attracted lots of attention with my clothes and my cars. Once I made a good salary, I was able to buy a house for my sisters in Havana. Now I could begin taking care of myself the way I had always wanted. I just loved nice clothes, and I took pride in the way I looked and dressed. To some day own a Cadillac convertible had been a long-standing dream of mine; now I had enough money to buy one. When I came to Chicago in 1951, I bought a Pontiac convertible. Then, at the end of the season, as I have mentioned, the people in my neighborhood sponsored a Day for me and presented me with a brand new Packard.

You may ask, why only convertibles? Why not!; I liked them. I loved the way they looked, and I loved putting the top down. I was partial to the color pink. My pink Cadillac convertible became my personal trademark. I would put the top down and feel simply great. Some guys like to drink, other guys play golf, still others enjoy hunting. I like driving convertibles. The Cadillac was the top car made in America, and I liked owning them.

At the end of the season, I'd drive my car to Miami where I would put it on a ferry and take it back to Cuba. The next year I would bring it back to the United States and trade it in. Usually I would trade the car in after I had driven it 9,000 miles. I would own two or three cars at a time, but I only bought one myself. The others were always given to me.

In Cuba, my car was special. A car like mine marked the height of success, and in Cuba, convertibles were rarely seen. Believe me, my ego or my self-esteem was never dependent on this. I never needed a convertible to feel important, but driving one just gave me a lot of pleasure. Remember too, that never in my wildest dreams did I ever believe I could own a Cadillac. Minorities never made the kind of money to buy such a car in Cuba. In January, my fellow countrymen honored me as Cuban Athlete of the Year. It was a feeling of triumph tempered with humility. How far I had come from the ranch of my boyhood—from the little town of El Perico to Major League stardom. I had seen and played against those great ballplayers I read about as a kid. Players like Ted Williams, Bob Feller, and Joe DiMaggio. I considered myself a lucky human being. I had been able to use well what God had given me. There is no greater gift in the world than that.

Earlier I mentioned that there was a lot of optimism in 1952, and that we didn't quite live up to expectations. This does not mean that the Sox didn't play good baseball, just that we might have played better. Again, we finished the year with a record of 81 - 73, the same as in 1951. We moved up a notch to third place. The Boston Red Sox, without Ted Williams, fell to sixth place. The Korean War was going on and Ted was serving another tour of duty as a Navy pilot. Our main rival for third place in 1952 was the surprising Philadelphia Athletics. Led by left hander Bobby Shantz, the American League's MVP in 1952 with a 24 - 7 record and a 2.48 earned run average, the Athletics turned in a record of 79 -75.

We may have moved up one notch in the standings, but we still finished 14 games behind the Yankees, who won their third consecutive American League flag and their third straight World Series title. We also finished 12 games behind the second-place Cleveland Indians.

Unlike 1951, we were unable to put together a sizable winning streak. We also had big problems hitting the long ball. In one stretch, we went to bat 99 straight times without producing an extra base hit. There were some high points. Nellie Fox led the American League in base hits with 192. Eddie Robinson's 104 runs batted in was one short of Al Rosen's league leading total of 105. Eddie was fifth in the League in total bases. For the second year in a row, the White Sox led the League in stolen bases. I stole 22 bases to lead the League for the second straight year. But it wasn't easy. Jim Rivera was right behind me with 21.

Defense and pitching are what carried us. We led the American League in fielding with a percentage of .980 and we committed fewer errors than any team in the league. Billy Pierce won 15 games and lowered his ERA to 2.57. Pierce also struck out 144 hitters, fourth best in the American League. Saul Rogovin and Joe Dobson won 14 apiece, with Dobson leading the staff with a 2.51 earned run average. Our staff also struck out 774 opposing hitters to lead the American League.

Although I was again selected to the American League All Star squad, 1952 was not one of my better years. It was one of my poorest, in fact. My average dropped to .281, my lowest until 1961 when I hit .280. I hit 13 home runs; three more than in 1951. But all my other offensive numbers dropped measurably: total hits, doubles, triples, slugging percentage, and runs scored. What bothered me most was my 61 runs batted in, by far the lowest total during my years as a regular player. The sophomore jinx, perhaps! But I'd rather think I just had a poor season. I wasn't happy about it at all; I made myself a vow to do better in 1953. It was a promise I would keep.

We had a good ballclub in 1953. In one of the most talked about trades that year, we sent our leading home run and RBI man, Eddie Robinson, to the Athletics for two-time American League batting champion Ferris Fain. It was a straight exchange between two of the League's top first basemen. We also had the services of Jim Rivera for an entire year. Our pitching really got a shot in the arm, when just before the trading deadline we obtained Virgil Trucks from the St. Louis Browns. Trucks whose 5-19 record in 1952 was deceiving— it included two no hitters and a one hitter—would win his first eight decisions with the Sox and propel us into second place by early July. We would stay there until the first week of September when we fell off a bit and finished the year in third place.

Our problem spot continued to be third base. With Hector Rodriguez gone, it seemed like everybody and his twin brother took a shot at the hot corner. We opened the year with veteran Bob Elliott, who in 1947 had been a National League MVP. Others who occupied third base that year were Freddie Marsh, Rocky Krsnich, Connie Ryan, former American League RBI champ, Vern Stephens, and even a guy named Minnie Minoso.

I played a total of 10 games at third base, but I was a solid left fielder now. I handled left field much better than I did the hot corner. Things were going great. I was hitting as well as ever; we were an improved baseball team. Then one afternoon I walked to my car. I saw something placed on the front window. It looked like a subpoena. But I still had trouble reading English, and wasn't sure, so I took it to the White Sox office to show it to Frank Lane. He looked at it; looked at me. Then looked at it again. "Minnie," he said. "This can mean big trouble." I was taken aback. To my knowledge I had never broken the law.

"Son!" Lane continued. "There's a certain young woman who says you're the father of her child. She wants money from you, big money!"

Minnie respected my toughness. But it was mutual, because it was one thing I remember about Minnie. You've got a lot of guys that don't have that toughness. The worst thing you could do to Minnie Minoso was to knock him down. He would jump up and then you were asking for trouble. He would give you the worst damn struggle you ever saw in your life. He'd hit a homer over the wall. The only way you'd get him out was to throw him out, because he'd hit a screamer off the wall.

You didn't scare Minnie. He was a tough son of a gun at the plate. If you threw too tight to some guys, they would respond by taking three feeble swings. You couldn't intimidate Minnie; it was like that old story to let a sleeping dog lie. Don't go and kick and wake that sleeping dog up. He's going to bite you. That was Minnie Minoso.

When I joined the Chicago White Sox in 1953, Minnie took me around and introduced me to all the players. Of course I knew them from reputation, but I didn't know them personally. Funny thing, but during my career I was never real close friends with any of the players, but Minnie and I always got along real well.

The year before I came to the White Sox, Doc Cramer and Minnie were very close. Doc kind of counseled Minnie. When I joined the ballclub, I became the player representative because I had been the rep in Philadelphia. Well, Minnie kind of adopted me and called me his "Number 3 Daddy." Frank Lane was Number 2.

I remember once when I was in the hospital and Minnie visited me. He had a bouquet of flowers with him and another big basket of fruit, which he had one of the nurses bring in. Minnie was real generous with people he liked. With people he didn't like, forget it. If he liked you, he would lend you $1,000. If he thought you were a horse's butt, he wouldn't lend you 15 cents.

Minnie would confide in me. He was very upset once, and I said, "Minnie, you really look down in the dumps."

"Ferris," he said, "I just don't understand. This girl she says that I am the Daddy of her kid. I'm not her daddy! I tell them, 'You look at Minnie, and you look at the kid, light hair and blue eyes, and how can you say I'm the baby's daddy?'" He was really hurt, I had never seen him so upset.

If Minnie was having a little trouble, and those stupid bastards threw at him, they were in trouble. He was going to score. I think I liked this so much in Minnie because basically I was the same way. Our relationship evolved, I believe, out of mutual respect. That's why I love Minnie Minoso. In a jam you're going to get 115 percent.

Ferris Fain, two-time American League
batting champion, 1951, 1952

9

REFLECTIONS AND
A FEW REGRETS

I hadn't been an angel. I am a man and I'm human. I was a young man back then, and I was also a single man. But I had never been with that young woman. And what happened to me in 1952 could happen to any man at any time, particularly one who is in the public eye.

The true story is that I was living in that south side hotel managed by Jesse Owens. Remember, I relinquished my room at the Lewis' to Hector Rodriguez in 1952. Hector was visiting with me one afternoon, when the desk clerk phoned and said there was a lady downstairs who wanted to speak with me. I excused myself and went downstairs to see her.

When I saw her, I knew who she was. She worked as a waitress at a restaurant on 63rd St. This was a popular restaurant, which was frequented by such high-profile athletes as Sugar Ray Robinson and Joe Louis. The owner would give a celebrity steak dinner for two to anyone who would hit a home run. I would talk to her a little when I was eating, then I would leave a tip when I left. That wasn't unusual; I was a baseball star, and all the waitresses liked to talk with me.

When I saw her in the hotel lobby, I asked her what she wanted. She told me she had no place to stay because her mother and father weren't in, and she had no key. I guess I believed her, but I made it clear that she couldn't stay in my place. That had always been my policy whether I was rooming with a family or was living in a hotel. So what I did was rent a room for her at the hotel. I told the desk clerk to give her a room and I'd take care of the bill. That was it. She thanked me, I never saw her any more that day or that night.

It was 1953, and the team was hot. We were due to play a big series against the New York Yankees when I found the subpoena on the car and took it to the ballclub. When Frank Lane read it, he turned it over to the team lawyer. There was no way the baby could have been mine. The woman in question was what we call "high yellow." She was a very light-skinned black woman, the type with a lot of white blood. The baby was extremely light as well. Certainly I have never been accused of having light skin, I am very dark. Anyone can see that.

There was a hearing, but the case never came to trial. She filed a paternity suit against me for half a million dollars. What I do remember is my lawyer told me to keep a very low profile. I would dress in big hats and sunglasses. It was like an old fashioned spy movie; I was incognito. My lawyer wanted me to stay away from the newspaper guys and the photographers as much as possible.

My teammates supported me all the way. One particular instance comes to mind. We were playing the New York Yankees in that big series I just mentioned. I was in the batter's box taking batting practice when a photographer who had been following me around tried to take some pictures. Ferris Fain jumped in front of the guy and told him in his inimical way that if he didn't scram, he'd break the guy's camera right then and there. Then he yelled to the other photographers not to take any pictures of me in uniform; only after the game when I was in my civilian clothes. In cases like this, Ferris Fain had a definite way with words. He proved time and again to be a real friend.

Something else happened during the Yankee series that surprised me in yet a different way. I was playing left field and this lady started shouting my name. Given my predicament, I decided it was best to just ignore her. But she wouldn't let up. She kept shouting my name. Finally I turned around expecting trouble. "Hey, Minoso!" she hollered. "Just forget about this lady who sued you. We trust you. Let's just beat those New York Yankees."

Eventually, the ugly incident was settled out of court. It was settled between the lawyers, and I never heard more about it. To date, I have no idea what the outcome was. The writers were gentlemen back then. They didn't hound me like they hound athletes today. There was no adversarial relationship between the writers and the players. Remember, too, we traveled by train and the writers traveled with us. We would eat together, play cards, and joke around during those long train rides between cities. One writer I was extremely close to was Wendall Smith of the *Chicago Herald American*. He was one of the few big-time black writers in Chicago and was my roommate on the road when I first came up. Wendall was a fine writer and a very nice man. I gained great respect for the writers back then.

I never saw that woman again. Yet one time, years later, when I was coaching for the White Sox—I believe it was 1976— a guy who hung around our team a lot when I was in the minor leagues at San Diego came to one of our games at Anaheim when we were playing the California Angels. We started talking and he said he had some kind of message for me. He told me he had a note from a woman who said she was the mother of my child. I read it. The note said that her daughter had grown up and wondered why her father was so black. She wanted me to talk to her daughter.

I took the note and burned it with my lighter. I don't know if it was another attempt to extort money from me, or whether she was just crazy. Looking back I think she was probably put up to the thing in the first place by the guy she was working for, in order to get money from me. Also she never had been my type of woman. After the case settled down, a few policemen whom I knew told me she used to party quite a bit in the town of Blue Island, Illinois with a lot of white guys, one of whom was the baby's father. The incident really hurt me, because the young kids in the neighborhood all respected me and looked up to me. I would never want to diminish myself in their eyes. The people tended to believe me, but the whole episode never sat well. Things like that never do.

I always preferred to room alone on the road. Because of the racial attitudes in those days, it was unheard of for a black and white ballplayer to room together. So in 1952, I roomed with Hector Rodriguez, and in 1953 with Bob Boyd.

Bob was our back up first baseman in 1953. His nickname was "The Rope." At 5'10" and 170 pounds he had a taut muscular body. Like Hector and myself the year before, Bob and I hung around a lot together. Being from Mississippi, Bob was quite sensitive about any racial slight. He became quite upset one day in Philadelphia after we had just come into town and were checking in the hotel. Bob happened to see a listing of the ballplayers and which players were in a given room. He took a closer look and saw, "Room 401—Minnie Minoso and Bob Boyd, Negro."

Bob was very angry. "Minnie," he said. "I don't like this, I just don't like this one bit!" I tried to calm him down by saying, "Bob, we are black. So what?" But I knew how hurt Bob was, so I called for the desk clerk. When he came out I said to him, "Sir! Whoever wants to find out if Bob Boyd and Minnie Minoso are black or white, tell them to pay and to come out to the ballpark to see. Not to put it down here." He insisted that he did not make these notations, that is how it came to the hotel. I said I didn't care how it got there, but that I never wanted to see anything like that again. I took my pen and scratched it out.

Usually I don't react like that. I did it for Bob, because I knew he was hurt; I really didn't care. I am black. That is a fact of life. I told Bob we didn't have to make apologies for who we are. Somewhere in the conversation I also added that as long as they don't call me "whitey" or "blondie" it's all right.

Now to show you how these things get out of context, when we returned to Chicago there was an article in *Jet* Magazine stating that Minnie Minoso said he is not black. A lot of people wanted to know. "Minnie, did you really say that?" they would ask. So I made a statement that all this was a bunch of "bull." I had never made such a statement. What I said was said only to make Bob Boyd feel better. What I had said in the hotel was "Yeah, we're black. But we are baseball players." That's what's important to me.

Bob Boyd did a good job for us in 1953 as a back up first baseman and outfielder. He played in 55 games and hit   a respectable .297. He must have impressed Paul Richards as well. He followed Richards to Baltimore in 1956, where he was the Orioles' starting first baseman for four seasons. Bob Boyd hit a career-high .318 in 1957, and closed his nine-year big league career in 1961 with a lifetime average of .293.

We finished the 1953 season in third place with 89 wins and 65 loses. Our 89 wins were the most by any White Sox team since 1920. The Yankees were out in front of everyone again with a 99-52 record and their fourth straight American League pennant. More important, we had closed the gap and finished only three games behind the second-place Cleveland Indians. We led the league in fielding percentage and in triples. For the third straight year we led in stolen bases. Billy Pierce was 18 and 12, and perhaps the best left hander in the League. He led the American League with 186 strike outs. He was second in the American League with a 2.72 ERA and second in shutouts with 7, two behind Bob Porterfield of the Washington Senators.

Virgil Trucks was nothing short of sensational since coming over from the St. Louis Browns. He was 15 and 6 in a White Sox uniform, and 20 and 10 on the year. He was second to Pierce in strike outs with 149, and right behind Billy with a 2.93 ERA. Billy Pierce and Virgil Trucks were the best right hander/ left hander pitching duo in the American League in 1953. What Richards had done for Billy Pierce in 1951, he did for Virgil Trucks in 1953. I said it before and I'll say it once more. There was simply no one better with pitchers than Paul Richards.

I promised myself to have a better 1953, and I did. Much better, in fact. I pushed my average up to .313, tied for third in the American League with Billy Goodman. Mickey Vernon and Al Rosen went down to the wire in 1953 for batting honors. It was the year Al Rosen came within an inch of winning the triple crown. Mickey Vernon edged him out for the batting title, .337 to 336, when Rosen failed to beat out a ground ball in his final at bat of the season. For the third straight year, I led the American League in stolen bases with 25, with Jim Rivera second again with 22. I raised my home run total to 15. Most important to me was the vast improvement in run production. I drove in 104 runs, and scored the same number. It was the first time I topped the 100 RBI mark.

With the false paternity suit behind me and a very good season in my pocket, I had a lot to look forward to in 1954. There was no question that I could play baseball with the best of them, and I was getting better each year. I had built a lovely home in Havana for my sisters, Juanita and Flora, where I would spend the winter months. They had both worked so hard. I kept my promise to my mother when she died that I would take care of my sisters. Juanita had been a cook in the employ of some wealthy families in Havana. Before I made enough money to take care of my sisters, Juanita would always bring food home for all of us. Flora cleaned houses and made less money than Juanita. In today's language, my sisters would be called "domestics."

Once I began making good money, I insisted that they quit working. There was no need to now; they could devote themselves to the children and to themselves. They could take care of the house on a full-time basis. Why should the sisters of a famous Major League baseball star have to work in the homes of other people? I felt strongly about that issue. Here everybody in Cuba knew me. My sisters deserved a better life, and the sisters of a hero who could drive a big Cadillac should not be doing domestic work.

In Cuban society, the man was the head of the household. So even if I was the youngest I carried a lot of weight. But I never abused my authority. Even today things are not like they are in our present American culture. The man has the final word 99 percent of the time; he is still the boss. It's this way in Miami today with Cuban families.

I've mentioned that I was chosen Cuban Athlete of the Year. But I never forgot who I was and where I came from. I was still Saturnino Orestes Arrieta Armas Minoso from El Perico, the same person who cut sugar in Cuba as a boy. I had no trouble handling success; I was just happy and enjoying where I was in life. It has always been difficult for me to pretend. I respond to people the same way, no matter where I am. Too many successful people—certainly many athletes—start believing their own publicity. They lie to themselves, and that is no good. Sooner or later in life you pay for self-deception.

I was also encouraged by an increasing number of Latin players who were making their way into the big leagues. Willie Miranda, who came up with Washington in 1951 and spent some time with the White Sox in 1952 before going to the Yankees and the Orioles, was an excellent defensive shortstop—one of the best. Bobby Avila was about to become the American League batting champion in 1954. Chico Carrasquel was still an All Star shortstop, and another Venezuelan shortstop, future Hall of Famer Luis Aparicio, was waiting in the wings. Sandy Amoros, who made that great catch in the 1955 World Series, was already playing for the Brooklyn Dodgers. Puerto Rican-born Ruben Gomez had just won 13 games for the New York Giants. And fellow Cuban Camilo Pascual, a right hander with a wicked curve ball who would win 174 ball games in his career, was a rookie with the Washington Senators in 1954.

I was not the only Cuban ballplayer on the White Sox roster in 1954. Mike Fornieles had won eight games for us in 1953, and was back for a second season. But it was Sandy Consuegra, who had been 7 - 5 in 1953, who would rewrite the Sox record book in 1954.

Sandy Consuegra was born in Porterillo, Cuba and came to the White Sox from the Washington Senators in 1953. During spring training in Tampa in 1954, Sandy was fooling around and cut himself with a spike. He needed six or seven stitches on his foot, and decided to rest at the hotel the next day. Sandy's absence did not go unnoticed by Paul Richards, who looked around the field and didn't see him. "Hey Doc!" Richards yelled to Doc Cramer.

"Where's Consuegra?" Richards told me to call Sandy at the hotel and tell him to get out on the field. He sent the trainer to pick him up.

Sandy thought Richards was nuts. He couldn't walk on his foot, much less suit up. Richards had other ideas. Sandy was wearing a pair of slippers, and Paul Richards had the trainer cut a hole in them. Then he constructed a platform from some wooden boards. He had Sandy sit on the wooden platform with his feet dangling and throw to the catcher. Sandy had to throw 15 minutes, then rest five minutes, and throw 15 minutes again. This went on every day in the hot sun. Sandy sat in the chair and threw for 45 minutes each day until the foot was healed. Sandy was in top form. Sandy, a relative unknown before the season started, had an amazing year, winning 16 games and losing only three, with a 2.69 ERA. His winning percentage of .842 was tops in baseball that year and remains the very best in Chicago White Sox history.

Needless to say, with Frank Lane running the show, there would be new faces in camp. One of the most interesting was that of Phil Cavarretta, former Chicago Cub great who played nineteen seasons on the other side of town. Cavarretta had been fired as Cub manager during spring training, and Lane immediately signed him for utility purposes. The old pro did his job well, hitting .316 for the White Sox in 71 games, many as a first-base replacement for the injured Ferris Fain.

There were other interesting acquisitions as well. In an attempt to bone up our third-base problem, Lane spent $123,000 to purchase the contract of former All Star and future Hall of Famer George Kell. Kell would divide the third base chores that year with Cass Michaels. In one of the year's big tragedies, Michaels was beaned by a pitch that fractured his skull, and he was forced to retire from the game at the age of 28. Chicago-born Johnny Groth also came to the Sox from the St. Louis Browns to patrol the centerfield turf for us.

Our pitching was especially strong in 1954. In addition to Pierce, Trucks, and Sandy Consuegra, Richards worked his magic on two previously unheralded pitchers, Right hander Bob Keegan who was 7 and 5 with the Sox in 1953, and left hander Jack Harshman, a converted first baseman, who had toiled a few years with the New York Giants. In a game against the Red Sox on July 25, Harshman set 16 batters down on strikes.

I felt as ready as I had ever felt for the start of the 1954 season. Keeping in good shape was always a priority with me; I refuse to abuse my body. I would take a drink now and then, but never in my life have I been drunk, and I've never taken drugs. I loved music and spent some time in the clubs, though not as much time as people thought. I spent much more of my leisure time at the movies. I am a big western fan.

Some ballplayers drank and played the town the night before a ball game. I felt they were fooling themselves. If you are not in top shape for a game, you not only fool yourself, you cheat the team. I don't claim to be perfect; I had my share of fun. But it is my feeling if you start lying to yourself, it won't be long until you lie to your manager and then to your teammates. I felt I owed it to everyone to be in the best shape I could be for a game. My teammates looked to me to hit and to play well. I'd have been doing them all a disservice if for any reason I didn't give them my best. Baseball was my profession, and I felt an obligation to give it my very best each day I was out there.

Nineteen fifty-four was an unusual year on many accounts. We won 94 games and still finished in third place. The Yankees won 103 games, more than any other Yankee team managed by Casey Stengel, and finished second. This is because in 1954, the Cleveland Indians established an American League mark by winning 111 games while losing only 43. In one of the great World Series upsets in history, the Indians would be swept in four games by the New York Giants in the 1954 October Classic. To show how lopsided the American League was in 1954, the Boston Red Sox finished in fourth place with a record of 69 and 85, 42 games behind the Indians.

Paul Richards had done a marvelous job once again. We actually split the 22 games we played against the Indians. Richards surprised us all in late August when he asked and received permission to negotiate with the Baltimore Orioles. Eager to escape Lane's shadow, he resigned as White Sox manager on September 10. Former St. Louis Brown's manager Marty Marion became the new Sox skipper. After the 1953 season, the St. Louis Browns were sold and moved to Baltimore, becoming the first Major League franchise to be moved since 1903.

Of course it was all Cleveland Indians in 1954. Bobby Avila won the batting championship, as Ted Williams did not have enough at bats to qualify for the title. Larry Doby led in home runs and runs batted in. Bob Lemon and Early Wynn topped the American League with 23 wins apiece, and Mike Garcia won 19 games and led the American League with a 2.64 ERA. The New York Yankees were still our same nemesis, beating us out of second place by nine games.

Nevertheless, it was a wonderful year for us, the best since I joined the club in 1951. Our pitching was marvelous. Billy Pierce slipped some to a 9 - 10 record, but he still tossed four shutouts and struck out 148 batters in only 188 innings, the best strikeout ratio in the American League. Virgil Trucks, with a record of 19-12 had another great year, just missing that 20-game mark for the second year in row. Bob Keegan went 16 - 9, including a no-hitter, Jack Harshman was 14 - 8, and of course, Sandy Consuegra was great with his league-leading 16 - 3 record. Our pitchers threw a total of 21 shutouts, the most in the Major Leagues.

For the third consecutive year, the Chicago White Sox led the American League in fielding percentage, committing the fewest errors in the League. And for the fourth year in a row, we topped the American League with 98 stolen bases. Nellie Fox tied Harvey Kuenn of the Tigers with 201 base hits to lead the American League.

I had my most productive big league season to date in 1954. I hit .320, second to Bobby Avila's .341 average. I led the American league in triples with 18 and in total bases with 304. I drove in a career high 116 runs, fourth best in the American League. I was second in runs scored with 119, second in doubles (29), second in slugging average behind Ted Williams (.535), and tied for second with Jim Rivera in stolen bases (18).

I had remained remarkably free of injuries in the past four years. Rarely did I miss a game. I was hit by more pitches than anyone in baseball, yet avoided serious injury. I would get the scare of my life in 1955 when I was decked in the head by Bob Grim of the Yankees. I was hospitalized for ten days and forced to miss 15 ballgames. And one other amazing thing happened that year. Unlike the previous years, the Chicago White Sox would find themselves involved in a genuine pennant race in 1955.

In the spring of 1955, I attended an exhibition game with my parents between the St. Louis Cardinals and the Chicago White Sox. That was the spring after I had my initial encounter with polio.

I was a White Sox fan. I went to the game with a White Sox t-shirt, a White Sox cap and my crutches. I was not quite six years old and was down by the dugout with everyone else trying to get autographs.

All of a sudden this ballplayer came up and handed me a baseball. He just gave it to me. It was a pleasant surprise for me. The player was a pitcher for the Cardinals named Tom Poholsky. I was just thrilled as any youngster would be. I remember turning around and showing the ball to my father, and I went back with my dad to thank him for the ball, and he said that another player had given it to me. He pointed to Minnie Minoso.

Minnie had given the ball to Poholsky to give to me. The reason was that apparently he didn't feel comfortable in Memphis, a segregated city, giving a ball to a white boy. Of course my father motioned him over and we thanked Minnie and talked with him. That started our relationship. We used to see Minnie when he came to Memphis with the White Sox and then with the Indians.

We went up to Chicago a few times and visited Minnie in the clubhouse. My father would give me a tie to give to Minnie as a gift. Minnie gave me a bat and he gave me a cap. Then we moved to Florida and California, and I would visit him in spring training just to say hello.

I read about Minnie attempting to play in that sixth decade in 1990. I passed a resolution in the Tennessee State Assembly praising Minnie for his anticipated sixth decade, and relating back to how sometimes people do small things that have an effect in a bigger way. One of those things was Minnie giving me that ball.

It opened my eyes to the evils of segregation, when a person who wanted to do something good and kind couldn't do it because of segregation. It taught me how foolish segregation was, and the evils associated with the separation of the races. In our State Legislature, I have been responsible for much of the civil and human rights legislation that has passed our Legislature. I encompassed that in the resolution which I presented to Minoso at home plate during the last year of the old Comiskey Park. It was a very proud moment for me.

I had called Commissioner Fay Vincent in 1990 about letting Minnie play in another decade. I introduced myself and explained how he could find an exception for the last year of a stadium; this being a situation of such historic significance. He said something like we don't want midgets batting, players parachuting into centerfield or other types of freaky exhibitions. He thanked me for calling.

Senator Steven Cohen, Tennessee State Senator

10

A SON IN
THE FAMILY

In 1955, my son, Orestes Jr., was almost three years old. This might surprise some readers, because I mentioned nothing of being married. The truth is that Orestes Jr. and my daughter, Cecilia, who was born in 1957, were born out of wedlock.

It was no secret that Julia Perez, the mother of both children, and I were not married. We had met in Cuba in 1947 when I was playing for Marianao. We were playing in a new park called El Cerro when I saw Julia and her sister in the box seats with the great Cuban boxing champ Kid Galivan. Kid Galivan would be welterweight Champion of the World one day and was known in fight circles for his damaging bolo punch. Galivan and Julia had been good friends for some time. She was very pretty and quite a nice lady; our attraction was almost immediate. I was introduced to her properly, and in time we became close friends. I met her sisters and the rest of her family when I started visiting her house.

So by 1952 we had been seeing each other for five years. She was more of a steady girlfriend than the others I was dating, which says a lot, because I was out of Cuba and in the United States for more than half the year. After that exciting rookie year in Chicago, I returned to Cuba for winter ball and we spent lots of time together.

We were winding down the '52 baseball season, when I got a call telling me that Julia was expecting a baby. My feelings were mixed. I was happy on the one hand, but very nervous and confused on the other. Truly, I didn't know what to do.

I returned to Cuba when the season was over. My son, Orestes Jr., was born on October 22, 1952. I loved Julia Perez, I really believe I did. But I was not ready to get married. I knew at the time that it would never work out for me. And if there is one thing I don't do well, it is to pretend. There was another factor; I was too carefree for marriage. I admit this freely. I also had obligations to my sisters. I had promised my mother before she died that I would take care of my sisters. Later my thoughts on this issue would start to change, but then my sisters were still my responsibility.

So I took care of Julia and Orestes, but still lived at home with Juanita and Flora. There was no big publicity. It was no secret who Orestes' father was, you bet there wasn't! Orestes Jr. was with me all the time. He was my first child and I was crazy about him. I had a little sleeper in my car and would take him to the ballpark with me. He had a little uniform like mine, with the same number on the back. As he got a little older, he would run with me in the outfield. We even made a commercial together for a vitamin company. I'll have much more to say about my family and children later. For now let's go back to Sarasota, Florida where the White Sox were training in the spring of 1955.

There were new faces in camp as usual. No Frank Lane team ever stayed the same for long. One of the best was big Walt Dropo. Dropo, who had one of the great rookie seasons ever in 1950 when he drove in 144 runs, came to us in trade with the Detroit Tigers. He hit .280 and gave us some much-needed home run punch. Ferris Fain who had played injured most of the '54 season was traded off to the Tigers. Another newcomer back for a second tour of duty was Jim Busby, our centerfielder from the original 1951 "Go Go" squad.

Our pitching was better than ever. "Superb" might be the appropriate word. Billy Pierce, Virgil Trucks, and Jack Harshman gave us three proven starters. Sandy Consuegra was there as a spot starter and relief pitcher. Connie Johnson, a hard-throwing right hander whom I used to call "Nat 'King' Cole" because of his striking resemblance to the great singer, was another starter with durability. The newest hero of our mound corps was right hander Dick Donovan. Donovan, who previously had not won a game with the Boston Braves and the Detroit Tigers, developed a slider, and by July 30 was pacing the staff with a 13 -4 record. Then a reported minor ailment of the stomach turned out to be appendicitis, and he would not pitch again until September. Dick Donovan's appendix may well have cost the Chicago White Sox the American League pennant in 1955.

I never paid too much attention to the MVP voting, but if I ever really had a shot at it, 1954 was the year. I realized that much of the time a player from a team that wins the pennant or a World Series title has an added boost in MVP voting. The Indians won in 1954, so I thought Larry Doby had as good a shot as anyone. Larry led the American League in homers and runs batted in. MVP honors went instead to Yogi Berra, who captured his second MVP award. Yogi was always a worthy candidate, but this particular year Larry and I both wondered why we had been overlooked. That year we both could make a legitimate claim to MVP honors.

Having said this, let me also say that I do not feel that I was cheated a bit by not playing with a pennant winner. I do know many ballplayers who need a World Series ring to feel that their baseball lives are complete. To play in a World Series, they will argue, is the most important thing in baseball. This was not true for me. Certainly it would have been nice to have played in a World Series, but to me the most important thing was to make the Majors in the first place; then to stay around enough years to have a good career. Look at Ernie Banks with the Cubs, all those years and not a single World Series. I would say there are lots of others who played 12 to 15 years in the big leagues without putting a World Series notch on their baseball belts. Call it fate; that's as good a word as any.

We missed Paul Richards in 1955. Marty Marion was a good manager, but the ball club wasn't the same without Paul. Personally I missed Paul a lot; but in this game very few stay in one place forever. Most of the players, I think, did not know all of what was going on upstairs in the front office. I certainly did not. They didn't bring it down on the field and that's how it should always be. A ballplayer's job should not be affected by what is going on anywhere but on the ballfield. Having problems at home is no excuse. When you are in uniform, your job is to play well.

So while we missed Paul Richards, we played as well as ever because we were professionals. Getting a new manager was like an orchestra getting a new band leader. It is the players' jobs to do their best every day and to utilize their talent well, no matter who is leading the band. In our era, if a manager did a pretty good job, you could generally expect to see him the next year. Today things are much different. A team changes managers as quickly as a catcher changes signals.

I remember the 1955 season well for many reasons. To begin with, I had a 23-game hitting streak, the longest in my big league career. Secondly we were involved in a real pennant race that year. We even found ourselves in first place as late as September 3rd. Finally, in 1955, Frank Lane left the White Sox organization. After eight years as White Sox general manager, and with five years remaining on a new contract, Frank Lane resigned his position. We were very close and I knew I would miss him; we had a special relationship. Frank and I would be together again in a few years, but then I would be wearing a different uniform. Always the master trader, Frank Lane was involved in nearly 250 separate deals involving over 350 players in his seven years with the Chicago White Sox.

It is common knowledge that I had a propensity for being hit by pitches. I believe I was hit nearly 200 times in my career. But none of them put me out of commission like a pitch thrown by the New York Yankees' Bob Grim in 1955. Let me say up front that I don't believe Bob Grim ever meant to hit me. Some pitchers did, but not Bob Grim. Grim had been a 20-game winner as a rookie in 1954, and I believe the only pitcher ever to win 20 games without pitching 200 innings. Bob threw a high, inside fastball to me. Normally I think I could have gotten out of the way, but it was getting dark in New York, and I couldn't follow the ball well. I felt an explosion in my head and went down; I was barely conscious. Nino Valdez, the heavyweight boxing champ of Cuba was in the stands. He jumped over the box seats into the field. "That's Minnie! That's my countryman!" I could hear him yell. Nino Valdez went to the clubhouse with me. He kept telling me everything would be O.K. He waited with me until the ambulance arrived to take me to the hospital.

I was trying to sleep in the hospital room when I opened my eyes and saw a guy by the door looking in. He had a woman with him and appeared as if he didn't want me to see him. But I recognized him; it was Bob Grim. He tried to leave, but I told him to come in. I said, "Come in, Bob. It's O.K." He really was shaken. "I'm sorry, Minnie!" he apologized. "I never meant to hit you. Please believe me!" He brought the woman in the room with him. She was holding onto his arm. I told him I believed him. It wasn't his fault, I assured him. It was a little dark, and if he really wanted to hit me he would have actually thrown behind me. I cleared things up, at least for the remainder of the year. However, tempers lingered, and the following year the White Sox and the Yankees became involved in one of the wildest bench clearing fights imaginable.

People often ask why I was hit so often with pitches. I think it was a combination of a few factors. One had to do with my stance. I crowded the plate, with my right foot actually closer to the plate than my left. I was an easy target. Remember too, I was a good hitter, and pitchers were not going to let me dig in. They too have to protect their turf. Baseball is a constant state of war between the batter and the pitcher. There were not all those rules back then to prevent a pitcher from brushing back a hitter. If you took too many liberties with the pitcher, or hit him hard, or tried to embarrass him, you could expect a really close shave the next time you came to bat.

There were some guys out there who just had it on their mind to throw at me. Jim Bunning was one who threw at me a lot, which was surprising because Jim and I played together with the Marianao club in Cuba. Once he hit me on purpose; this I know. I was taking batting practice and hit one 360 feet over the fence in left field. I looked at Jim Bunning, who was going to pitch against us, and told him I was going to do that again when I faced him later. "No way, Minoso. No way!" he shouted back to me. He was wrong. When I came to bat, I hit a home run in precisely the same place. The next time I was up, he delivered a pitch right under my chin. He didn't hit me, but boy was I mad. I took a feeble swing at the ball and let go of the bat so it would fly in his direction. He got the message. I usually didn't do things like that; but I was hot under the collar. In more ways than one, I might add.

There was another pitcher who threw at me a lot. He was Willard Nixon, a southern boy from Georgia who pitched for the Boston Red Sox. My usual habit after I was hit was to pick up the ball and throw it back to the pitcher underhand. This especially annoyed him. It was my way of rubbing in that old "Jungle Jim" Rivera line, "You can't hurt Minnie with that garbage you are throwing." Funny thing, but many years later I ran into Willard Nixon and he apologized for throwing at me so much. He had softened a lot. He said he was born in an area of the south where he was expected to do things like this. The best way to fight pitchers who threw at me was to get up and hit the daylights out of the next pitch. Once I got on base, I would find a way to score. I didn't try throwing punches like these guys do today. There is too much of that today, and it is plain silly. My way was much more productive, and, I might add, more satisfying.

We battled the Yankees and Indians right down to the wire in 1955. On September 3 we enjoyed a half-game lead. This was the latest date the White Sox were in first place since September of 1920. Our pitching, defense, and speed remained intact. Yet in 1955 we displayed some power as well. We hit more home runs than any prior White Sox club. One game that comes to mind was April 23, 1955, against the Kansas City Athletics. We knocked out 29 hits including seven home runs to beat Kansas City 29 - 6. We tied a major league record for most runs scored in one game. I played my part, hitting one of the seven home runs and scoring five runs.

We flirted with first place for a while, but at the end of the season we finished in third place again, five games behind the Yankees, and two games behind the second place Cleveland Indians. Billy Pierce was just sensational, far better than his 15-10 might indicate. He led the Major Leagues with a 1.97 earned run average, the only time in the 1950s that a pitcher had an under 2.00 ERA. Billy threw six shutouts and lost many heart breakers. Casey Stengel made him the American League's starting pitcher in the All Star Game, although Billy's record was one game under .500 at the time. Billy struck out 157 batters, third best in the American League. Herb Score in his rookie season with the Cleveland Indians fanned a total of 245 hitters.

Dick Donovan finished the year at 15 - 9. Trucks had another good year with a 13 - 8 record. Jack Harshman was 11-7. Our main guy in relief in 1955 was right hander Dixie Howell—his full name was Millard Fillmore Howell after the American President—who finished with an 8 - 3 record. Nineteen fifty-five was also the last season in a White Sox uniform for Harry Dorish.

Harry was the unheralded, but most steady relief pitcher on our club for four years. Harry was traded to the Baltimore Orioles early in the '55 season. In his four seasons with the White Sox, Harry was credited with 36 saves and compiled an overall record of 36 wins and 20 losses.

We hit 116 home runs in 1955. Not a particularly high number, but quite high for a Chicago White Sox team of that era. Walt Dropo led the team with 19, and Sherman Lollar had 16. George Kell had a fine year, hitting .312 and leading the club with 81 runs batted in. Nellie Fox hit .311, fourth best in the American League, and his 198 base hits were two shy of Al Kaline's total of 200. Like Herb Score, Al Kaline set the baseball world on its heels in 1955. Just two years out of high school, the 20-year-old Kaline led the American League in hitting with an average of .340.

I played in only 139 games, my lowest total as a regular player. The beaning and the hospitalization took its toll; I had only missed one game in the previous two seasons. My average fell 33 points to .288. My run production dropped as well to 10 home runs and 70 runs batted in. The White Sox finished the season with a record of 91 - 53. It was a good showing for first year manager Marty Marion. We also led the American League in hitting with a .268 team average. For the fifth straight year, we led the League in stolen bases. Jim Rivera led all American League base runners with 25. I was second with 19.

For the second straight year, the Chicago White Sox won 90 games, and because we were a real pennant contender, there was a newfound excitement. What if Dick Donovan had not undergone surgery? What if Minoso had not been beaned and hospitalized? Such "iffy" intangibles make baseball the interesting game that it is.

The winds of change were in the making though. It started with Lane's resignation on September 21, in response to a public reprimand by Chuck Comiskey over remarks made by Lane to the League's supervisor of umpires, Cal Hubbard. Both Frank Lane and Paul Richards, the two architects of the "Go Go" Chicago White Sox, were now team history. The winds of change would surface on the playing field as well, a subtle but troubling indicator that some of our original cast might soon be treading different pastures. It started in 1956 when one of our true stalwarts was traded away. Chico Carresquel was traded to the Cleveland Indians in exchange for Larry Doby.

The reason I flew to Chicago to interview Minnie and other Latinos is something that isn't too well known in baseball circles. This is Minnie Minoso's position within the history of Latin players. Before Minnie came on the scene in the late forties there had been around 50 Latin players who had played the game, all of them light skinned because of the racial policies. None of them had ever made a real big impact on the game until Minnie. He really put Latin players on the map in Major League Baseball.

He could hit. He could run. He could throw. And he played the game with such unbelievable style. Because of him and others who came up at that time like Chico Carrasquel, and later Aparicio and Clemente, scouts really started going after Latin players. A number of players like Orlando Cepeda, Tony Perez and Tony Olivia, who came up after Minnie and are very familiar to fans, look to him as a hero, even as an idol who showed them the way. He is like a father or a grandfather to the generation of Latin players who have come since. I firmly believe —and the research I did preparing my work bears this out— that those who came after him owe Minoso a debt of gratitude for opening the door and making Latin players legitimate in the Major Leagues.

When I met him I was taken by something else, which I feel is the essence of Minoso. Here is a man who grew up very poor, and lived in a very impoverished part of the country. The people he knew pretty much lived their lives picking sugar cane. He spoke to me about racism in his own country. That there were just places where blacks could not go. And yet he was able to lift himself out of that and come to the United States at a time when racial laws and segregation prevailed in this country. He passed through all this without ever letting it taint him in any way. He stayed clean all these years and never allowed himself to be dragged into the mud, or to allow hatred or self-hatred to become part of his personality.

Despite his humble beginnings, he transcended not only race, but class as well. There is an inner pride which makes him very comfortable with who he is and what he is all about. He held on to what he is and never allowed himself to be changed. The funny thing is I never saw him play. He retired as an active player in 1964, and I was born in 1965. Yet through my research and speaking with those who know him and those who played with and against him, I really came to respect who he is and what he stands for.

To me he is just a remarkable man.

Marcos Breton, The Sacramento Bee

11

THE WINDS OF CHANGE

The 1950s had entered its second half , and the Chicago White Sox were now genuine pennant contenders. Since 1951, when Frank Lane and Paul Richards first resurrected the baseball landscape on the south side of Chicago, old faces went and new faces came. Yes, there were lots of changes, that was precisely what Paul and Frank were all about, but the "Go Go" style of play always remained the same. We played winning baseball by melding speed with defense and pitching, and by adding some occasional power now and then. Of our 1951 squad, Jim Busby, Eddie Robinson, and Saul Rogovin had been traded elsewhere, although Busby came back in 1955 for one year. Sherman Lollar and Jim Rivera came to the club in 1952, joining Billy Pierce, Nellie Fox, Chico Carrasquel and myself, to form the nucleus of our ballclub.

In 1956, Chico became the first to find employment elsewhere. In November 1955, after five great seasons, the four-time American League's All Star shortstop was traded with Jim Busby to the Cleveland Indians for outfielder Larry Doby.

Larry's credits were well known. He was a genuine slugger who twice had led the American League in home runs and once in RBI's. It was nice being with Larry after all these years.

Larry and I went back a long time together, back to the Negro Leagues when I was with the New York Cubans and Larry with the Newark Eagles. We were later teammates during my brief time with the Cleveland Indians.

But it was sad to see Chico leave the club. We were more than teammates; we were good friends. Waiting in the wings to replace Chico was another brilliant shortstop from Venezuela named Luis Aparicio. The White Sox were so sure of Aparicio's potential that they were able to let Chico go in clear conscience.

Luis Aparicio impressed me from the start. He had worked out with the team in the past during spring training. Some of the ballplayers concluded that he was a relative of Chico's getting in some spring practice. He had good hands and a good arm; I thought he had a fine future. Aparicio's strong point was his speed; in this way, he was more in the true "Go Go" mold than Chico. He was also going to cover more ground because Chico had slowed up some due to his bad knees. Of all the great ball players the White Sox had during the 1950s, Luis Aparicio is the only one with extended years of service to have made it all the way to Cooperstown and the Hall of Fame. Early Wynn is a Hall of Famer, but he was with the club only five of his 23 Major League seasons.

Another new face on the team, and one of my favorite guys, was Sammy Esposito. Sammy was a local kid from Fenger High School in Chicago and a joy to be around. We got along real well and teased each other mercilessly. Sammy was a handsome guy in the traditional Italian mold. He would dress spiffy and spend lots of time combing his jet black hair. He looked the part of a man about town, a real ladies man, and I used to call Sammy "the pimp," which of course he wasn't. Sammy and "Jungle Jim" would pal around together, always joking and laughing with each other. Sammy was a good ballplayer, a real hustler on the field. His presence on our roster gave us one of the best utility men in the game. During one memorable four-game series with the Yankees in late June, Sammy showed his particular mettle by contributing heavily in a four-game sweep of the World Champions.

Billy Pierce, Dick Donovan, and Jack Harshman were our big three on the mound. Virgil Trucks, after three outstanding years in a White Sox uniform, was traded to the Detroit Tigers.

To pick up the slack, the White Sox obtained veteran right hander Jim Wilson from Baltimore. But the real coup was in landing Gerry Staley from the New York Yankees. Staley had been a starter and a winner for the St. Louis Cardinals in the early 1950s. Now his forte was mainly as a relief pitcher. Staley's acquisition would pay great dividends, especially in 1959 when the bullpen team of Turk Lown and Gerry Staley closed the door on so many late inning rallies and played such a huge role in the White Sox 1959 championship season.

Ballplayers usually prefer hitting in certain ballparks. My two favorite parks were Griffith Stadium in Washington D.C. and Briggs (Tiger) Stadium in Detroit. I played in both the old and new Griffith Stadium, and hit particularly well in the old Stadium. There was nothing to bother you there; the ball really traveled. I hit a lot to the left center field alley, so I always liked a park with lots of space out there.

Detroit was a hitter's paradise. It was far and away the best park to hit in. There were no distractions for a hitter to contend with. I liked Fenway Park in Boston, too. It was a good field with very good grass. But Fenway could trick you, and it took a little getting used to. It was easy to get derailed by the "Green Monster," the tall, inviting left field wall.

The "Green Monster" teases hitters. It looks so appealing, so easy to hit. Because of this, hitters try to pull the ball and end up dribbling it to short or third. This is what happened to me. When I first came up, I would try to pull the ball and ended up playing an abbreviated game of pepper with the shortstop. Paul Richards set me straight. "Minoso, why the devil are you trying to pull the ball? I just want you to hit away straight. Will you please?" I said "O.K., Paul! I'll try." Richards was right. The next time at bat I homered over the center field fence about 368 feet away. From then on I never tried to pull the ball in Fenway. I just went up to hit. A good hitter must know how to adjust to the park he is playing in.

Yankee Stadium was a different story; it was the hardest park for me to adjust to. Down the lines it looked so easy. But it is tough, because if you don't hit it down the lines, you are in trouble. The ball stays in the air forever and can be easily caught. Pitchers would give you the line like they did in Boston, but they would pitch you differently. I always had a warm spot in my heart for New York. I played three years for the New York Cubans, and always enjoyed coming back. Yankee Stadium was a good ballpark with a very special tradition. I just never liked to hit there.

I felt I had something to prove in 1956. I wanted to show the fans that the fractured skull was fully healed and no longer a hindrance. I wanted to improve on my 1955 numbers, which were not vintage Minoso. Many of the old faces were gone, but there was still that special feeling of camaraderie among the players. Of the eight regulars on the 1951 squad, only Nellie Fox and myself were in the starting line-up in 1956. Out of the entire pitching staff, only Billy Pierce remained.

We started well and by June we were breathing down the necks of the New York Yankees. On June 22, the Yankees came to town for a four-game weekend series. What transpired was a weekend of dramatic thrills the likes of which Comiskey Park fans have rarely seen. We swept the Yankees four games that weekend, as some of our less-heralded players became instant heroes. Sammy Esposito, pitcher Jim Wilson and Dave Philley, whom the Sox had traded away in the deal that brought me to Chicago, did most of the big damage.

Bad feelings between the two clubs lingered from the previous year, when I was decked by Bob Grim. This time Grim hit Dave Philley in the second game. We had had enough. The bad blood spilled out onto the field, and a free-for-all melee occurred. Tempers were hot. With the likes of Billy Martin, Hank Bauer and even an aging Enos Slaughter the New York Yankees were a rough, tough bunch of guys. They were fighters. But our guys refused to take a back seat in the exchange. We wouldn't be pushed. The following day, Billy Pierce and Gerry Staley polished off the weekend with a 14-2 and a 6-3 double header sweep of the World Champs. There was lots of celebrating.

Yet this was as far as it went. It was business as usual after that. The Yankees were still the Yankees. Mickey Mantle was tearing the League apart on the way to a banner Triple Crown season and the American League MVP Award. Hank Bauer emerged as a power hitter of some repute, along with first baseman Bill Skowron, a Chicago boy from Weber High School. Allie Reynolds, Vic Raschi, and Eddie Lopat were gone. The acknowledged ace of the staff was now Whitey Ford. Johnny

Kucks, Tom Sturdivant, Bob Turley, and Don Larsen provided the Yankees with a well-rounded rotation of starting pitchers.

It was tough overtaking the Indians, too, although we were getting closer. The Indians' pitching staff was still the best. Anchored by Bob Lemon, Early Wynn, and Herb Score, Cleveland boasted a talented trio of 20-game winners. Score was 20-9 with 263 strike outs in his second big league season. He was being hailed as a left handed Bob Feller, a pitcher with a Hall of Fame future. It all ended the following year when Herb Score was hit in the eye by a line drive off the bat of Gil McDougald. He would stick around for a few more years, but was never the same again. I have faced many pitchers in my day, and I have seen even more. But only Bob Feller and Nolan Ryan could throw a baseball any harder than Herb Score. Sandy Koufax was unbeatable in his day, a consummate pitcher once he learned control. He threw fast, but no faster than Score. Bob Feller, Nolan Ryan, Sandy Koufax, and Herb Score, two right handers and two left handers, were the fastest pitchers I have ever seen in this game.

The 1956 season was a little disappointing. We had won more than 90 games in 1954 and 1955. In 1956, our won-loss record dropped to 86-69. We finished 12 games behind the Yankees, and one game behind the second-place Cleveland Indians.

Pitching, defense, and speed had again carried the day. We led the American League in stolen bases for the 6th straight year, and in fielding percentage for the 5th year in a row. Billy Pierce had another great year. Billy was 20-9 and led the American League with 21 complete games; he was second to Herb Score with 192 strikeouts. Jack Harshman was 15-11, and Dick Donovan finished the year with a 12-10 record.

Larry Doby supplied some needed power, leading the club with 24 home runs and 102 runs batted in. I came back nicely. I led the team with a .316 average, hit 21 home runs, and drove in 88 runs. I was tied for the League leadership in triples with 11, and was third in runs scored with 106.

It was our rookie shortstop, Luis Aparicio, who stole the show in 1956. Luis hit .266, fielded brilliantly, and led the American League with 21 stolen bases. He was named the American League Rookie of the Year. The big change was still ahead. Try as we might, we couldn't seem to lift ourselves higher than third place. Perhaps it was time for a managerial change, so thought Chuck Comiskey. In late October, Marty Marion tendered his resignation as skipper, and Al Lopez, who had guided the Indians to one pennant and five second place finishes in six years, was named the new manager of the Chicago White Sox.

It is not easy for me to judge Al Lopez as a manager. I really wasn't with him long enough to have formed a definite opinion. Truly, his record with the Cleveland Indians was an outstanding one; he was a proven winner. He was also not a total stranger. Remember, he was the Cleveland manager in 1951, the year I was traded to the Chicago White Sox. Al must be given credit for allowing me the opportunity to prove my worth as a Major League player. Early in 1951 we were playing an exhibition game against the New York Giants. I was sitting in the bullpen with a few of the guys when Lopez came over and took a look around. He gazed my way. "Minoso," he asked, "did you ever play first base?" I told him I hadn't, but I would try. He said he wanted me to play first for Allie Clark. For some reason he was angry at Clark, a reserve outfielder and first baseman, who soon would be traded away.

Then suddenly, the bases were loaded. Lopez called time out and told me to pinch hit for Clark. I went to the plate and hit a grand slam home run. When Luke Easter was hurt, I started playing first base. I was playing first base much of the time before the Indians traded me to the Chicago White Sox a short time later. So Lopez helped me establish myself as a Major League ballplayer. However, in later years, my feelings about Al Lopez would become tinged with ambiguity and doubt.

Lopez did a good job in 1957. We moved up to second place, the first time since 1920 that any White Sox team had been that high. Realizing that we had problems at the corners, Lopez experimented with Jim Rivera at first and Bubba Phillips at third. When that didn't work out, the Sox traded Dave Philley to the Tigers for Earl Torgeson. Burly and bi-speckled, "Torgy" was one tough cookie. A hard-nosed veteran, he spent many years in the National League with the Boston Braves, and played first base on the Braves' championship team of 1948. I remember Torgeson for quite another reason. He once made a complete fool of me.

We were playing the Tigers and I was on base. Earl was the first baseman. I never knew him well, only that he had a reputation as a tough competitor and an aggressive ballplayer. When he politely said, "Minnie, would you please step off the base so I can kick the dirt from the bag." I said "Sure! No problem!" Well there was a problem, a big one. Guess what was in Torgeson's hand as soon as I stepped off the bag. He was holding the baseball. Torgeson simply tagged me on the spot and I was out. Wow! Did I feel ashamed.

There were two outstanding additions to our club in 1957. One was outfielder Jim Landis. Landis originally signed as an infielder, but learned the outfield so well, that he was soon being compared favorably as the defensive equal to Joe DiMaggio in his prime. The other great addition was catcher Earl Battey. Earl who was up very briefly in 1955 and 1956, saw some playing time in 1957 as a back-up catcher to Sherman Lollar. Battey had caught Paul Richards' eye years earlier, but had the misfortune of playing in Sherm Lollar's shadow for too long. Once he was traded to the Washington Senators in 1960, Earl quickly established himself as one of baseball's best all-around catchers.

We got off to a great start in 1957, our best since 1951. We held first place until the end of June, and our six-game lead on June 8th was the largest by any White Sox team since 1919. The New York Yankees were our target. We were optimistic that this could be the year. I was having one of my best seasons, and was confident that we could win it all. Nellie Fox, as usual, was among the League's top hitters all year. Nellie Fox and Luis Aparicio gave us the best keystone combo in the American League. Billy Pierce and Dick Donovan were pitching beautifully and were capable of beating the best on any given day.

Some habits die hard. Once again we had what now had become our yearly fist fight and brawl with the New York Yankees. This one was a real humdinger. On June 14th, Yankee right hander Art Ditmar plucked Larry Doby. The usual words were exchanged, and then the benches cleared. Dropo grabbed Slaughter and fists were flying from all directions. When it was over neither team got off unscathed. Fines of $150 apiece were leveled at Larry Doby, Walt Dropo, Billy Martin and Enos Slaughter for their parts in the melee. We were backed to the core by our front office. "The Yankees have been bullying their opponents long enough," said White Sox vice president John Rigney. "I'm glad it happened!"

Bullies or not, the New York Yankees could not be stopped on the ballfield. At the end they were once again American League champs with a record of 98 - 56. We finished in second place, eight games behind. We distanced ourselves well from the third-place Red Sox who finished eight games behind us. An interesting fact that year was that Paul Richards' upstart Baltimore Orioles had become a .500 ballclub after only three years, and finished only one game behind the fourth-place Tigers. The fading Cleveland Indians fell to 6th place in 1957, their lowest finish since 1946. Bob Lemon and Mike Garcia were clearly on the downslide, Early Wynn fell to 14 and 17, and the loss of Herb Score was devastating. That marvelous pitching staff that made the Cleveland Indians perennial pennant contenders for a decade now was no more. In need of rebuilding, the Indians turned to Frank Lane to get things going again. Lane became the Indian's general manager. I, too, should have payed more attention to this particular front office move.

We finished the year with a record of 90 - 64. Once again we led the American League in fielding percentage and in stolen bases. Billy Pierce was 20 - 12, and Dick Donovan was 16 - 6. Pierce and Donovan recorded 16 complete games apiece to lead the American League. Jim Wilson had his best year with a record of 15 and 8. Nellie Fox hit .317 and became the first player in White Sox history to lead the American League in base hits. Luis Aparicio took stolen base honors again with 28.

I had one of my best years; everything went well. The Gold Glove Awards were originated in 1957, with one given at each outfield position. Willie Mays, Al Kaline, and myself were the first three outfielders to win Gold Gloves. It was the first of three Gold Gloves that I would be awarded.

I also had quite an All Star game that year. Hardly anybody at Busch Stadium in St. Louis noticed when I trudged into left field to replace Ted Williams. I drove a double off the centerfield wall in the top of the ninth to score Al Kaline from first base, in what proved to be the winning run in the American League's 6 - 5 victory that year. Then in the last of the ninth, I broke a National League rally with a great throw, gunning down Gus Bell at third base. With two outs, I speared Gil Hodges' hard line drive with a fine running catch to end the game, and to end a three-run ninth inning and preserve a 6 - 5 American League

"Two number 9's." Ted Williams and I at Municipal Stadium in 1959. He was the greatest hitter that I have ever seen.

My Rookie Year with the White Sox, 1951. How excited I was to finally be playing in the Major Leagues! In my rookie year I batted .326, second in the American League. I led the AL in triples with 14, and in stolen bases with 31. I was second in runs scored with 112, and placed fourth in MVP voting. It was a great year.

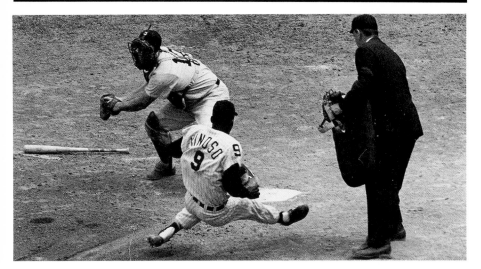

Sliding into home was always a great feeling. From 1951 through 1961, I scored more than 100 runs four times and more than 90 runs nine times.

My daughter, Marilyn, and I celebrating her sixth birthday in Mexico in 1969. At that time I was managing a team in Gomez Palacia, while I still continued to play winter ball. This was also the year that divisional playoffs were first instituted in the Major Leagues.

How fortunate I have always felt to be associated with the Chicago White Sox. It is a first-class organization run by first-class people.

"Seems like old times." Here I am, back in a White Sox uniform in 1976. At left is my old mentor and favorite manager, Paul Richards. Holding the bat is Al Lopez, the manager of the team every time I got traded; and next to him is Frank Lane, my "Papa Number Two."

I was always known for my sharp clothes and my flashy cars. Back in Cuba, I never dreamed I would ever own a Cadillac, and I took great pride in trading in for a new one every year. Some people like to gamble, some drink, some chase women. For me, it was cars and clothes.

I was honored on "Minnie Minoso Day" in Miami in 1976 by, among others, the former president of Cuba, Prio Socorra (right). Next to me is Edelia, my first wife. My many public commitments and her unfounded jealousy were factors in our estrangement and eventual divorce.

I have always loved and appreciated spending time signing autographs and talking with children. Here I'm presenting a ball to a little leaguer in Puerto Rico.

My life in baseball has opened many doors and has allowed me to meet some wonderful people. Here, I'm at a reception hosted by Vice-President Bush in Denver in 1984. It was held after an Old Timers' Game in which Vice-President Bush played and got a base hit on a line drive to center field off of Milt Pappas. I was greatly honored when Bush later sent me two pairs of cuff links with the presidential seal as a symbol of our friendship. I was also very honored when President Reagan sent me a letter of congratulations when my #9 was retired by the White Sox.

Here I am with my good friend, David Forbes, at his birthday party in 1992. I met David when I went to his house after I found out he had leukemia and had asked for my autograph.

Gerry Healey, president of the Minnie Minoso Fan Club, presents me with an autographed ball from his softball team in 1992. The fan club was founded in 1992 and has well over 1,000 members representing 15 states and three countries. I really appreciate the encouragement from all of the people who have followed my career through the years.

I am so grateful for the love and support I have always received from the Cuban community in Miami. Here I am thanking them for a "Minnie Minoso Day" in 1992.

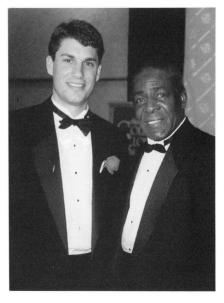

"The torch passes." I won three Gold Glove Awards in my career. Here I am chatting with White Sox third baseman Robin Ventura, 1993 Gold Glove recipient, at the awards banquet in New York City.

ORESTES MINOSO,JR 1B-OF

I often wonder what Orestes Jr.'s (left) baseball career might have been like had I been around to help guide him, instead of managing baseball in Mexico. Perhaps my daughter Cecelia's son, Lorenzo, (below, left) or my son, Charlie, (below, right) will one day have their own baseball cards.

My wife, Sharon, and my son, Charlie, make me happier than I have ever been in my life. I feel so very lucky to have them! Our age and race differences have been no barriers to our happy marriage.

My agent, John Wasylik, and I met while walking our dogs. Our friendship and working relationship have meant a great deal to me.

In 1980 I had five commemorative bats, one for each of my decades in baseball. Now that I'm a "six-decade man," I realize how blessed I am to have done the one thing I loved most in the world and made a good living at it. How many people can say that? I have been a very lucky man. This could only have happened in the United States of America, land of freedom and opportunity.

victory. I ran with the ball in my hand all the way to the dugout, where I asked Casey Stengel to autograph it for me. Casey did. It was only the second time in his seven All Star games to date that Casey managed a winner.

I knew I had been an important cog in the White Sox rise to second place. My stats spoke for themselves. I hit .310, drove in 103 runs, and tied for the League lead in doubles with 36. I was third in hits (176), tied for third in RBI's, and tied with Jim Rivera for second in stolen bases. In fact, Luis, Jim, and I were one, two, three in the stolen base department in 1957, giving the Chicago White Sox a clean sweep for the year.

Things could not have been better. I was an acknowledged baseball star. I had fame and popularity. I found a real home in Chicago; everybody knew me there. I was proud to be playing for the Chicago White Sox, one of the top teams in baseball. I had given my best always, and without false modesty my record looked quite good. In seven seasons with the White Sox, I hit better than .300 five times. I drove in more than 100 runs three times, and scored more than 100 four times. I led the League in triples three times, and in stolen bases three times. I led once in doubles and once in total bases. I headed back to Cuba for winter ball with Marianao, happy to see my family and my friends. The last thing I expected in the world was to be traded.

Suddenly the boom was lowered. I picked up the paper one morning in December—December 4th to be exact. What I read stunned me. I had been traded to the Cleveland Indians along with Fred Hatfield for Early Wynn and Al Smith. I had no idea such a trade was pending. I tried to clarify things in my mind, but nothing seemed to make sense. Then a thought crossed my mind, a fleeting thought this time. It had been the second time in my career that I had been traded: in 1951 with the Cleveland Indians, and now in 1957 with the Chicago White Sox. Both times it came as a total surprise. Perhaps it was just a bit coincidental, but both times the manager of the club that traded me happened to be Al Lopez.

The winds of change had blown full circle.

The thing that I remember about Minnie is that he was a winner. He was a run producer and he scored runs. He was an aggressive hitter and an aggressive base runner. With all these things he did physically, he was also a leader. He led by example. For some reason you just liked to watch him play, and he just brought that out in everybody else.

When Minnie came to Cleveland in 1958 we were working for Frank Lane, and he would trade anybody and everybody. So you were never surprised when there was a trade made by him. Lane thought an awful lot of Minnie; he would call him his son. And he'd say it in very endearing terms

Bobby Bragan was our manager at Cleveland the first part of 1958 and he thought the world of Minnie. He kept alluding that he was our best player in spring training, and we had a pretty good ballclub, including Rocky Colovito. I was also with Minnie with the White Sox in 1961; so I played with Minnie on two ballclubs, Cleveland and the White Sox. He not only was a hell of a player, he was a joy to be around. When you have a guy like him, everybody else just seems to fall in line. A lot of players didn't play with the same enthusiasm as Minnie, but he just loved the game so much that he couldn't play it any other way. Heck, I was a fan of his when I was sitting on the bench and not pitching. I enjoyed watching him play.

A lot of folks don't know that I first ran into Minnie in the Coast League when he was playing for San Diego and I was playing for the Los Angeles Angels. We knew he was a big league ballplayer at the time. I could tell that the first time I saw him swing a bat. He is one of my favorite people whom I played with all through the years.

Cal McLish, pitcher for the Cleveland Indians 1956-1959
Chicago White Sox, 1961

12

TO CLEVELAND AND BACK

The World Series That Almost Was

When I first heard I was traded to the Cleveland Indians, I felt that I had fallen into the ocean. In those days you developed a real emotional attachment to a club and the fans. We were not ballplayers for hire like today. We didn't sell our bat to the highest bidder. We had a loyalty that doesn't seem to exist now. Baseball is a different business today; the world has changed and so has baseball. True, we did not have the mobility and freedom that today's ballplayers have.

We did not have free agency, multi-year contracts, or high-powered agents. We could not veto a trade or dictate terms to the management. But we did have loyalty and friendship, a love for the game, and a burning desire to play. We held dear the tradition and professionalism of the sport. We wore our uniforms with pride and dignity. We kept locker room business within the confines of the locker room. Sure, things have changed. In some respects, perhaps for the better. But the pendulum of change seems to have gotten off kilter and has swung too much in the opposite direction.

So as badly as I felt, I kept my mouth shut. My only job now was to give the Cleveland Indians as much of myself as I had given to the White Sox. And what more fun could I have than to tangle with Frank Lane again over salary negotiations.

It was the same old story. Minnie Minoso and his "Papa Number Two" playing a game of cat and mouse over how much I should be paid. One thing I knew for sure is that Frank Lane wanted me. The deal that brought me to Cleveland was the first he had made as general manager. So when he sent me a contract that I found unacceptable, I had no compunction in not signing it immediately. Instead I put the contract in my pocket and brought it back to Tucson where the Indians were training. Frank Lane called me upon my arrival and we had lunch together. I made $40,000 with the White Sox in 1957. I had a fine year and felt I was entitled to a $15,000 raise to $55,000. Lane offered me $45,000. He held firm at that figure.

I would always bring back a large box of cigars from Cuba. By now that big Cuban cigar that I was smoking had made me dizzy, but I still held out for the $55,000 I originally requested. He applied more bait. "I'll tell you what, son! If you have a good year I'll give you a new Cadillac El Durado convertible." After all these years I learned the bargaining techniques of Frank Lane. "Daddy," I said, "you should know better than that. How do I know what you mean by a good year?" I explained that I could hit .999 but drive in only 99 runs, and by his interpretation that might mean a bad year, because I didn't drive in 100 runs. Frank Lane explained that a good year was to bring people into the park. He expected me to talk with the kids as I had in Chicago. If that was what he meant, it sounded easy as pie. I signed the contract for $45,000, and of course the promise of a new Cadillac if I delivered.

What Lane wanted to do with the Indians was to build his team around young Rocky Colovito and myself. Rocky, he felt, was coming into his own. He wanted my bat in the line-up to help him. We were his nucleus. He would have given half a ballclub for the two of us, he contended. Yet as he had stressed, he wanted more than our bats. Rocky and I were to be goodwill ambassadors. It meant taking care of people after the game. To walk with people and sit in the park with the kids. He wanted us to show kids how to be gentlemen. Sure, Frank Lane needed our bats, but he needed Colovito and I for public relations.

The Cleveland Indians were a team in transition in 1958. The strongest card was the pitching staff, consisting of promising youngsters like Mudcat Grant and Gary Bell, and some seasoned veterans like Ray Narleski, Don Mossi, and Hoyt Wilhelm. The emerging ace of the pitching staff was 33 -year-old Calvin Coolidge Tuscahoma McLish. Cal McLish would lead the club with a 16 - 8 record and an under 3.00 ERA. The following year Cal would do even better.

Larry Doby had been traded by the White Sox back to the Cleveland Indians, the same team where ten years earlier he had become the first black to play Major League baseball in the American League. It was also good to be reunited with Chico Carresquel, now a part-time shortstop with the Indians. Mickey Vernon, a two time American League batting champion, was winding down his playing career with Cleveland, as was former batting champ Bobby Avila, now in the last year of his ten-year career with the Indians.

There was also the guy that got away. In mid-1958, Lane traded 23-year-old Roger Maris to the Kansas City Athletics. The rest is history. The Kansas City club operated like an unofficial farm club to the New York Yankees. The St. Louis Browns served a similar role for the Chicago White Sox in the early 1950s. After one season with Kansas City, Roger Maris was traded to the Yankees. In 1960 Maris hit 39 homers, led the League in runs batted in, and was chosen American League MVP. In 1961, Roger Maris shattered the grandest record of all, breaking Babe Ruth's mark of 60 home runs in a season. Roger Maris' record 61 home runs in 1961 has yet to be bettered.

The deal went well for us too. Kansas City sent Cleveland an outstanding ballplayer, the versatile Vic Power. Power may well have been the best defensive first baseman in the game. Yet he could also play good second and third base as well. Also included in the deal was Woody Held who would do so much the following year when the Indians made a run for the pennant. Vic Power did a great job with his bat too, hitting .317 in a Cleveland uniform and .312 on the year.

I well recall the first time I came to Chicago to play in Comiskey Park. I was a Cleveland Indian now, and the feeling was strange to me. I admit there was a touch of bitterness toward the Sox management for having traded me. As usual, the fans gave me a warm welcome back. The fans were always in my corner in Chicago. I had heard that the organization sustained a lot of disfavor from the fans after the trade. I was friendly with my old teammates before and after the game. We joked and kidded around a lot. The White Sox had a good team, but my job now was to do all I could to beat them. When the game started, the White Sox were the enemy. It was strange to face Billy Pierce, my teammate for many years, and one of the best pitchers in the game. In all the years Billy and I were teammates, we had never faced each other, even in batting practice.

Midway through the season, with our record standing at 31 and 36, Joe Gordon replaced Bobby Bragen as the Cleveland manager. We played better than .500 ball for the remainder of the year, to finish the 1958 season in fourth place with a 77 - 76 record. I was satisfied with my work that year. I hit .302, with a career-high 24 home runs and 80 runs batted in. Rocky Colovito was just sensational. Rocky hit .303, with 41 homers and 113 runs batted in. His 41 home runs were just one short of Mickey Mantle's league-leading total of 42, and his .620 slugging average was the best in baseball. Cal McLish had the best year of his career, pacing the pitching staff with a 16 - 6 record and a 2.99 earned run average. The New York Yankees coasted to their fourth straight American League pennant and their tenth league title since 1949, ten full games ahead of the second-place White Sox. There didn't seem to be any way to stop them.

At contract time, I felt I was on thin ice. True, I had hit over .300 and had 24 home runs. But did my 80 runs batted in still constitute a 'good year' to Frank Lane? I wondered. Frank Lane clarified the matter immediately. "Son!," he said "You had quite a year. Here is $7,000. Go buy yourself a new Cadillac."

I was a little surprised. "Daddy, you must know I didn't drive in my 100 runs."

"Things are just fine," he assured me. "To me you drive in 150 the way you play."

In 1959, for the only time in my career, I had a genuine altercation with a manager. We were playing in Chicago shortly before All Star break; it was the final game of the series. In the seventh inning, we had men on first and second, and I was up.

Billy Pierce was pitching for the White Sox and he had a 3 - 2 count on me. Billy threw me a half-speed slider. If I had taken it for a called third strike, I would have looked foolish. Instead, I swung and foul tipped the ball. Sherm Lollar held on to it for strike three. Lollar then fired the ball to third to cut down the man on second who was trying to steal, and they had a double play.

After the game I asked Joe Gordon for permission to stay in Chicago during the All Star break. I was not selected to the All Star squad that year. I had an enjoyable three-day rest. When I returned to Cleveland, I was met at the airport by a friend. He told me he had read in the paper that Joe Gordon was going to rest me. I wondered why Gordon wanted to do that. I had plenty of rest, and wanted to get back on the field. His answer was only that Gordon felt I needed a rest.

We were playing the Boston Red Sox. The next day I arrived at the ball park to find that I wasn't in the line-up. Boy was I mad! Here I was leading the team in almost every department, and I find myself on the bench. Like I said, I was angry, so angry that I took a pencil and slashed out the line-up on the official score card. Eddie Stanky, who was one of our coaches, was sitting next to me. "Minnie!" he said with a look of surprise. "Why did you do that?" I simply said, "Eddie, in all my career I have never been benched. I don't understand this!" Knowing my state of mind, Stanky let the matter drop.

In the eighth inning, Gordon told me to pinch hit for Mudcat Grant. He said that this is what he was saving me for. I hit the ball 400 feet, and it was caught by the center fielder. I ran into the dugout, up the clubhouse stairs and into the locker room. I quickly got dressed and exited the ballpark. When one of the players asked if I wasn't staying till the end of the game, I told him I had done my duty. And I left.

Gordon didn't say anything about it. I don't know if he even knew. What he did the next day was to tell me to change my swing. He wanted me to chop on the ball. To swing down. It was the kind of swing that worked for him. It would never work for me. He had me in the line-up however. I was leading off.

Later in the game I came to bat with the pitcher on first base. I hit the tar out of the ball, a long home run. I took off around the bases, but the pitcher in front of me was just trotting, "Hey, Minoso," he said. "You're running, man!" I told him to pick up the pace or I was going to pass him and one of us would be out. He crossed the plate with me right behind on his heels. When we got to the dugout he yelled to me again.

"Minoso, you're crazy! You almost passed me. You almost stepped on me. Did you know that?" I snapped back, "Sure! I know. I'm the lead off man, and the job of the leadoff man is to run, even if he hits a home run, and the guy in front of him had better run too."

Joe Gordon said, "Nice going Minnie, but you didn't swing like I told you." That did it. "Look Joe!" I said. "How many Joe Gordons are there in the League? There is only one, right? But there is only one Minnie Minoso in the whole world. Minnie Minoso. I'm the only one." I told him it was too late to change. If I was a rookie, then maybe I'd listen. But for most all my career I had been among the top ten hitters in the American League. "Joe!" I explained. "I can't change. I'm going to hit the way I always have."

I remained the lead off man for a number of weeks. Then with about seven games left at the end of the season, he inserted me in the clean up slot. Being in the lead off slot may well have cost me 100 runs batted in that year.

The real surprise in 1959 was that the Yankees were stopped cold. They temporarily fell flat. On the 20th of May they were in last place. The '59 pennant race was a battle between the Chicago White Sox and the Cleveland Indians.

It was an interesting year at Cleveland. Frank Lane went shopping in the trade market as usual. He obtained Billy Martin from Kansas City for pitchers Ray Narleski, Don Mossi, and two other players. He traded Vic Wertz and Gary Geiger to the Boston Red Sox for Jimmy Piersall, and obtained Tito Francona from the Tigers in exchange for Larry Doby. Getting a chance to play on a regular basis, Francona hit .363, but lacked enough times at bat to qualify for the batting title. We had a good starting rotation with Cal McLish, and youngsters Gary Bell, Mudcat Grant, and rookie Jim Perry.

Rocky Colovito picked up where he had left off the previous year. On June 10th, Rocky tied a Major League record by belting four homers in a single game. Rocky, now one of baseball's premier sluggers, led the League with 41 home runs and drove in 111 runs. Woody Held had a great year. Woody, who came to us in the Vic Power/Roger Maris deal, was originally an outfielder. He took over shortstop down the stretch, and pounded out 29 homers.

But the year belonged to the Chicago White Sox. After allowing us an early lead, they plugged enough holes and began a surge in June and July. On the 12th of July they took over first place and never let it go. It was pitching, defense, and speed again. Thirty-nine-year-old Early Wynn won 22 games to lead the Major Leagues, and won the American League Cy Young Award. Bob Shaw topped the American League in winning percentage with a record of 18 - 6. The bullpen tandem of Gerry Staley and Turk Lown saved 29 games between the two of them (a large number in those days).

Sherman Lollar hit 22 home runs to lead the Sox. The White Sox were the only team in the American League to hit less than 100 home runs in 1959. In fact, at one stretch, the White Sox went to bat 306 times without hitting a home run and 70 innings without putting together two doubles in one inning. But they could really run. Luis Aparicio tied a White Sox record set by Wally Moses with 56 stolen bases. Center fielder Jim Landis, a defensive gem, stole 20 bases. The White Sox led the American League with a 3.29 earned run average, and the team's 113 stolen bases were 47 more than their nearest rival. The joke around the League that year was that the White Sox offense consisted of a walk, a hit, and a sacrifice.

Nellie Fox was the only White Sox regular to hit over .300, batting .306 and winning the American League MVP Award in 1959. A feeble offense, perhaps. But they used it as well as anyone ever has. The White Sox record in one-run games was outstanding, they won 35 and lost only 15. Chicago White Sox fans back then will not forget the night of September 22, 1959 in Cleveland's Municipal Stadium. This was the night the sirens sounded all over the Windy City. Vic Power bounced a game-ending double play ball to give the White Sox their first American League pennant in 40 years.

It is a bit surprising how many people still think I was a part of the 1959 Championship team. It is a testimony to my long association with the team, and the wonderful "Go Go" era that gave the city so many years of exciting baseball. Few people, however, know that I was almost traded back to the White Sox before the 1959 season ended. The deal had been arranged by Frank Lane and Bill Veeck, who had taken over the controlling interest of the White Sox in March 1959.

It was, in baseball lingo, a "done deal." I was ready and more than willing, but maybe I was a little too able. The week before the deal was to take place, I went on a tear. I drove in something like 13 or 14 runs, and my average jumped from .292 to .306. The problem was that Lane couldn't deal me now. "If we come back to Cleveland without you, Minnie, they will kill me," Lane said. He assured me I would go back to the Sox after the season was over. He was as good as his word.

On December 6, 1959, while I was in Cuba, I heard that I had been traded to the Chicago White Sox for catcher John Romano, first baseman Norman Cash, and third baseman Bubba Phillips. So thrilled and appreciative was Bill Veeck to get me back that the White Sox voted to give me a World Series ring, because I was denied the 1959 Championship season. It has been suggested by some that had the deal gone through as planned, my bat in the White Sox line-up might have changed the outcome of the World Series, which the White Sox lost in six games to the Los Angeles Dodgers. An interesting notion, but one whose answer we will never know.

My second and final season with the Cleveland Indians was a good one. I hit .302, placing me among the American League's top five hitters, with 32 doubles, 21 home runs, and 96 runs batted in. The Indians led the American League in hitting, runs scored, slugging percentage, and in home runs with 163. A nice season to be sure, but the good news was I was going home. I was returning to the Chicago White Sox.

But before I continue with that story, let me first digress to say something about an event that occurred on New Year's Day 1959, an event that would forever change the course of my life. On January 1, 1959, Fidel Castro took over the reigns of government in my native Cuba. Things would never be the same again in the land of my birth.

To me, Minnie was a hero. I saw him play when I was a little kid in Cuba, where he played against my brother who played for Havana. Once a week, I'd catch the train and travel the 90 miles to Havana to watch them play. Minnie was a legend in Cuba.

Unfortunately, I never had a chance to see him play in the United States because I signed in 1961, but I saw him play in his prime in Cuba. It was like mentioning Ernie Banks in Chicago. If you mentioned Minnie Minoso in Cuba, you would get the same reaction.

I felt badly for him, because before Castro took over, he was a very wealthy man in Cuba. Right in the center of Havana there were high rise buildings about six or seven stories, which in Cuba is pretty high. I saw them when I was a boy and came to see the games. They belonged to Minnie, and under Castro the government took them over. He also had apartment buildings and one of those taxi lines, but he just left everything after Castro took over. He didn't want to stay.

Every year he would bring a brand new Cadillac to Cuba, and he was the only one driving a Cadillac in Cuba in those years. I used to go to the ballpark and my brother would point out Minnie's Cadillac in the parking lot. I began thinking, "Maybe one of these days this can happen to me." I wanted to be like Minnie, and my first year in the big leagues was in 1965. Minnie was managing in Mexico by then.

It's amazing that a guy his age can run, can field, and can move. He has more energy than a 25 year old. Knowing Minnie, he could have played in that sixth decade game last year. He doesn't wear glasses; he has eyes like a 25 year old kid. One time at bat he can swing the bat as well as anyone else. We are getting older, but we know what to do when the ball is coming, because we have more experience. I think he should have had the chance to play. I think it would have been good for baseball to have let him play six decades.

Minnie Minoso is unbelievable. I'm 50 now, and I hope God gives me the kind of body Minnie has when I'm in my late 60s.

Jose Cardenal

13

CUBA, CASTRO, AND THE LATIN CONNECTION

I am not a politician, I am a ballplayer. Politics was never my game, baseball was. That is why I could withstand the changes in the Cuban government. Fulgencio Batista, a military officer, took power in Cuba in 1934 and dominated Cuban politics for the next 25 years. The one political party that truly worried me, however, was the Communist party. I never bought into its message that it really cared about the people. What I believed instead was if it ever took power, the material possessions that hard-working people had earned would be taken away.

When Fidel Castro took the reigns of power on New Year's Day 1959, he fooled a lot of people. Call it a gut feeling, but I was always suspicious of him. I kept quiet at first, but kept an eye and ear open as to where his government was heading. When I became convinced beyond doubt that he would take all freedom away from the Cuban people, I made up my mind to leave. I started the ground work in the summer of 1960, six months before I left Cuba for good. When I left in February, 1961, my new bride, Edelia, came with me. My sisters, Juanita and Flora, remained in Cuba. So did my father, Carlos. I would not see any of them again. My concerns about the Castro government proved well founded. In December, 1961, Fidel Castro officially decreed that he was a Communist. The Cuban people lost their freedom, and my family and I lost nearly every stitch of property we owned. We were allowed one piece of property only. The rest was confiscated by the government.

I'll talk in more detail about my marriage, my family, and exodus from Cuba later in the story. But now I'd like to mention another by-product of the Communist government in Cuba, the devastating effect it had on the future of Cuban baseball players.

Many people don't realize that there was always a steady flow of Cuban baseball players in the Major Leagues. It started in 1911 when the Cincinnati Reds signed two Cubans: infielder Rafael Almeida and outfielder Armondo Marsans. Almeida played three years with the Reds and hit .270. Marsans, a speedy outfielder who batted .317 with the Reds in 1912, played until 1918 and hit .269. In the next six decades, 116 Cuban players came to the big leagues. At first the flow was steady but slow. Before World War II, roughly 20 Cuban players had made it to the Majors. The best known were Dolf Luque and Mike Gonzalez.

Adolfo Luque, called "The Pride of Havana," won 27 games for the Cincinnati Reds in 1927, and 194 games over his 20-year big-league career. Mike Gonzales, also born in Havana, was a National League catcher for 17 years and managed briefly in 1938 and 1940 with the St. Louis Cardinals. In the 1946 World Series between the St. Louis Cardinals and the Boston Red Sox, Mike Gonzalez was the third base coach who waved Enos Slaughter around third base, when Slaughter went from first to home on a two-out single in the last of the eighth inning, for what proved to be the winning run in the Series.

The Washington Senators had a scout by the name of Joe Cambria. We called him Papa Cambria because he signed so many Cuban ballplayers. For this reason, the Senators had more Cuban ballplayers than any Major League team. In 1950 alone, six Cuban-born pitchers came up with the Senators. One of them was Carlos Pascual, the older brother of Camilo Pascual, later to become one of the American League's best pitchers and the best curve ball pitcher in the Majors. Cambria, who learned to speak Spanish, scouted for 25 years in Cuba. One of his most successful finds was a Venezuelan pitcher Alex Carrasquel, the uncle of Chico Carrasquel. Alex Carrasquel recorded a record of 50 wins and 39 losses for the Senators between the years of 1939-1945, compiling an 11-7 record in 1943.

The 1950s were the golden age of Cuban baseball. From 1949 through 1960, Cuba won the Caribbean World Series seven times. U.S. tourists vacationed in Cuba, the night life was thriving, and baseball was flourishing. Fans would fill the stadium wearing the blue of Almendares, the red of Havana, the green of Cienfuego, and the brown of Marianao. Fans whistled and shouted and clapped their hands to the tune of team songs. It was pure energy and emotion.

All this changed once Fidel Castro seized power. He expropriated all U.S. owned property, including sugar mills, oil refineries, utilities, and banks. He seized the private land and businesses of the Cuban people as well. Many Cuban families fled to the United States, including the parents of Jose Conseco and Rafael Palmeiro. Since then, only a handful of Cuban players became Major Leaguers, and like Canseco and Palmeiro, they were born in Cuba and raised in the United States.

An interesting story is that of Jose Cardenal who had an outstanding big league career and is now coaching for the St. Louis Cardinals. Jose came to the United States for the first time in 1961, the year of the Bay of Pigs invasion. He signed with the Giants when he was only 16 the following year. The Giants, however, knew that it would be difficult to get him out of Cuba, so they had placed him with a family in El Paso, Texas even before they signed him to a contract.

Cuban-born players have had exceptional Major League baseball careers. I have already mentioned Sandy Amoros, Sandy Consuegra, Camilo Pascual, and Jose Cardenal. There are guys like Tony Perez, Leo Cardenas, Tony Taylor, Tony Gonzalez, Pancho Herrera, Cookie Rojas, Tony Oliva, Bert Campaneris, Joe Azcue, Diego Segui, Orlando Pena, Luis Tiant, Mike Cuellar, and more recently Jose Conseco and Rafael Palmeiro. I'd say that is quite an All Star team. Another guy who has done well is Jose Martinez, who was signed about the same time as Cardenal, and is now first base coach of the Chicago Cubs.

I have mentioned that every winter I would go back to Cuba to play for Marianao. A lot of Major Leaguers came to Cuba to play winter ball. Freddie Martin played for Havana, Max Lanier played for Marianao, and was later traded to Almendares. Two Major Leaguers later pitched for Marianao. Jim Bunning, who would win over 200 games pitching in both the National and the American Leagues, and Bob Shaw who helped pitch us to the Caribbean World Series title in 1958, then won 18 games for the Chicago White Sox in 1959.

Dick Sisler, son of the great Hall of Famer George Sisler, played for Havana. I remember he broke in against us by hitting three home runs. We lost the game 3 - 2. Some people still recall that it was Dick Sisler's three-run homer against the Dodgers in the final game of the 1950 season that gave the Philadelphia Phillies their first National League pennant in 30 years.

Danny Gardella and Sal Maglie played for Cienfuego. So did George Altman, who had some good seasons with the Chicago Cubs and St. Louis Cardinals. Sal Maglie was a friend of mine and a wonderful guy. I was saddened to read of his recent death.

Walt Moryn, a hard-hitting outfielder for the Chicago Cubs and the guy who made that great ninth-inning catch to preserve Don Cardwell's no hitter in 1960, played for Almendares. So did Chuck Connors who is better known as "The Rifleman" in that popular TV series. He used to take me a lot of places when he played at Los Angeles in the Pacific Coast League and I was with San Diego.

Here in the States, each team has its own ballpark. Earlier, two clubs might have shared the same park such as the Cardinals and Browns did in St. Louis. In Cuba, however, the four main teams shared El Cerro Park in Havana. So with each person having a favorite team, things could become pretty boisterous. We always had our own fans, but say we were playing Almendares for example; the Havana fans might be rooting for us, too. The fans could get pretty rowdy, because some people would gamble, even though it was against the law. So naturally, if you got a big hit you were a hero, that is for the people who win. For the people who lose, you become a bum. They might yell all kinds of names at you and at each other.

This kind of thing had a big effect on my father, who came to see me one day. He was in the stands when some fans were calling me very nasty and bad names; one guy even mentioned my mother. This did not sit well with my father, to say the least. My daddy became furious; he started yelling back at the guy. I could hear my dad telling the guy he'd kill him. After the ballgame my father said "Look son, I don't think I'm going to come to the ballgame any more." He said he never had done anything wrong, but maybe he would if he came back and heard those names again. He knew I wouldn't like him doing anything wrong.

I told him I understood. But I also told him some realities of the game. One day you are a hero, and the next day you are the bum. As long as they didn't hurt me, they could yell anything they wanted. The same people who were yelling those names at me from the stands would be friendly to me after the game. They really weren't going to kill me, I reminded him. I said that in America I played in eight different parks. Here I played all my games in El Cerro, so there were bound to be people in the stands who would give me a hard time.

The two top teams when I began playing professional ball in Cuba were the Almendares Blue and the Havana Red. The other two teams were the Cienfuego Elephants, and my team, the Marianao Tigers. At the time, the Marianao Tigers were a last-place club. By the mid-50s, we had come into our own and won the pennant in 1957 and 1958. We began improving once we moved from the old El Tropical Stadium to the new El Cerro Stadium. Originally the only professional park in Havana was El Tropical. In 1946 the new park was built at El Cerro. So for a short time we had two professional leagues, the Federation League, which played their games in El Tropical, and the Cuban League, which played in El Cerro. Havana, Almendares, and Cienfuego each had a team in both Leagues. Within a year, the Federation League folded, and a lot of those guys found themselves without a job.

The Marianao team only drew about 350 people when we first played in El Cerro. The Stadium held 35,000 people, and we could virtually count the fans. But as we improved in the 1950s, we started to fill the house. Not only did we win the Cuban League pennant in 1957 and 1958, we won the Caribbean World Series as well. In 1957, Jim Bunning pitched two of our five victories as we took the Series title. In 1958 ,we defended our title as I won League batting honors with a .311 average. Juan Pizarro, who later pitched so well with the Chicago White Sox, struck out 17 batters one game, pitching for the Puerto Rico Caguas.

I can't emphasize too strongly how popular baseball was in Cuba. It was the biggest sport in the country during the pre-

Castro days. But if Castro curtailed the flow of Cuban ballplayers to America and the Major Leagues, the doors were wide open for talented baseball players from other Latin American countries.

The first Latin American actually to play Major League baseball was a native of Colombia by the name of Louis Castro, who played some infield for the Philadelphia Athletics. Little more is known about him. There is a small blurb about him at Cooperstown that reads, "Louis Castro played 42 games with the Philadelphia Athletics and disappeared."

Luis Olmo was one of the first Latin players to gain big league stardom. A native of Puerto Rico, Olmo led the National League in triples in 1945 for the Brooklyn Dodgers, drove in 110 runs, and hit .313. In 1946, Olmo took Jorge Pasquel's offer for more money and jumped to the Mexican League with fellow Major Leaguers Mickey Owens, Max Lanier, and Danny Gardella. When the Mexican League toppled in 1947, Olmo, like the rest, was barred from the game. When the ban was lifted, Luis Olmo played one more year with the Dodgers and two years with the Boston Braves, before retiring from the game in 1951.

Orlando Cepeda, another Puerto Rican, became a truly great Major Leaguer, a genuine candidate for the Hall of Fame, where I feel he should be. Orlando did it all. He was the National League Rookie of the Year in 1958, National League home run and RBI Champion in 1961 with the San Francisco Giants, and the unanimous choice for MVP with the St. Louis Cardinals in 1967. In fact the San Francisco Giants of the 1960s were knee deep with outstanding Latin ballplayers. Hall of Famer Juan Marichal, one of baseball's truly great pitchers, was born in the Dominican Republic. He is now the Oakland A's scouting director in the Dominican Republic.

The Giants also had a talented trio of Dominican-born brothers, Felipe, Matty, and Jesus Alou. Felipe Alou, of course, has done very well as manager of the Montreal Expos the last two seasons. Jose Pagan from Puerto Rico was the shortstop for the San Franicsco Giants when they faced the Yankees in the 1962 World Series. Pagan also played on the 1971 World Champion Pittsburgh Pirates.

In many ways, the most celebrated Latin ballplayer was Roberto Clemente. Clemente is a national hero in Puerto Rico, and has a high school named after him here in Chicago. Roberto had a rifle for an arm. The only three right fielders I have seen with comparable arms were Bob Kennedy, Carl Furillo, and Rocky Colovito.

Tony Oliva, as most people know, is a compadre of mine from Cuba. In 1964, Tony became the first rookie in Major League history to win a batting championship. It was the first of three batting championships he would win. He also led the American League in hits in five different seasons. Tony's is an interesting story. He was originally brought to this country by the Minnesota Twins, who actually released him. He was waiting to return home to Cuba when the Bay of Pigs invasion occurred in 1961. All the flights were canceled and Tony was stranded here. Two Latin scouts then told the Twins they might as well keep him because he had a six-month visa. Three years later, Tony won the American League batting championship as a rookie. Today he manages in Mexico during the winter months.

If Tony's story is a happy one, the story of another Cuban Zoilo Versailles, is very sad. Zoilo, it may be remembered, was the American League MVP in 1965 when the Twins won the American League crown. The first Latin player to win an MVP Award in 1965, Zoilo Versailles has been forgotten in many circles. After he won his MVP Award, he was not allowed to travel to see his family in Havana because of the broken U.S.-Cuban relations. The Castro government had stifled that. Recently I read Zoilo succumbed to financial ruin. Bitter, angry, and needing money he sold his MVP trophy and his other awards to collectors and has spent years now in abject poverty. A sad case of misspent talent.

I get a great thrill when I hear how I paved the way for future Latin ballplayers. Those like myself who were black had to deal with both racial discrimination and a language barrier. Sure it made things more difficult, but never impossible. I always felt that I was defending my uniform each time I put it on. To me, it was like defending the American flag. I respected my uniform, and I wore it as if I was representing each Latin country. My dream was always to come to the United States, and once I was here I fell in love with this country. It may have been more difficult for me than for some others, but in the United States, you have the opportunity to develop and make the most of your full potential. I never let the word discrimination hold me back.

Likewise, I don't like to hear it from others as an excuse for failure.

When I came to the United States, I was surprised and a bit amused to hear some black ballplayers tell me that I didn't understand prejudice and discrimination because I was Cuban, not black. What nonsense! Without mentioning names, I told these players to look at me and then tell me I am not black. Cuba was not the racial paradise some might want them to believe. Just as in the United States, there were many sections of Cuba, and many neighborhoods, where you only saw white people. Baseball too, beneath the professional and semi-professional level, excluded blacks. And here in this country, the signs in restaurants and buses prohibiting blacks applied as much to me as it did to them.

Fortunately, things are easier for the young Latin ballplayer of today. I am happy to see more Latin American ballplayers making it to the Big Leagues. I read recently that there are over 100 Latin-born ballplayers playing Major League baseball as of this year. They come from many countries: The Dominican Republic, Mexico, Nicaragua, Panama, Puerto Rico, Venezuela, and even Cuba.

Many of us so-called pioneers are still active in the game. Orlando Cepeda is doing community relations work with the San Francisco Giants; Chico Carrasquel, as I mentioned earlier, is doing color commentary for the Chicago White Sox on Spanish language broadcasts; Vic Power recently retired as a scout for the California Angels and is conducting free baseball clinics for Puerto Rican youngsters. And I am enjoying my work immensely, making personal appearances and doing public relations for the Chicago White Sox and private appearances through Sports Personality Associates of Chicago.

What I tell kids all over the country is never to use the words "I can't!" Tell yourself that you *can*, no matter what obstacles you think are in your way. Respect yourself and your work. And work hard, there is no substitute for that. Then if you have the talent, you will make it, and you will be proud of the way that you did.

I hear that today, one out of every four ballplayers signed is foreign born. Around 600 Latin American ballplayers are signed to professional contracts each year. Unfortunately, only about a dozen make it past Double A ball. Yet things are improving. Approximately 1,000 Latin American ballplayers have made it to Major Leagues during this century. Perhaps more could have if they hadn't been discouraged by a language problem. Yet just taking a look at the Major League rosters today shows the progress that has been made.

Ruben Sierra, Rafael Palmeiro, Mario Soto, Roberto Alomar, Sandy Alomar Jr., Jose Canseco, Carlos Barega, and young slugger Juan Gonzalez. On the north side of Chicago there is Jose Bautista, Jose Guzman, Rey Sanchez, and Sammy Sosa, with the Chicago Cubs. On the Chicago White Sox roster there is Wilson Alvarez, Joey Cora, Ozzie Guillen, Roberto Hernandez, and Julio Franco.

Yes indeed! It has been a long journey from the sugar fields of Cuba to where I am today. And it only could have happened in this great land of freedom, The United States of America. This I believe with all my heart.

If anyone was born to be a ballplayer, it was Minnie. He was the consummate pro. His professional life was totally outstanding. He didn't miss games; he was always on time. He did what he loved doing. Two especially applicable descriptions about Minnie are that he was a very joyful person and was wonderfully childlike. That does not mean childish. Truly, he loved what he was doing. I'm quite sure in his life there was pain, but he talked about this to only a very few people. Many times his heart was heavy, but when you are a pro— and that is a very important word in our family— you don't inflict that on your public.

There was great dignity to Minnie. He was a terrible chauvinist, but that I can understand. First, because of his culture, and second because of the era in which he lived. On the other hand, he had the most wonderful way of being courtly toward women. I don't care if they were 108. Only Hank Greenberg and my husband Bill had that wonderful innate manner of treating women. Minnie was a lover in the truest sense of that courtly tradition.

Sometimes you hear people say that he has stayed around too long. Anybody who says that doesn't know what is going on. This wonderful dignity about Minnie precludes anyone trying to patronize him, if they knew him at all. Bill and I always felt honored that Minnie took us into his life and trusted us. I always felt that Minnie carried the burden of his people as his life was going on, much more than some realized.

The timing is just right for a book on Minnie. He always made it appear like it was a piece of cake, but it wasn't. The fact that he could make it appear that way is the sign of a true pro. There should be a tremendous interest in his story. It's really wonderful that so many people who have known Minnie from all avenues of life, and in some way have been a part of his life, have contributed to the book.

Mary-Frances Veeck

14

CHICAGO, THE CRITICS, AND A BIT OF CAMELOT

There was a new feeling in the air. The Fifties had passed into the pages of history, and a new decade was upon us. Dwight Eisenhower was in the last year of his two-term presidency. Before the year would end the country would have a new Chief Executive-elect, John F. Kennedy. Young, articulate, and handsome, for so many he was perceived as the embodiment of a new America.

For baseball player Orestes Minoso, 1960 marked the start of the second decade in the Major Leagues. It meant a return to the city of Chicago, where in 1951 I first achieved big league stardom. Then I was the first black athlete to play Major League baseball in the Windy City. I had gone there speaking very little English, knowing only the tools of the baseball trade. Now a decade later so many things had changed; I was older, and the color barrier had been broken, not only in Chicago, but through the entire Major Leagues.

During the 1950s, black ballplayers such as Sam Hairston, Bob Boyd, Hector Rodriguez, Connie Johnson, Earl Battey, Larry Doby, and Al Smith had worn a Chicago White Sox uniform. On the North side of town, Ernie Banks and Gene Baker broke the color line for the Chicago Cubs in 1954. In the ensuing years, "Toothpick" Sam Jones, Monte Irvin, Tony Taylor, and George Altman found employment in the friendly confines of Wrigley Field. In 1955, Elston Howard became the first black to play for the New York Yankees, one of the last teams to break the color line. In 1957, black infielder John Kennedy had his debut with the Philadelphia Phillies, the last National League team to break the color line. Finally in 1959, utility infielder Pumpsie Green became the first Black player to wear a Boston Red Sox uniform, as the Red Sox were the last Major League team to break the color barrier.

The Chicago White Sox lost the 1959 World Series in six games to the Los Angeles Dodgers. It was the last year any Chicago baseball team played in the World Series. In order to bolster an offense that scored less runs than any American League team except the sixth place Baltimore Orioles and the last place Washington Senators, Bill Veeck engineered a series of trades designed to put more muscle into the line-up. Promising outfielder Johnny Callison was traded to the Philadelphia Phillies for third baseman Gene Freese. Freese hit 23 home runs and had a .500 slugging average with the Phillies in 1959. Then in April of 1960, Earl Battey and Don Mincher went to the Washington Senators for slugger Roy Sievers, who had led the American League in home runs with 42 homers in 1957 and hit 39 more in 1958.

Bill Veeck took a lot of heat later for making these trades, including the one that brought me back to Chicago. His critics say that he bankrupted the White Sox future by trading such talented young ballplayers. Yet Bill Veeck knew better than anyone that he could not win another pennant with the same 1959 team. He wanted another pennant in 1960 and he went after it, feeling that his team desperately needed more power in the line-up. Hindsight is a marvelous commodity, especially when you are not the one making the decisions. They are fodder for the newspapers and arm chair critics. But how many teams today do the same thing. If they want to win, they go for the here and now. Look no further than the Chicago Cubs in 1984. Dallas Greene traded for Rick Sutcliffe. It worked, and the Cubs won the division. But in the deal, he traded away a young outfielder named Joe Carter.

Much has been said of letting Norm Cash get loose. In 1961, Cash won the American League Batting Championship and had one of the greatest seasons in the last 35 years. But remember, Cash was dealt to the Tigers not by the White Sox, but by the Cleveland Indians, who traded him to Detroit for third baseman Steve Demeter. Demeter never lasted in the big leagues.

If anything was responsible for the White Sox third place finish in 1960, it was a combination of two factors. First, the New York Yankees were back on beam and would win five consecutive American League flags. In fact , in 1963, the White Sox won 94 games and still finished 10-and-a-half games behind the Yankees. Secondly, the Sox pitching tailed off quite a bit in 1960. Early Wynn and Bob Shaw, the two big winners in 1959, fell to 13-12 and 13-13 respectively. The young pitching staff of Paul Richards' second-place Baltimore Orioles led by the lively young arms of Chuck Estrada, Milt Pappas, and Steve Barber was just simply better. It was a final, but fruitful testimony to the genius of Paul Richards.

Finally, the White Sox remained a first-division club for eight more years, coming with one game of winning the American League flag in 1964. Then they battled down to the wire in 1967 in one of the most exciting pennant races ever, before they blew it all in the last week of the season and finished in fourth place, three games behind the surprising Boston Red Sox. Yes, Bill Veeck traded away some genuine talent, ballplayers who would do quite well in the future. But to lay the failure of later years at his feet alone is far too simplistic.

One final point should be made; for eight more years, the Chicago White Sox would remain a first-division club. Eight years is a long way for any organization to see ahead so clearly, but the Chicago White Sox remained as competitive as any team in the American League until 1968. The "Go Go" era officially ended in 1967, but by then the Chicago White Sox had been a first division club for 17 straight seasons. With the exception of the New York Yankees, no other American League club could make such a claim. No post-World War II Chicago sports team even comes close to matching this record.

For my part, I gave the White Sox one of my best years. I came to play in 1960 , and play I did. I led the American League with 184 base hits. I was second to Roger Maris with 105 RBI's. I was third in the American League in hitting at .311 behind Pete Runnels and Al Smith. I was third in doubles, in runs scored, and in total bases. I hit 20 home runs and stole 17 bases. I was chosen to start for the American League in the All Star Game. I hit two opening game home runs against Kansas City and drove in six runs. Not too bad for what some pundits called a "fading" Minnie Minoso.

In this game of life, there are some people who are simply so unique, so very special, that no words can do them justice. To me, Mr. Bill Veeck was such a person. I cannot say enough about him. From that moment of impetuous youth when I yelled, "Hey boy! Get that ball," way back in the spring of 1949, until the day he died, he gave me nothing but respect and kindness.

I have never stopped appreciating what he did for me; how much he always stood in my corner. He brought me back to the White Sox in 1960 and gave me the best contract I ever had, far more money than I ever made before. In those days you didn't say publicly what you made. It was generally a secret, and you didn't mention it to anyone. With all the passing years I still won't quote an exact figure. Let's just say that my contract with the White Sox was in the $70,000 range. But I did not disappoint him. As I indicated, I put together an excellent 1960 season.

What made Bill Veeck so extraordinary, was his identification with ordinary people. Translated to the arena of baseball, this meant the ordinary fan. He had a built-in disdain for all forms of pomposity and pretense. For this reason, and because he was a consummate showman, he often outraged other owners. If he was controversial, he always had the best interest of the fan in mind. He never called me Minnie; always to him I was Orestes. Even when I was on a different team, he would pass me in the park and say, "How are you, Mr. Minoso?" or "How are you, Orestes?"

Bill Veeck respected me, not just as a ballplayer, but as a human being. When I was going through marital problems in the 1970s, he and Mary-Frances were the only people who knew the extent of the pain inside me, but they never told anyone else. I remember well his love for Cuban food. He would call us at our north side apartment, and ask my wife and myself if we would cook up some rice, chicken and black beans, and come over for dinner. Either Edelia or I would cook a big pot, and we'd drive to his south side home and have a wonderful afternoon with the Veecks. Bill Veeck is someone I have never forgotten; and I never will as long as there is a breath of life in me.

When the White Sox began the 1960 season, only Nellie Fox and Billy Pierce had been with the team from the start of the" Go Go" era nine years earlier. After averaging 19 wins a year from 1956 through 1958, Billy's record fell to 14 - 15 in 1959, the first time since 1950 he had a losing season.

But I faced Billy in 1959, and he was still a good pitcher. Why Al Lopez bypassed Billy by refusing to give him a World Series start remains anyone's guess. The left hander who had pitched so beautifully for the White Sox through most of the 1950s, the greatest left hander in the history of the club, was given only four innings of relief work during the entire World Series. Billy has never said much about this to me, he is too much a gentleman for that. But I think he was quite hurt. Nellie, of course, won MVP honors in 1959, a worthy tribute to a wonderful career. His .306 average was the sixth time in nine years that he topped the .300 mark, and the eighth time he had more than 186 base hits.

Too much has been made of the contention that we had become a team of slow-footed sluggers in 1960, that we had sacrificed speed as well as youth. Sure, neither Roy Sievers or Big Ted Kluszewski, whom the Sox had obtained from the Pittsburgh Pirates for the 1959 pennant drive would light up the base paths. Nor would Sherman Lollar who was winding down his durable career with the club. But the fact remains that we led the American League in fielding, and actually stole more bases in 1960 than we did in 1959. In 1960 we stole 122 bases, nine more than during the pennant-winning year of 1959. For the tenth straight year the Chicago White Sox led the American League in stolen bases, with Luis Aparicio leading the League with 51, Jim Landis was next with 23, and I chipped in an additional 17.

There is more to remember about the 1960 season other than falling to third place. Bill Veeck literally lit up the park with the world's first exploding scoreboard. And boy, did I make it explode that first day. What a thrill! On April 19, 1960, I celebrated my return to the Chicago White Sox and christened that scoreboard by hitting a fourth-inning grandslam home run. Then hitting a second solo shot in the ninth inning to break a 9 - 9 tie. Later in the year, I would hit the longest home run in my Major League career by blasting a pitch from left hander Bud Daily more than 500 feet over the left field wall at Comiskey Park.

Again, we started well, and held first place early in the year. But the Yankees were back, there was no doubt about that. With newly acquired Roger Maris to complement Mickey Mantle's big bat, the Yankees had become a powerhouse again. Mantle and Maris would be one and two in the American League in home runs with 40 and 39—a portent of what would be the following year, as the Yankees knocked out 193 home runs, 43 more than the Detroit Tigers.

Before the largest crowds of the season, the Yankees swept us four games the weekend of June 17-19 to all but dash any hope of repeating in 1960. The Yankees would take the American League flag in 1960 with a 97-57 mark, but this time drop the World Series to the surprising Pittsburgh Pirates as Bill Mazerowski hit that dramatic ninth-inning World Series homer in the seventh game, and the Pirates became the unlikely baseball champions of the world.

More surprising were Paul Richards' Baltimore Orioles, who passed us up the last two days of the season to finish in second place with a record of 89-65. We finished a disappointing third with an 87-67 record. While we won seven less games than the year before, we were still 20 games over .500 and 11 games ahead of the fourth-place Cleveland Indians.

Billy Pierce came back nicely with a 14-7 record to lead the staff in wins. The big pitching surprise of the season was left hander Frank Baumann who came to the White Sox from the Boston Red Sox. Baumann finished with a 13-6 record, and led the American League with a 2.67 ERA. Early Wynn and Bob Shaw whose combined records in 1959 were 24 games better than .500, were only one game better than .500 in 1960. Gerry Staley had a 13-8 record, all in relief. Shaw and Staley would be gone early in 1961. Tough Early Wynn, in the twilight of his great Hall of Fame career, would win only 15 more games the next two seasons before finally getting that cherished 300th Major League win with the Cleveland Indians in 1963. A gritty competitor was Early Wynn.

Two baseball legends said goodbye to the big leagues in 1960. The first left the team he managed with unprecedented success. The second said farewell to the game of baseball where he had few, if any, equals. The New York Yankees out-hit the Pittsburgh Pirates .338 to .236 in the 1960 World Series. They outscored the Pirates 55 to 27, and they leveled the Pirate pitchers with a 7.11 ERA. Yet the Yankees lost the Series. Not taking defeat easily, they fired 71-year-old Casey Stengel who had won nine World Series in 12 seasons as Yankee manager.

Also at the end of the season, Ted Williams— without question the greatest hitter I ever saw— retired from the game with a lifetime average of .344. Williams, who homered in his last Major League at bat, hit his 500th home run earlier that June. Few players in all of baseball history could have matched him as a hitter. No one since has even come close.

There was hope in the country when President John F. Kennedy threw out the first ball on April 10, 1961, as the White Sox opened the season in Griffith Stadium. There was something new in baseball too; the American League had been expanded to 10 teams, with the addition of the California Angels and a new team in Washington, still called the Senators. The old Washington Senators moved to the Twin Cities to become the Minnesota Twins.

Our starting line-up was almost the same from the previous year. There were two changes: Al Smith had moved from right field to third base to replace Gene Freese who was sent to the Cincinnati Reds in a deal that brought pitcher Cal McLish to the White Sox. In right field instead was 25-year-old Floyd Robinson, who in 1962 would establish a White Sox record with a league-leading 45 doubles. The big addition to the club was left handed pitcher Juan Pizarro. Pizarro, a native of Puerto Rico, had little success with the Milwaukee Braves. He came to the White Sox in 1961, struck out 188 batters, and led the pitching staff with a record of 14 - 7.

We started out poorly, and on June 10 the White Sox were in last place. Bill Veeck was ailing, and on that date he sold the club to Arthur Allen, a Chicago businessman. The following day, Hank Greenberg, who was running the front office traded Bob Shaw and Gerry Staley to Kansas City for third baseman Andy Carey, outfielder Al Pilarcik, and pitcher Ray Herbert. Herbert, who would win nine games in '61, became a 20-game winner in 1962.

After the trade, we started to surge, winning 12 in a row. We finished the season in fourth place with a record of 86-76, our worst finish since 1951, and 23 games behind the New York

Yankees. In Ralph Houk's first year as skipper, the mighty New York Yankees—behind Roger Maris' 61 home runs and Mickey Mantle's 54— hammered out a Major League record 240 home runs. They won 109 ball games and lost only 53. The Detroit Tigers' 101 wins would have been enough to take it all in most seasons. They finished second, eight games behind Maris, Mantle, and Co.

The "Camelot" of the Kennedys would shortly pass from the scene. The tranquility of those years would soon be shattered by a presidential assassination, a war in a far-off place called Vietnam, more assassinations to follow, and a rebellious assault by much of the country's youth on the values that were dear to me and to many others.

The baseball era in Chicago, which I knew and loved, was also drawing to a close. In June, "Jungle Jim" Rivera was released by the White Sox. The guy who made a patent out of exciting play and head-first slides was picked up by Kansas City, where he ended his ten-year big league career at the end of the year.

In November, Billy Pierce was traded to the San Francisco Giants for pitchers Dom Zanni and Eddie Fisher. Billy's 186 wins are the most recorded by any White Sox left hander and the fourth highest in White Sox history. He pitched 35 shutouts and his 1,796 strikeouts still stand as a club record. But Billy wasn't through. In 1962, Billy Pierce helped pitch the Giants to the National League pennant with a 16 - 6 record; the best of his career. Billy retired from baseball with a record of 211 wins and 169 losses. We can only wonder how many more wins there might have been, had he been backed with the type of sluggers that were constantly in the New York Yankee line-up, or even the Indians and Red Sox in those early years.

There was another trade, too. In early December, I was driving back to an old-timers dinner and reunion held at a club near the Illinois/ Wisconsin border. I was headed there from McCormick Place where I was holding a clinic on hitting for some kids. I switched on the car radio; that's when I heard of the trade. The White Sox had traded me to the St. Louis Cardinals for first baseman Joe Cunningham. It was a true shocker. Just like 1951 and in 1957, there was no warning. Not even a bit of speculation that I might be going. And just like in 1951 and 1957, Al Lopez was managing the ball club that traded me.

15

MARRIAGE AND A
BITTERSWEET FAREWELL

Everything had changed in 1961. The trade to St. Louis was just the proverbial icing on the cake. My life changed totally for other reasons. In 1961, I was married. It was also the year I left Cuba, the land of my birth, never to return again.

Edelia Delgado and I met in 1958. It really was love at first sight. Anyone who has felt it knows what it's like: sheer magic. I had always enjoyed the company of women. As a single man, I had known many. I made some mistakes in judgement; to that I readily admit. I was not perfect. But life is something we learn about only through our mistakes and experiences. Yet through it all, I was never dishonest; I never pretended. Before Edelia, marriage had been something I just wasn't ready for. I knew that. As long as I was single, I felt I could be free. I don't believe I have anything to hide in discussing the women in my life. I have never said a bad word about any woman who has been my girlfriend or my wife. There have been problems, but never bad words.

My bachelor ways changed with Edelia. Once I knew for certain that there was no one else I wanted to be with, then throughout our formal courtship and our entire 20-year marriage, there was never another woman. In later years some real problems would develop between us. We would eventually separate, and in 1977 we were divorced. But in 1961, there was no indication that we would not be together forever.

I first set eyes on her at El Cerro, the ballpark in Havana. I was playing left field for Marianao, when I noticed her in the crowd sitting all the way by the right field bullpen. She had long black hair. Edelia was a light-skinned Cuban woman who looked Mexican or Italian; she was very pretty, like a movie star. At the end of the inning I said to Juan Izaguirre, one of the coaches, "That's a beautiful young lady over there." Juan looked at me strangely as I pointed her way. "You mean you can tell from here?" he asked. I answered, "Sure I can!"

She was the stepsister of Orlando Contrara, the rookie pitcher who was hurling for us that day. I asked him if he could get her telephone number for me. He did, and I put it in my pocket. After the game she was standing by the clubhouse door, but it was Orlando, her stepbrother, not me, whom she was waiting for. The only reason she came to the game was to see him pitch.

A group of ballplayers went out that night to a social club. The president of that club wanted to register a team in the Amateur Federation of Havana. Edelia came along with us. From there we went to another club where there was music and dancing. Edelia was the only lady with us, so when the music started, I asked her to dance. That was it; we didn't stop. We fell in love on the spot, right then and there.

We went together for three years. Once she visited me in Tampa for spring training during her first visit to this country. We became engaged following the 1960 baseball season, and I returned to Cuba in October, where we were married early in 1961.

The wedding was in a little Catholic church in Havana. It was a wonderful wedding. We then had three lovely days together at the Hilton Hotel in Havana, before leaving for Mexico on our official honeymoon. It was more than a honeymoon, however; it was to be our final goodbye to our country. We had made up our minds. We left Cuba in February of 1961, and neither of us would ever return again.

For months now, I'd been making plans to leave Cuba. Things had gotten worse. By the end of the year, Castro would drop all pretense and declare himself a Communist. He would take all freedom from the people just as I had feared. Yes, Batista governed as a dictator and Cuba had its problems. But I never believed for one moment that the way to cure these ills was to take away other people's property and their hard-earned savings. The plight of the poor has never been made better by punishing the more well to do. This was about to happen in Cuba, and it was time to leave my country and to cut all ties.

I recall vividly the day Fidel Castro took over the government in Cuba. An increasing number of people had turned away from Batista and his military rule. I never involved myself in the politics of my country; I respected the head of state even if I did not like the man himself. I feel much the same here in the United States. There have been presidents whom I have not cared for at all. Yet whoever holds the office is the president of all the people, and I always show the proper respect that the office commands.

I indicated earlier how Communism always worried me. At first, Fidel Castro posed as a friend and liberator of the Cuban people. He won lots of supporters, many of whom were willing dupes who needed to believe, rather than being actual Communists.

I remember well January 1, 1959, when a whole group of his followers were making their way from the mountains to the Army base at Colombia. They marched through Oriente picking up more and more people along the way; now they had reached Havana. Edelia, my friend Ti Ti, and I were bringing food to Edelia's father who was working at the Fire Department. We were blocked by the big military parade that had now reached the streets of Havana. There was one army car after the other. These were made up of the guerrillas who fought with Castro in the mountains. I was in my Cadillac going nowhere it seemed, when one of the militia people spotted me. I knew him. "Hey, Minoso! Hey, Minoso!" he yelled waving to me. "Join us. Come on. Come on. Come on!"

I left my car and was about to jump in the back of one of the passing trucks. Then I looked more closely. Suddenly I knew that this wasn't right. I sensed something. Perhaps it was a premonition. I turned to one of the others whom I knew. "Something is wrong," I said. "This is a Communist group." These were Castro's supporters. They were the guerrillas who had been in the mountains with him for two, three, or four years. They had marched into every part of the city. I quietly dropped back and returned to my car with Edelia and Ti Ti.

I said nothing more to anyone, but I knew in my gut how tough this was going to be. Like we say in baseball, I knew I had my work cut out for me. I started thinking about leaving Cuba, but I wouldn't tell anyone. I began laying the groundwork, so that those in the family who wanted to leave could come with me. I had a gnawing feeling all along that the Cuban people were soon going to lose all their freedom.

Of course I also knew how hard it would be to say goodbye. We were a close family, but I never talked politics at home. My sisters, I am sure, did not agree with my strong stand against Castro. I'm not sure what their political leanings were, but I do recall that Juanita was very happy the day Castro took over. Since my two sisters lived together and thought much alike on most things, I would imagine Flora had the same sympathies too.

No, we didn't talk politics, but we sure played a lot of dominoes. Every night after the ballgames, we played dominoes until three or four in the morning. It would take me about fifteen minutes from the park to drive home. I could get a little excited, and sometimes drove faster than I should have.

Once a policeman stopped me for speeding and pulled me over. "Hey, Minoso! What's going on? What's your hurry?" I said that there was an emergency back home, and I had to get there as quickly as I could. He began laughing and shook his head. "I know your big emergency, Minoso. You're heading home to play dominoes with those sisters of yours." He gave me a warning as I started the ignition and began pulling away from the curb. "Minoso!" the policeman shouted again. I turned my head to see what he wanted. "Be careful!" he yelled.

There were so many nights that we played dominoes, My two sisters, my friend, Ti Ti , and I. And believe me, we took our game seriously. Juanita was divorced at the time and had a son. Flora was not married, and remains single today. I don't remember her ever having a boyfriend. She never wanted to stray too far from our house once she wasn't working. They were my older sisters, and I was their little brother. But in the house I was the big guy.

Yet my sisters did not attend my wedding, which both hurt and disappointed me. I never knew why for certain. Maybe they were jealous; Edelia was so very pretty. Maybe they felt that Edelia would take up too much of my time. Perhaps they felt that

I would forget them, and she would take me totally away from them. They had been used to having me around as the man of the house for a long time now. Once I, too, had been very jealous when my father had remarried.

After my wedding, I returned back to the house; I wanted to leave something with them before I left. Perhaps this was just an excuse. When I arrived my sisters were sitting outside on the porch. I looked at them as I walked in. I said something like, "Ah huh! You didn't show!" They said, "No!" "No problem!" I answered.

But truly, there was a problem. I don't know how things would have been between us had I come back to Cuba as in the past. I left them well provided for, and the house remained theirs. But as long as Castro controlled the government of Cuba, I knew that I would not come back. It was a closed chapter.

My suspicions proved well founded and hurtful. The government confiscated everything except the home that we lived in. I had invested in property, and owned a number of apartment buildings. They took everything. We were allowed to keep our house. That's it. They confiscated whatever else we had.

The saddest and most difficult goodbye was to my father. It was very tough. He was a quiet man, a very respectable man. Carlos Arrieta was a true gentleman; he was respected by everyone. My father knew what it was like to travel through much of life alone. I think that is what he showed me, and what he always wanted me to know. He wanted me to be independent, to be able to take care of myself and not rely on others.

But there was so much more I learned from him, too. He taught me not to try to pretend in life, and to remain true to myself. He wanted me to look at the world realistically. He taught me never to live beyond my means, to live on what money I had, and not to be extravagant if I couldn't afford to be. He impressed upon me from an early age never to think I was better than anyone else; but also never to think that anyone was better than me. It's still a good lesson. If we all felt that way, the world would be a better place. This is the attitude that helps me live my life day by day. What my father did for me was to tell me the truth.

When I said goodbye to him, I didn't think it would be the last time we would see each other. I don't think in terms of last times. But he understood my leaving. He told me to do what I had to do and he wished me the best, that everything would be all right. "Are you sure?" I asked. He told me he was.

I stressed that I didn't want him to work anymore. To take it easy is what I insisted. His retirement was fixed, I had seen to that. His check would come every month. He was remarried and had a house in Camaguay, where his sister also lived. There was the house in Havana with my sisters and the ranch in El Perico. Truly, I had hoped that he might visit me in Mexico, and from there I could make plans to take him to the United States. But Cuba was his home. He had never been out of Cuba; it was his only world, the only place he knew and understood. He didn't want to leave. He must have known my feelings, because he said something to me before I left, which I will never forget. He said, "Son! I never was a politician. I'm never going to be a Communist. So don't worry!"

I would never see my father again, but he was never far from my thoughts. I never forgot our times together, either. We would tease each other like a couple of kids. Remember, I was his little baby; he never hit me or beat me. When I did something wrong and he wanted to punish me, he would get a piece of rope and then hit the ground. The people watching would scream,

"Oh, look what that man is doing to that poor boy! He's going to kill him." My brother, Cirilo, would say, "Don't worry about it. He's not hitting him at all. He loves him. He's just hitting the ground."

People used to say we looked quite a bit alike. Even with the difference in age, people often mistook us for brothers. I was very proud of him, and he was proud of me. But it wasn't just my baseball career; he was not a real baseball fan. He didn't brag, and he never tried to impress people with his famous son. My sisters were the baseball fans, but they were fans only from the house. My father went to a game, but my sisters never did.

There is one thing I remember particularly well when I think of my father. I would buy clothing material in Cleveland and bring it back with me to Havana. Once I took my father to the tailor. The tailor fit him and I ordered three suits for my father and three suits for myself. The tailor was so impressed.

"Carlos," he said to my father. "I've never seen anything like this. You have such a good son." But my father couldn't understand why I was spending this kind of money on him. "I don't need all this," he told the tailor. "This is silly!"

I just looked at my father and said. "Look here, Carlos! You just keep quiet and let him take your size." It worked; he got three new suits. We would often dress up, Carlos and Orestes—father and son—and go out together. He liked music, and many times we'd go dancing! There were lots of good times with him that I have not forgotten.

Another time I tried to give him some money. He never wanted to take it, and when I handed it to him, he let it drop on the floor. He just wouldn't take it. I'd say, "Look, 'Lencho' (that is what people called him affectionately), what's the matter. Don't you like me." He would say, "I love you, son!" Then I grabbed him and pretended I was going to wrestle him to the ground. I got him close to the floor. "Orestes," he said. "You be careful. If you ever beat me, I'm going to cut this hand of yours and you will never be able to throw another baseball." We had so many good times like this. Everyone loved to see the two of us get along so well.

My father died in 1977. I was coaching with the Chicago White Sox at the time. I got the sad news the day after Larry Doby replaced Bob Lemon as White Sox manager, and I was informed that Tony La Russa was taking over the first base coaching job and I was going to do public relations work with the White Sox.

In all his life, my father had never driven a car; he always drove horses. Cars, he thought, were not worth driving. He liked the old ways of doing things. He lived by the old-fashioned values, and he died that way. This was Carlos Arrieta, my father.

Edelia and I were not the only ones to leave Cuba. When I returned to the United States in the spring of 1960, I brought Orestes Jr. back with me. Of course, he needed someone to look after him during the season, so my friend, Nancy Locada, flew in from New York and took Orestes Jr. back with her. Just one of so many times that Nancy was there when I needed her.

Nancy had been my very dear friend from the time I first arrived in New York in 1945 to play for the New York Cubans. She lived in the top floor apartment of the same building where Alex Pompez and the New York Cubans had their headquarters. Her family owned a grocery store. Years later when I was with the White Sox, Nancy would bring us food whenever we came to town. Nellie Fox just loved the mangos she'd bring us. He could hardly wait to get back to New York for some more. She has remained the best female friend I have ever had. She is still there for us today if she is needed.

My sister, Juanita's, son and daughter came with me too. So did my brother, Cirilo's, daughter, Julia. I had promised Cirilo's wife that I would look after her. She lived with us in Chicago. Eventually she met a man whose work was in Puerto Rico. They were married, and today the two live in Puerto Rico. Juanita's son, Damaso Santa Cruz Minoso, was 16 at the time. I helped get my nephew a job at Comiskey Park, and 30 years later, Damaso still works at the park with the grounds crew.

Juanita's daughter, Marian, was twelve years old, and she lived with us as I raised her as my own daughter. She died tragically in Mexico ten years later. My daughter, Cecilia, arrived in America a short time later with her mother. Julia had married a very nice gentleman, and the family settled in the city of Evanston, Illinois. They still live in the same area.

I waited nervously in Mexico until I received a phone call from Ernie Carroll telling me that my family had landed safely in Chicago. What a wonderful feeling of relief! Ernie Carroll was the chief cook and ran the commissary at Comiskey Park for years, and he was also my right hand man and very good friend. He had arranged an apartment for us on South Drexel Boulevard in Chicago. Needless to say, I brought a large household back with me. But as luck would have it, I was traded to St. Louis at the end of the year, and we would have to move once more.

But for the moment, I was just thrilled that my family was safe in Chicago. It was a cause for celebration. I phoned a friend, and we celebrated the good news with a couple of beers. The next day it was off to Sarasota and spring training.

What I love about Minnie is he never changes. What I got a kick out of is at a recent Fantasy Camp, Minnie cooked all his own meals. He loved doing it. He loves Latin food; whenever we would go out together, we'd never go to an American restuarant. All of his success never changed him one ounce.

Minnie and Nellie Fox were like second fathers to me when I came to the White Sox. Those two, Minnie and Nellie, were probably the most instrumental for my learning the ways of playing the game, and also my realizing how good people are. Now that's a great combination. Those two had that extra drive that made them such great ballplayers. Both those guys worked so hard at the game. They were just such great role models.

I was 23 years old, really kind of shy and bashful, so a guy like me needed people like Minnie to make me feel at home. But the whole organization was so great. Unlike a lot of other guys, they weren't worried about you taking their jobs. Their attitude was "Hey, if you play better baseball, you are going to help me." The White Sox had this special quality of belonging together. Other teams may have come close, but I don't think any were quite like we were.

Today you see two ballplayers eating together, it's a miracle. Heck, we had nine or ten guys gather together to get something to eat and take a belt. It was really a beautiful group of people, lots of classy people. But none classier than Minnie.

Jim Landis, outfielder, Chicago White Sox, 1957-1965

16

THE TWILIGHT YEARS

After the 1961 season, I was traded to St. Louis. I never knew why, but I was very surprised. It was also a big disappointment, because I had just brought my family here the year before. I thought I was going to be here quite a while and end my baseball career in Chicago.

As I mentioned, I learned of the trade on my car radio. I was stunned. There was never any inkling that the trade was in the making. Nineteen sixty-one was not one of my best years, but by any standard, it was a good one. I had played in 152 games, hit .280, drove in 82 runs, and had scored 91 runs. I also picked up my second and third Gold Gloves in 1959 and 1960. In today's market, that would warrant a $3 million contract, at least. Joe Cunningham was a good hitter, having batted .345 in 1959. But in 1961, he hit .286, with seven home runs and 40 runs batted in. Ironically, Joe had come in from St. Louis to attend the same banquet I was driving to when I heard the news. Like me, he had no idea about the trade. When we saw each other, I said, "Joe, good luck! I hope we see one another in the World Series. And I'll try like hell to beat you guys when we get there!"

Sure, I was hurt, darn hurt. But I didn't say anything; I never asked the White Sox the reason. That was not the way of a professional baseball player. There were some things you had to swallow in this game. Everyone who has played it knows that this is part of being a major leaguer. Still, after the trade, I spent a lot of days not answering the phone. I didn't want to talk about it; and I told my wife not to answer any calls either. Then I started thinking that it wasn't right; I was acting like a kid. If they didn't want me, forget it!

So it was off to St. Louis to meet with General Manager Bing Divine. We got to the point where I signed my contract with him. He said, "Minnie, the only one on this club who is making more money than you is Stan Musial."

The manager of the Cardinals in 1962 was Johnny Keane, a real gentleman, and a fine man. Johnny replaced Solly Hemus midway in the 1960 season, and he was a good man both on and off the field. He was the type of manager I always liked to play for, the old-fashioned kind who knew every aspect of the game. He concentrated on the players and like Paul Richards, Keane didn't play favorites. Everyone was the same, whether you were the star or a journeyman. Everybody was treated the same way.

Of course, the big name with the Cardinals was still Stan Musial. He was a great ballplayer and a good person as well. Unlike some of the great athletes I have known, Stan was not the kind of guy who thought he owned the whole world. He was a humble man, and also a very good-looking guy who dressed nicely. He could be a comedian of sorts, too.

I recall when I was recuperating after my harrowing head injury in May, 1962. I was activated in late July, in time for the team's west coast swing. Boy did Stan keep me amused! He was great with card tricks. We'd be on the plane and he would do unbelievable tricks with a pack of cards. Like a magician, he could make cards disappear and jump from the bottom to the top of the deck. I said, "Now wait a minute, Stan, how did you do that?" Then he'd do it again. "Stan," I said, "It's no wonder no one can get you out. Why don't you show me how to do those tricks, and then maybe I can hit the way you do!"

The St. Louis Cardinals were a good baseball team in 1962, just a couple of years away from being World Champions. With Bill White at first, Julian Javier at second, and Ken Boyer at third, the Cardinals had a solid infield that could hit as well as field. White hit .324 and drove in more than 100 runs, while Ken Boyer hit 24 homers and drove in 98. The pitching staff was anchored by Larry Jackson, Curt Simmons, Ernie Broglio, and Bob Gibson, soon to become one of the best right handers ever, and a great Hall of Famer. With an outfield of Stan Musial, Curt Flood, and I, and a record of 84-78, we may well have been the best sixth-place team ever.

But my walls came tumbling to the ground in less than a month. On May 11, 1962, we were playing the Los Angeles Dodgers. What happened that day resulted in the most serious injury of my career. I fractured my skull and broke my wrist chasing a line drive off the bat of Duke Snider. The bases were loaded, and Johnny Keane moved me in. In the American League, I would have been playing deeper; I always preferred moving in to chasing back for a fly ball. But being new in the National League, I moved in. Those were the days when going from one league to another was like two different worlds. Before the advent of free agency and wholesale inter-league trading, players often spent their entire careers either in the National or the American Leagues; it was rare to see service in both.

Duke Snider hit a long, lazy fly ball. I was running like the devil and I kept on going and going. Suddenly I ran into the left field wall. I was unconscious and taken out on a stretcher into the clubhouse. When I awoke, I wanted to go back to the field to play. I was out of my mind; I was sitting in the clubhouse, and I was saying that I was ready to play. Someone replied, "Sure, Minnie! Tomorrow."

Then the ambulance came and I was rushed to the hospital. I was unconscious for four days. When I woke up I saw my wife, Edelia, and I said, "What are you doing here? You look like you're in a daze." She said she had been there for four days watching me. She said the doctors wanted to operate on me, but she would not sign to allow it. She told them that it was my wish that if I ever got hit badly enough in the head and anyone wanted to operate, not to let them do it; that I wanted to die in my uniform. That was my wish. Edelia brought some medicine, and it stopped the bleeding. The doctors asked her if she ever studied medicine. She had; as a young girl, she had been a nurse.

I never doubted that I would be back playing baseball. I'd work out at home until I felt I was ready to play again. I returned to the active list on July 29, but was used only sparingly. Stan Musial moved to left field and hit .330. It was Stan's last big year. In 1963, his average fell to .255. At the end of the year, he retired from the game and a marvelous 22-year career that was spent entirely with the St. Louis Cardinals. Even with Bill White, Julian Javier, Ken Boyer, Curt Flood, and Stan Musial in the everyday line-up, the Cardinals finished the year 17 1/2 games behind the San Francisco Giants, who defeated the Los Angeles Dodgers in a three-game playoff to capture the National League flag, an indication of just how strong the National League teams were that year.

Things never worked out after my injury. I played in only 39 games, went to bat less than 100 times, and hit an anemic .197. The following year, the Cardinals sold me to the Washington Senators for $30,000 and a minor league player to be named later.

The Washington Senators were a sorry lot in 1963. They should not be confused with the old Washington Senators of Harmon Killebrew, Earl Battey, Bob Allison, Camilo Pascual, Jim Kaat, and Co. who left Washington in 1961 to become the Minnesota Twins. The new Senators, under manger Mickey Vernon, finished a distant last in the American League in 1962 with a record of 60 - 101, and would do worse in 1963, finishing last again with a 56-106 record.

I opened the 1963 season for the Senators in left field. I had two doubles in the opener off the Orioles' Steve Barber. We lost the opener to Barber, 3 - 0. I led off in the ninth with my second double, but was left stranded. I was in the line-up the second day, but the third day, I did not play. Shortly, Gil Hodges took over the team from Mickey Vernon, and I was used only against left handers. I didn't like the idea at all; I was not ready to be a utility player.

But these things we have to accept, because it is a part of baseball. Chuck Hinton, the Senators' big power hitter would ask me why Gil Hodges wasn't playing me more, and I could only tell him that I was not the manager. I was new here, and maybe there were things to learn. Sure, I had hard feelings; I could still play, and the Senators were a weak team. But I had to swallow my pride; and I didn't say a word to anyone. Players didn't open their mouths back then like many do today. You took your medicine, and you didn't cry about it.

Realistically, I knew that I was becoming a part-time player. Lots of things go through your mind, but I couldn't let it consume me. I didn't know that the Senators had ideas of grooming me to manage one of their minor league clubs. Part-time work was not the answer for me; it never was. I played in 109 games for the Senators in 1963 and hit only .229. I played out my option year with the Senators. They released me in October, with the condition that I could report for spring training the next year.

While my numbers slipped on the ballfield, 1963 turned out to be a very happy time for my family. In May, my daughter, Marilyn, was born in Washington D.C. How well I remember that day. I was looking at my new daughter through the glass where the other fathers were gazing at their newborns. On my right, I saw a nice-looking man with light, wavy brown hair and a pleasant smile looking at his child. I thought I knew him; at least I knew that I had seen him somewhere before. Then I recognized him. Shortly, he too, would write his name into the pages of history. The man standing next to me looking so attentively at his newborn child was Bobby Kennedy.

Early in 1964, I got a call from Bill Veeck, who was living in nearby Baltimore. Bill invited Edelia and me to visit with them for a couple of days. While we were visiting there, Bill received a phone call from White Sox General Manager Eddie Short. In the course of the conversation, Short asked Bill if he knew where Minnie Minoso was, and what he was doing. Veeck replied that I just happened to be there, and he handed me the phone.

Eddie was very direct. He asked me if I'd like to come to spring training with the White Sox in Sarasota. I answered that indeed I would. I reported to Sarasota in March 1964, worked very hard, and I made the team. I was just thrilled. Was Short's phone call to Bill Veeck an accident of timing, or did Bill Veeck in his inimical style arrange all of this himself? I have often wondered.

It was a vastly different White Sox team in 1964. A special era ended officially on December 10, 1963 when Nellie Fox, the last of the original "Go Go" White Sox was sold to Houston in a waiver deal. Six times, Nellie hit over .300 for the Sox. Two more times he hit over .295. He won three Gold Gloves for fielding, and *The Sporting News* named Nellie baseball's outstanding second baseman four different times. Nellie Fox was the American League's Most Valuable Player in 1959, and six other times he was among the league's top ten players for League MVP honors. Nellie was one of a kind; he left us all far too soon. His early death saddened everyone who knew him.

Gone from the team as well was Sherman Lollar. Durable as they came and often vastly underrated, Sherman was one of the best catchers of the day. For twelve years with the Chicago White Sox, Sherman was our quiet leader, our unofficial captain on the field. He was a blessing to White Sox pitching staff in the

1950s, all of whom respected him immensely. As with Nellie, Sherman Lollar passed from the scene all too soon.

Two more White Sox mainstays were no longer with the club in 1964. Luis Aparicio and Al Smith were traded to Baltimore early in 1963 for shortstop Ron Hansen, third baseman Pete Ward, outfielder Dave Nicholson, and pitcher Hoyt Wilhelm. It was great having Hoyt and his baffling knuckleball on our side for a change. There was no other pitcher who ever gave me the same trouble for so many years as Hoyt Wilhelm. Eddie Lopat was a close second, but no one could make me look as bad at the plate as Hoyt Wilhelm.

The White Sox had pitching in 1964, great pitching to be sure. We had the best young arms in the league. Rookie Gary Peters had played out his option with the White Sox in 1963, and only came north with the club because lefties Juan Pizarro and Frank Baumann were hurting. Gary won 11 games in a row, finished with a 19-8 record, led the league with a 2.33 earned run average, and was the American Rookie of the Year. Gary Peters was even better in 1964, posting a record of 20 - 8, tops in the American League, a 2.50 ERA, and 205 strikeouts.

By now, Juan Pizarro was one of the best left handers in the game. He went 16 - 8 in 1963, and like Gary Peters, Juan was even better in 1964. Pizarro put together an excellent 19 - 8 record, and a 2.56 ERA with 162 strikeouts. Young right hander Joel Horlen was just outstanding. He lost so many close games that he gained the nickname of "Hard Luck." Horlen's record in 1964 was 13 - 8, but his ERA of 1.88 tells the real story. With Hoyt Wilhelm and Eddie Fisher in the bullpen, you would have to look a long way to ever find a better Chicago White Sox pitching staff. The entire pitching staff carried a combined ERA of 2.72.

Yes, I made the team in 1964, but I hardly saw any playing time. By mid-season, Eddie Short told me that the club wanted to bring up a young ballplayer and asked me to go down to play at Indianapolis. After all those years, it was back to the minors. I was told they would bring me up in September, which the club did. I didn't like the idea at all, but really had little choice. Had I not agreed, I knew that I would probably have been released.

I was playing third base and hitting well when I was called back up. To beef up our sagging offense, the White Sox also acquired Bill Skowron from the Washington Senators and Smokey

Burgess from the Pittsburgh Pirates. Smokey, it may be recalled, was baseball's premier pinch hitter.

So I came back to the White Sox in September as a player and part-time coach. Our pitching was keeping up in the race, neck to neck with the New York Yankees. The offense was hurting and was weak and non-productive. We had trouble scoring runs, yet for some reason I was rarely used. I was brought back in September to help us win a pennant, or so I thought; yet I wasn't allowed to do that. I wasn't the only one who was puzzled; most of the other guys were too. Bill Skowron in particular questioned me all the time. "Minnie! You are one of the few guys here that can move a runner along. You've been around. You know the tricks. You are a run producer. The team has trouble scoring runs. What's wrong with them? If you play, we can win this thing. You can bunt. You can move a man to third base. You can still hit!" But I didn't play.

I never had words with Al Lopez, but he just wouldn't play me. Remember, in those days, the manager held a lot of power on a club. I can't forget how that '64 season ended either. We took four straight games from the Yankees in August. Then we closed out the year by winning nine straight. But the New York Yankees won their last ten games to take their fifth straight American League title. They finished with a record of 99 - 63. We finished one game behind at 98 - 64. I came to bat only 31 times, 22 of them as a pinch hitter. To this day, with a pennant on the line, I don't know why Lopez didn't use me more.

However, if my playing days were numbered, there was always the possibility of coaching. Johnny Cooney had announced his retirement at the end of the year, and the guys on the team were real encouraging, cheering me on all the time. Most really believed I would be Cooney's replacement in 1965. I helped in various coaching capacities all year, and I knew and understood the players. It all made good sense. At the end of the year, I went up to Lopez. "Al, " I said. "If you decide to integrate your coaching staff, I would be privileged to coach for you next year." Lopez said he would certainly give the matter some thought and get back to me.

Twenty days later, I was given my outright release by the Chicago White Sox! There was no coaching job!

When we lived in Mexico, it was a family thing to go to the games. He used to dress me up like a little baseball mascot. My dad was playing for and managing a team. My sixth birthday was celebrated in the ballplayers' dugout after the game. Baseball is so much of my dad's life. The pasison he had for baseball was so real. We could be driving somewhere and he saw a baseball game going on, he'd stop the car. He'd either get involved or somehow end up playing in the game.

Now that I have grown older, I wish I had the passion for something like he had for baseball. It was incredible. That's what has kept him looking so young. You see the players today with athletic directors and ten or fifteen coaches, and you think how he did it all alone. He had discipline and passion. Those are two words that describe him best. I remember having to cover my ears as a little girl, because he could get so mad at the umpires. He had such a strong voice that you could hear it all over the park. As a manager, he'd be out of the game quite a bit for arguing. But he always respected the umpires and their job. Yet somehow he'd find a way to stay and direct the team even when they ejected him from the game. The fans loved it because he really cared.

I think my dad was as popular in Mexico as he was in this country, especially in the little towns. It's incredible, but sometimes when I speak to friends of mine who live in Mexico City and they happen to mention that they know me, the older generation gets real excited. They used to call him "The Black Charro." When they would win a championship, he used to come out of the dugout with this beautiful Charro black hat. He used to come out of there like a bullfighter. He'd walk around and the people would go crazy. They loved him.

Marilyn Arrieta, Minnie's daughter

17

MEXICO

"O.K, Minnie, I'll let you know!" That is what Al Lopez told me after I made it clear that I would like to replace Johnny Cooney as a full-time White Sox coach. Nobody let me know anything. I found out that I was released by reading the newspapers. There was not a phone call from either Al Lopez or Eddie Short. My Major League career had ended with little more than a blurb in the papers.

What followed was one of the darkest times of my life. I thought I was part of the White Sox organization; I knew the organization was a part of me. In some ways, it was like losing a parent. I was crying inside, but never let anybody know. That is why people thought I was so strong. I never let on when I was bleeding inside.

I would experience similar feelings of despair again in 1976 when I was back with the White Sox as a first base coach. My marriage to Edelia was falling apart. Any man who has experienced these painful happenings certainly knows the stress and strain involved in such legal procedures. Only Bill Veeck and Mary-Frances knew how shattered I really was. Again, I never said anything publicly, I had the old ethos of the professional baseball player. What happens in the clubhouse, remains in the clubhouse. Similarly, the home is your domestic clubhouse, and you don't take your personal problems on the field with you. So I continued my first base coaching duties, coaching and chattering all the time. I even surprised Bill and Mary-Frances, both of whom wanted to know how I could sustain my chatter in the coaches box, when I felt so badly inside. "Orestes," Bill Veeck said to me. "How can you do that? You stand there and do your job like you are the happiest guy on the whole team."

After my release from the White Sox in 1964, we continued living in Chicago. I was forgotten quite quickly; the only ones who made a big deal over my release were the fans. For the second time I felt my world was over. But unlike in 1951, when Cleveland traded me to Chicago, there were no histrionics or instant heroics to soothe my pain. Winter was setting in and with every drop of snow, with every falling degree of temperature, I only felt worse. Finally Edelia told me quite frankly that sooner or later I would have to come to terms with being out of baseball.; that I would have to adjust.

Since 1962, I had been doing public relations work for S&H Green Stamps. It gave me an opportunity to get back into the world. Shortly after Christmas, I made a trip to Denver for the S&H Company. By the time I came back, I felt so very lucky to be a part of the world I had.

On the return flight we encountered heavy snow storms, making it very tough to land. The plane kept circling and circling; I thought that I had had it. That we would never make it to the ground. When the plane finally landed, I was so happy I said a prayer. Suddenly, my other travails seemed small.

This was not the first time I encountered a harrowing experience in the air. Back in 1955, the team had taken a flight from New York to Baltimore. The plane ran into real trouble, and we were all scared out of our minds. I was sitting with Virgil Trucks, Sandy Consuegra, and Connie Johnson. I was holding a medallion that I have always worn around my neck, and praying like the devil. My mother had given it to me as a good luck charm. Sandy Consuegra told me to pray for him, too. He was very worried for his wife and kids, and I told him, "Sandy, we better pray for us. They are safe on the ground, we are the ones who are in trouble. If this plane doesn't land, their lives will eventually go on. Our lives are finished."

When we finally made it to Baltimore, Connie Johnson, my friend and pitching teammate who looked like Nat King Cole, began saying prayers in all directions. The team had a meeting the next day. We were told that anybody who did not want to fly could use other means of transportation. Connie, Virgil Trucks, and I took the offer to heart. The three of us took a long and relaxing train ride to Kansas City.

I relate these two stories to explain how I was able to get myself back together and to stop feeling sorry for myself. I was alive, and I had a lovely wife and a wonderful baby girl. So instead of sulking any further, it was time to get on with my life.

I had been receiving phone calls from Mexico for a while. They came from a gentleman by the name of Jesus Carmona who was general manager of the Charros de Jalisco club in the Mexican League. But I hadn't seen fit to call him back. Now after my frightful episode, I was just so glad to be alive. I made up my mind to contact him and to speak with him, and he asked me if I would consider playing baseball in Mexico for his team, which was located in Guadalajara. He asked if I could come out there and help them. The owner of the team, Albaro Lebrija, insisted the team needed a player of my abilities. I asked him how he knew where to reach me. It seems that my old buddy and teammate, Jim Rivera, had played for him and told him that I was available, still fit, and could help them out.

I said I would come out to Guadalajara, but there were some further conditions, questions that I insisted he answer. First I asked if I could wear my old number, "Number 9" on the back of my uniform. He assured me it was waiting for me in Guadalajara. I asked him if there were any Cuban ballplayers on the team who returned to Cuba to play winter ball. This was no joke; I was very serious. I did not want to be associated with any Latin ballplayer who in any way supported a Communist government. I was very angry by this time. The Castro government had taken every bit of property that I had owned.

So I packed my clothes and drove my car from Chicago to Guadalajara. I bucked a heavy blizzard along the way but was able to arrive in Laredo, Texas intact. Then I cleared my car through customs, established my visa credentials, and headed on to Guadalajara. The following month, Edelia arrived with my daughter, Marilyn, and my niece, Marian. I had everything ready for them including a new apartment in Guadalajara.

I played for the Charros de Jalisco club in the Mexican League for three years. Then they moved me to Orisaba to be a player/manager at the minor league level. The Charros represented the entire state of Jalisco, although our home stadium was in Guadalajara, a truly beautiful city with near ideal weather. The Mexican League was composed of eight teams and played during the summer months from April through August. There was winter ball in still a different league, the Mexican Pacific League. So I was able to play baseball throughout the whole of Mexico.

When I first came to Mexico, I was called Orestes "Minnie" Minoso. But almost immediately they started calling me *The Charro Negro* (The Black Charro). I bought a lovely home in the suburbs, with a swimming pool and lots of room. We needed all the room because soon Edelia's mother and father came to stay with us, as did Edelia's sister and her four children. We enrolled Marilyn in a Catholic parochial school, where Spanish became her first language.

Truly, I never thought of my playing Mexican ball as a step down. I think of only one thing when I play baseball; that I am a professional baseball player, which means I play the game with the same intensity anywhere I go. It was not that I didn't miss the Major Leagues; but it was no longer there for me. This was a new life and a new challenge. Wherever you play baseball, you must think the same way you did during your glory days, otherwise things won't work out well. The same rule applies to the game of life as well. People should know this beyond all other things, because in life nothing is forever. We all find this out sooner or later.

So I loved playing baseball in Mexico. It was in my blood here just as it had been in the United States. I lost almost all contact with the people I had known in America. Mexico was my home now. I had begun a new life and soon became a very busy man.

I was well paid in Mexico. My salary was in the $25,000 range, which allowed me to live in comfort. There were quite a few black ballplayers in Mexico. They came from America, Cuba, The Dominican Republic, Panama, etc. Each team in the Mexican League was allowed to "import" three players. By "import," it was meant that each team could have three non-Mexican players on its roster.

I was able to see a good friend whom I had not seen in many years. After his one season with the Chicago White Sox, Hector Rodriguez settled in Mexico. He was now manager of a minor league team in Mexico. I had always felt that the White Sox gave up on Hector too soon. But the years had been good to him; he looked well and was getting along fine. We would run into each other from time to time during my years in Mexico, but when I returned to the United States we lost contact with each other again. Occasionally, I have tried to get in touch with him, but I have been unsuccessful.

I could still play baseball and had good, productive years in Mexico. My first season with Jalisco I hit .360 with 14 home runs and 82 RBI's. I led the Mexican League in doubles and in runs scored. I lost the batting championship to Emilio Sosa who played for Poza Rica and hit .365. Someone later told me that a mistake had been made in compiling averages and I actually hit .375, which would have given me the title. But officially the title was Sosa's, and I was runner-up. In 1966, I was again in the running for batting honors, hitting .348 for Jalisco, although I was hindered most of the year by a fractured finger, which put me on the disabled list for more than a month.

During the winter months of 1966-1967, I had my first shot as a player/manager with the Orizaba club, a minor league affiliate of the big club at Jalisco. Here I was given a chance to work with kids; the 17-, 18-, and 19-year-old youngsters. I enjoyed managing and tried to employ much of what Paul Richards had shown me when I was a youngster myself. Anyone who has ever managed knows there is no greater thrill than to watch raw, young kids develop into complete baseball players. I had a nice season with the bat too. I let the kids do most of the playing, but in 100 at bats I got 35 hits for a .350 average. Included among those 35 base hits were seven doubles, three triples, and five home runs.

When it comes to youngsters, no thrill is bigger than seeing your own son develop into an outstanding ballplayer. Here I can relate to such baseball fathers as Ray Boone, Bobby Bonds, and Ken Griffey. Orestes Jr. was a fine athlete, even as a little boy. As an eleven-year-old boy in Evanston, Illinois, the local newspaper gave him quite a write-up. Bob Cullen, his Little League coach in Evanston called him a natural-born athlete and credited him with being responsible for his team's first-place standing. Actually Orestes Jr. received his first glove when he was two years old, and was playing in the Midget League in Cuba when he was six.

He became a star athlete at Evanston Township High School, and by the time he graduated he was considered one of the top prospects in the state. He signed with the Kansas City Royals and was sent to play Class A ball in Florida. However, things didn't work out. He had a disagreement with the organization, whom he felt did not give him enough of a chance to show what he could do. When the Royals did not ask him to spring training, he decided to call it quits.

From 1967 through 1969, I continued as player/manager for the Puerto Mexico team. Actually, the Orizaba club had changed locations and had moved to the town of Puerto Mexico. It was still the minor league affiliate of the big team in Jalisco. Always working with the youngsters, I played only part time at Puerto Mexico and even more sparingly when I made appearances with Jalisco.

In 1970, the Charros wanted me to try to revive baseball in the town of Gomez Palacio. There hadn't been a team there for 16 years. The last person who tried to re-establish baseball there was Martin Dihigo, the great Cuban Hall of Famer and my boyhood idol. I would manage at Gomez Palacio for four years and also continue to play winter ball each year.

I left the Charros organization after the 1973 season and spent most of the next two years with the team at Puerto Vallarta, which was just a four hour drive to my home in Guadalajara. I played first base, and my first year with the team we won the pennant. In the play-off series against Compostella, I played an instrumental role. It was a best-of-seven series and we were leading Compostella three games to two. In Game Six, I hit the home run that won the title for us. At the award ceremony, some of my younger teammates carried me on their shoulders. Later I was asked to make a speech. It was just a marvelous thrill.

I played in the little mining town of Cananea as well, where I was a coach and a batting instructor. I mention Cananea in particular, because my son, Orestes Jr., played on the team too. Orestes Jr. lived with his mother in Evanston, but he always kept in touch. As I have indicated, he was an outstanding high school athlete in both baseball and football. He arrived in Mexico after playing outfield for Class A and Double A teams in the Kansas City organization. Before Orestes came to Mexico, he tried to reach me. He called Edelia and told her that he wanted to come to Mexico, and Edelia called to give me the news. I told her to tell Orestes Jr. not to do anything until he first reached me, but he never called. He just took a plane and came out here.

He showed up at Leon, a lower-level minor league team where I was managing. He couldn't play there because he was far too advanced. This was essentially a rookie league. That's why he hooked on with Cananea. He was quite a sensation at Cananea, hitting five grand slam home runs in two-and-a-half months.

The following year, Orestes Jr. came to play for me at Puerto Vallarta. This little, picturesque Mexican town just loved winning. In fact, the Puerto Vallarta team would win three consecutive pennants, and each time the town feasted and celebrated for three days with outdoor dancing, eating, and drinking. To say they took their baseball seriously would be an understatement.

The Puerto Vallarta club was encumbered by the rule that allowed a team only three non-Mexican players on its roster. It so happened that the two other non-Mexican players decided they wanted to play elsewhere, thus there was room for both Minosos, Orestes Jr. and I, to play on the same team again. The League was set up differently than most baseball leagues in the United States; there were two separate half seasons.

Technically, a team might finish last the first half of the year, but if it finished first in the second half of the year, a team could still get into the World Series. That's just what happened to us. We were a young team and started out poorly. We had trouble adjusting during the first half of the year and finished last. In the second half, we turned things around totally and won it all. Father and son were together in the line-up. Orestes Jr. batted third and I batted fourth. I will never forget how we won the game that clinched that second half-season title for us. It was high drama, the stuff from which movies are made.

It was the seventh inning. We were one run behind with two runners on base. Orestes Jr. came up and hit one out of the ballpark for a two-run lead. As my son crossed the plate, I shook his hand. Then I stepped up and hit the ball out of the park in exactly the same spot. The crowd just went wild. The "Black

Charro" and his son hitting back-to-back home runs to give Puerto Vallarta a three-run lead in the seventh inning. Everyone was ecstatic. We won the game and went to the World Series. Then we went on to take the World Series in seven games. The "Black Charro" and son. We did it!

But there were also big problems in managing your own son. You have to walk the thin line of not showing favoritism on the one hand, and not overcompensating by being unduly harsh on the other. Again, we can apply that old familiar theme. The officer's son joins his unit and the officer goes to great lengths to demonstrate that he is just another trooper, often making it rougher on him.

Orestes Jr. was a fine outfielder. His throwing arm and his fielding ability were probably better than mine, and he hit with power. Truly, I believe that he had the potential to be a solid major league player. However, a combination of bad luck and lost opportunities got in the way. Often I wonder if I had been in the United States to guide him, instead of in Mexico during the time his baseball career was in limbo, if things might have turned out differently.

A particular instance of that old father/son clash occurred over a missed sign. We had a player who made a habit of missing signs. He missed a bunt signal when we were losing by a 3 -2 score, and I removed him from the game. The following day, my son came to bat. We had a man on first and I flashed him the bunt sign. Instead of bunting, Orestes swung away and bounced into an easy double play. Either he missed the sign, or he just plain didn't listen. At the end of the inning, he began walking up the dugout steps to go in the field. I told him to stay where he was. I pointed a finger at him "You're on the bench! You missed your sign."

He was very upset and angry with me. Orestes thought I was trying to show him up in front of the fans. I told him he better hold his mouth; I was the boss on this team, and the same rules applied to everyone. The incident was very upsetting to me also. With the score tied, the game was called due to darkness. After the players cleared the bench for the clubhouse, I remained in the dugout, sulking some over what happened. A few fans had remained in the ballpark and walked over to the dugout. They let me have it. I was far too rough on my son they said, and they insisted I should not have taken him out of the game.

A baseball team is one big family. At least that is the way it should be. A manager cannot show favoritism, not to a brother, not to a son. To no one! I never would want to hurt my son, but as a manager I would not be doing a good job if I didn't respond to him as I would any other player.

All did not glitter at home either. Our family experienced a tragedy that touched us all so deeply. In 1971, my niece Marian, Juanita's daughter, committed suicide. I had raised her and loved her as a daughter since she first came to the United States with me in 1961 as a child. She was an older sister to my daughter Marilyn, who just worshipped her. There was never any inkling that she might do such a thing. She never said anything to me or my wife. Now thinking back, I recall that her moods changed very quickly. Edelia would try to talk with her, but she never said much. We know for certain no drugs were involved; she was never involved in that sort of stuff. Nor was there any indication of a broken romance.

On that terrible day I was on the road, and Edelia was shopping in Lorado. My niece was at home with my mother-in-law and my daughter. She was talking with grandma, and then excused herself, put her arms around Marilyn and hugged her, and went upstairs. After a while, grandma became concerned and called to her, but heard nothing. She called again She went upstairs to her room and opened the door, and there was my niece dead on the floor; she had swallowed a bottle of pills. It was a dreadful and awful blow to all of us, but especially to young Marilyn who was totally devastated.

On a more positive note, something unbeknownst to me was going on in Chicago. Remember, I had lost contact with most of the people I had known. The White Sox, it seems, had lost something like $8 million since 1970. John Allen announced he would entertain offers to sell the club, but there were few takers. There was one, however, a genuine surprise. With rumors flying high that the White Sox were headed for Seattle, Bill Veeck made a bid to buy the club. The American League owners turned a deaf ear to Veeck's bid, but they gave him an additional week to raise the required revenue. Of course, no one believed he could raise an extra $1.2 million in just a week, but Veeck did just that. The impossible had happened. Bill Veeck had control of the Chicago White Sox. One week later, Paul Richards was named manager, replacing Chick Tanner who had guided the White Sox to a fifth place finish in the six team American League West.

It was December 1975. I was resting in Puerto Vallarta when the phone rang. It was Roland Hemond, the general manager of the White Sox. He said that Bill Veeck had been trying to reach me for three days, and he wanted me to rejoin the Chicago White Sox as a coach for the coming year. I was thrilled and elated beyond belief; then suddenly a thought hit me. During those dark days of 1964, Bill Veeck had asked me if I would like to work for him if he would have another Major League club one day. I replied, "Bill, I would work for you wherever you are." The years had passed and I had totally forgotten our little exchange. Time often has a way of making words disappear. Sure, I may have forgotten. But Bill Veeck never did. After eleven years far from the Major League scene I once knew, Bill Veeck was bringing me home. I was going back to Chicago to wear a White Sox uniform once again.

In 1976, while playing for the California Angels, we began a three- game series with the Chicago White Sox. I remember reading in the papers that Minnie would be activated for the Saturday game.

Sid Monge at that time was a young pitcher. I was playing third base that day and Monge was in command of his pitches. Minnie hit a line drive single to left field to celebrate his fourth decade in baseball. The next hitter made the third out. My first thought as I left the field was to run over, shake his hand and congratulate him. I was impressed to say the least. This from a man in his fifties. He had hit a rope.

Bill Melton, Chicago White Sox, 1968-1975

18

THE WINDS OF CHANGE
KEEP CHANGING

Of course, Bill Veeck never did things in an ordinary way. But then, there was nothing ordinary about Bill Veeck. The man who gave baseball its first midget, its first exploding scoreboard, and Chicago its last World Series entry had another surprise waiting in the wings. I was that surprise!

When Roland Hemond told me about my good fortune that December, I wanted to shout about it from the highest steeple. However, I was told to keep the news of my return a secret for the next month. Veeck, it seems, was going to announce my hiring at a banquet being thrown by the Chicago Baseball Writers who were honoring Bill with the Comeback Award. It was to honor Bill Veeck for buying the White Sox and rescuing the team from a possible sale to another city. But there had to be something else for him; another special feature. I was it. Not only would he announce my return to the White Sox at the banquet, he would present me in person. He told the press and the reporters that he would bring a "mystery man" with him. Just who this "mystery man" might be, he would leave for them to speculate.

I kept the news secret. Well almost. I did tell my son, Orestes Jr., when I returned. We embraced and cried happily. The big event took place in January 1976. Clearly the announcement of a "mystery man" only helped stimulate the coverage. When I arrived at the airport on the day of the banquet, I was met by my good friend, Ernie Carroll. I was incognito from that point on. Ernie whisked me away to the Back of the Yards Inn where I was instructed to stay in my room and talk to no one. Earlier in the day, I had been in the lounge when Bill Veeck called the hotel. Where was I? he asked Ernie Carroll alarmingly. Under no condition was I to leave my room. For the remainder of the day, it was the joy of room service.

Finally Ernie came for me. He gave me an oversized coat and a big hat, so I wouldn't be recognized when we drove to the Palmer House in downtown Chicago where the banquet was being held. Shortly after the banquet began, I was escorted downstairs to the Grand Ballroom where the event was going on. Soon the Chicago sports fans, the writers, and an overflow crowd would know the identity of Bill Veeck's "mystery man."

I later read that there were lots of guesses, and some actually hit upon my name; but they were only guesses. Nothing had been confirmed. When Bill Veeck was being presented with his Comeback Award he announced to the crowd: "The fellow who is really entitled to this award is a gentleman named Orestes Minoso." In high theater fashion I was escorted from the back of the Grand Ballroom by Ernie Carroll. There was a standing ovation; and when I reached the podium, Veeck presented me with the William Wrigley, Jr., "Comeback of the Year Award," the same award that had just been given to him moments before.

It would be an interesting year, with a twinge of *deja vu*. Here I was back with the Chicago White Sox. Paul Richards was again the manager, and he would start the season with two coaches who had played for him 25 years earlier. I was one and the other was Jim Busby, the fleet-footed centerfielder from the original 1951 "Go Go" White Sox team. There might have been another coach as well. Sadly, Nellie Fox had been struck down by cancer a short time before. Otherwise he, too, would have been asked to return as a coach. Yet Bill Veeck made it very clear that this was not a play on nostalgia. Both Busby and I, he insisted, were fine baseball men.

Needless to say, this was a double treat, because I was working for my old mentor, Paul Richards. But Paul was sorely minus the same talent he had in the 1950s. We had some good young players, and we were trying to work with them. Brian Downing, who would later have such fine years with the California Angels, was our catcher. We had a good double-play combo with Bucky Dent and George Orta. Bucky was traded to the New York Yankees early in 1977 for outfielder Oscar Gamble and pitcher LaMarr Hoyt. It was Bucky Dent's three-run homer in the 7th-inning playoff game against the Boston Red Sox, which erased a 2 - 0 Red Sox lead and gave the Yankees the East Division title. From there they defeated the Royals to gain the American League Pennant. Then they wrapped up the 1977 World Series in six games against the Dodgers, with Bucky Dent being the Series MVP.

The little-known LaMarr Hoyt would eventually emerge as the ace of the White Sox staff, and win the American League Cy Young Award in 1983 in pitching the Chicago White Sox to the American League West title.

In 1976, though, the Sox pitching was poor. Our three main starters in 1976 were Rich Gossage, Bart Johnson, and Ken Brett. Gossage, who was 9-17 in 1976 as a starter, was traded to the Pittsburgh Pirates where he became a standout relief pitcher. Then it was on to the New York Yankees and true big league stardom.

The only high point of the season was a ten-game winning streak in late May. By season's end, Paul Richards was plain tired. He told me that he would like to turn the club over to me. Yet he was skeptical, because he knew we didn't have much going for us, and a terrible record such as ours would not look good on my managerial resume. I told Paul to take it easy, and that the coaches would carry the load. Paul refused to quit. He stuck it out until the end when we finished the 1976 season in last place with a record of 64 - 97. In 1977 he was replaced by Bob Lemon.

Paul Richards retired from baseball. He returned to his home town in Waxahachie, Texas, to be with his family and to play golf. It was on the golf course where he died of a heart attack in 1986. Somehow I think that's where he would have wanted to be at the final fadeout. Paul Richards has too often been ignored when the pundits list baseball's best managers.

On September 10, 1976, I was put on the active White Sox roster in time for a weekend series with the California Angels. In doing so, I became the third oldest player to take an official turn at bat in the Major Leagues. Only Satchel Paige and Nick Altrock were older. I also joined Ted Williams, Early Wynn, and Mickey Vernon as the only players to perform in four decades.

My physical skills were every bit intact, and they still are today. If there were any doubters back then, I showed them by lining a ball into the stands during batting practice. I did not play on the 10th against Nolan Ryan, because Richards wanted me to have righty/lefty advantage against Frank Tanana. So the big day was Saturday, September 11, 1976. It was the first time I stepped to the plate in Comiskey Park in 12 years. I was hitting ninth in the order as the designated hitter. My first at bat was with one out in the 3rd and Kevin Bell on base with a triple. Truly, it was a proud and nostalgic moment for me. As a rookie 25 years earlier, I made my first plate appearance with the White Sox against Vic Raschi. Visions of those great "Go Go" years flashed before me.

Things were far less heroic this time. I struck out on three pitches. I couldn't get the bat around fast enough on the first pitch and grounded it foul. Then I swung and missed the next two pitches, both breaking balls. My second turn came in the fifth inning. With Bell on base again, I swung at Tanana's first pitch and popped it to second. In my final at bat, I took Tanana's first pitch and then flied out to right fielder Dan Briggs.

It had been a hitless comeback. Admittedly, my timing was off. The great milestone came the second day. We played a double header against the Angels. I was in the line-up once more as a designated hitter in Game One. Left hander Sid Monge was on the mound for the Angels. I opened my stance a bit and slashed Monge's first pitch, a fastball, into left field for a single.

With that line drive, I became the oldest player in major league history to hit safely. Satchel Paige and Nick Altrock were both pitchers and did not get hits. It was a momentous and happy occasion for me. As I trotted back to the dugout, Angel third baseman Bill Melton ran over to congratulate me. Umpire Dave Phillips was also applauding.

The good times did not last long. Sadly things were starting to become stormy at home. My marriage was failing, and I knew it, but I didn't know what to do. It is difficult to pinpoint exactly when a marriage stops working. You always want to think of where and why it went wrong; you look for the "maybes" and the "what ifs." But you can "maybe" or "what if" yourself to death and still not know much more.

Part of the problem I believe was that Edelia was going through a very rough change of life. For some reason she started getting jealous. I was always popular and enjoyed being around people. Women would come up to me and say 'Hi, Minnie!' Then they might kiss me on the cheek or hug me. I was gracious; this was a part of my public persona. But there was never another woman as long as Edelia and I were together. I always made it quite clear that I was committed to Edelia, just as I am committed totally to my wife, Sharon, today. Throughout our entire marriage, I was in love with Edelia. I loved my wife.

But there was something inside her that she could not tackle. I told her time and again that she was the only woman I ever married. I had married her for a reason; and that reason was that I loved her. Marriage was based on trust, I reminded her. I trusted her and she must trust me. To keep on like this would just hurt her and hurt me as well. No matter what I said or did, however, she just would think in a different way.

These problems began in a small way when we were in Mexico. But these episodes seemed to pass. Then when we returned to Chicago, it started building up again in a big way. I was popular; I was a local hero. And I was Minnie. Those things could not be helped.

By 1977, things were deteriorating rapidly between us. Her problem was jealousy, unfounded jealousy, and there didn't seem to be anything I could do. Sometimes I would come home and play cards with her mother. Grandma was living with us in Chicago as she had in Mexico. Even this bothered her, so we stopped playing cards for a few days. Then she started asking me if I was mad at her mother.

In public it appeared that we were happily married. We'd go out together and socialize, but at home our estrangement worsened. I was being torn open inside, but except for Bill and Mary-Frances Veeck, the outside world never knew. On the ballfield and in the coaches box, it was business as usual. I never dreamt that our marriage would come to this; these were things that happened to other people, not to us. All this was very hard on our daughter. How can you expect a young teenage girl to understand? But on the ballfield, the chatter and cheering continued. And in 1977, the Chicago White Sox had a lot to cheer about.

Let me pause now to say a few words about the 1977 Chicago White Sox, or the "South Side Hitmen" as they were called. No White Sox team in history hit as many home runs. In fact, no White Sox team has even come close. In 1977, we hit a total of 192 home runs. Only the Boston Red Sox as a team hit more than us. It was just unbelievable. Our pitching was mediocre, but time and time again, after spotting our opponents a large lead, we unleashed our big bats and came roaring back. We were the "South Side Hitmen," and how the fans loved us!

Late in the previous year, Bill Veeck said that things would be different in 1977. Boy, was Bill right. Truly, we may have been one-year wonders, but what wonders we were in 1977! The two heroes that year were Richie Zisk and Oscar Gamble, both of whom signed one-year contracts in 1977. Zisk, who had many good years with the Pittsburgh Pirates, hit 30 home runs and drove in 102 runs for the White Sox. His sidekick for the year, Oscar Gamble, began his career with the Chicago Cubs in 1969, and was traded to the White Sox by the New York Yankees. Gamble, who only once hit as many as 20 home runs in a season, clubbed 31 for the White Sox in 1977. The next year both Zisk and Gamble would be gone: Richie Zisk to the Texas Rangers and Oscar Gamble to the San Diego Padres.

The White Sox had only one .300 hitter that year. Ralph Garr hit .300 right on the nose. Inclusive of Zisk and Gamble, the Sox had nine players with double digit home runs. Third baseman Eric Soderholm came to us from the Minnesota Twins and hit a career high 25 home runs. Others with ten home runs or more included Chet Lemon (19), Jim Spencer (18), Lamar Johnson (18), George Orta (11), Jim Essian (10), and Ralph Garr (10).

The White Sox actually held first place from July 1 until August 14. There was a new fight song as well. With each home run, organist Nancy Faust would lead the crowd to a rousing chorus of "Na-Na-Hey-Hey Goodbye." Crowds turned out in numbers to cheer the South Side Hitmen. But when it was all over, the White Sox finished in third place with a 90-72 record, 12 games behind the Kansas City Royals and four games behind the second-place Texas Rangers. The following year the 'Hitmen' were history. The White Sox record dropped to 71-90 in 1978, and hit only 106 home runs on the year.

On a less happy note, my marriage was about to become history. Nineteen seventy-eight was a particularly tough year for me. In mid-season, Larry Doby replaced Bob Lemon as White Sox manager, and I guess I had hoped it would be me. Larry had been brought in as a hitting instructor, but had no managerial experience. I had managed all those years in Mexico under a multitude of conditions and situations. But in some ways Doby's appointment made sense. It was Bill Veeck who allowed Larry to become the Major League's second black ballplayer, and the first black to play in the American League. Now Larry would become only the second black manager in the game. One day later, I was informed that the White Sox were moving me upstairs to do public relations and make personal appearances for the club. Taking my place as first base coach was a young fellow with a law degree who would soon go on to be a great manager. His name was Tony La Russa. One day later, I received another bit of very bad news. It came by way of letter. My father Carlos Arrieta had passed away in Cuba.

The death of my father hit me hard, but my faith allowed me to sustain these types of losses. I am Catholic, and have a strong belief in God, and in times such as these I am able to cling onto my faith. But it was at home that another loss was in the making. By the end of 1977, Edelia and I separated. She took Marilyn and her mother and moved to San Diego, and by early 1978, our divorce was official.

Financially I was left with very little. I don't believe for a moment that Edelia wanted to hurt me, nor to make things unduly hard for me. She spoke very little English, and her lawyer did the talking for her. His was a contingency agreement, so I don't feel I have to say much more.

At first her lawyer wanted me to pay $ 3,000 a month. My salary with the White Sox was less than $20,000. Her attorney said that I made extra money on appearances, and that I didn't have to spend anything on meals or other functions.

I remember once in front of the judge I said that the lawyer was trying to ruin my life. I would make payments, I insisted, but only as much as I could. The judge replied that if I didn't pay the $3,000 dollars a month, he would put me in the county jail. I told him he might as well do just that, because I didn't have that kind of money.

Another time I told the judge that Edelia's lawyer was no more than a criminal protected by the law. The judge asked me if I had ever been to school to become a lawyer or if I ever studied law. I said "Your Honor, I don't think you have to go to any kind of school to tell the truth." I think the judge was impressed by that. At the start of our procedure, he had asked Edelia what kind of man I was. She said I was a very nice man. And that I had never as much as raised my hand to her. She insisted only that she no longer wanted to be married to me. That she just wanted to live by herself.

Finally I received a more sympathetic judge. He was rather shocked by what I had been ordered to pay. At this time the figure was far less than the original $3,000 a month. He was surprised, he said, because he knew real millionaires who were not paying as much as that. Finally we settled for $1,500 a month.

Another judge even thought this amount was too much. I knew I could pay it. With difficulty perhaps, but I could pay it. And I did, religiously every month. The judge was willing to reduce my payments to $1,000, but I told him that this would not be enough to sustain them. I said that as long as I was working, I'd be able to pay the $1,500 . The first thing I did with my check at the start of each month was to send money to Edelia and my daughter Marilyn. When Edelia passed away suddenly in 1990, my legal obligation ended, but each month I still send money to Marilyn in San Diego to help take care of Edelia's mother, who is 90 years old and an invalid.

Financially, things were tough for me, tougher than they had been in years. I had many obligations; to Edelia, to my daughter, and to myself. Yet I managed to live within my means. My father, you might remember, preached that lesson all his life. He taught me well, to live with what I had. So at least I was prepared when financial hardship came my way.

I continued working for the Chicago White Sox and doing some public relations work for a beer distributor. Slowly I began putting my life together. I was better able to do so because of the friendship of a wonderful family who lived in Joliet, Illinois. Jose Cardenal introduced me to Mary Lou Russ and her family. Mary Lou has one son and four daughters. The whole family befriended me at a time when there was much pain inside me. Their home became my home away from home. I am even the godfather to young Jimmy, who is the son of Mary Lou's daughter Diane and her husband Jim Bartholomew.

The years were passing quickly toward a new decade. I was 55 years old, an age when some men start looking toward retirement. Others look backward to lost dreams and misspent youth. They focus and lament on lost opportunities and faded dreams. I can't live life that way. Sure, I was a little older, but I had been around long enough now to have gained one of life's greatest treasures, a little wisdom.

So I turned my back to the past and looked forward to brighter days ahead. Not even in my most blatant optimism, however, did I imagine all that was in store for me. There was a new road ahead that would give my life an entirely new meaning.

19

LIFE BEGINS AT 60

The first time I saw Sharon Rice was the Thanksgiving weekend of 1984. Call it fate. Call it coincidence. But I really believe at the time I met her, I was looking for someone to make my life the way it is now.

Because the Thanksgiving weekend officially starts the Christmas season, the city of Chicago was having a Grand Christmas Parade to usher in the Holiday Season. There were lots of celebrities and lots of floats. In fact one of the celebrities was a young woman whose career was just starting to surface. Her name was Oprah Winfrey.

I was representing the Chicago White Sox. The celebrities were due to meet at The Little Corporal, a restaurant and lounge on the corner of Wacker Drive and State Street. Sharon had driven in with her girlfriend from Lake Geneva, Wisconsin, that very morning. Her friend was the manager of the bar, and Sharon had come just to keep her company and to watch the parade.

It was about ten in the morning and the celebrities were arriving to find out which float they were riding on. I walked in with a young man who was one of my godsons, the son of a dear friend of mine. I called him 'El Torro' because he was built like a miniature Ted Kluszewski—the big muscular first baseman who could clout a baseball a mile. He was to be riding on the float with me. As soon as I walked in, I saw Sharon at the corner of the bar looking at the TV and sipping a soft drink. Somehow I knew that I wanted to meet her and to see her again.

I was being swarmed by people wanting autographs, everybody but her. She had no idea who I was; the name Minnie Minoso meant absolutely nothing to her. I told her girlfriend behind the bar to bring her a drink.

"This is from Minnie Minoso," her friend said, handing her the drink.

"Who's he?" Sharon asked. "Who's Minnie Minoso?"

Her friend, a Hispanic woman, knew who I was. She told her to please accept the drink, if only not to be rude. I walked over to her and introduced myself, and she didn't know me from the man on the moon. What impressed her at first was that I was looking after a young boy. I mentioned that I had to take him home after the parade, but it would be nice if she'd still be there when I returned. I made it a point to stress that I'd be back.

That's how it started. That is how I met Sharon Rice, the woman who would one day become my wife and the mother of our five-year-old son, Charlie Orestes. True to my word, I returned to the restaurant, and Sharon was still there. Later she told me she was very surprised that I really returned. I asked her if she would like to go to Chinatown for dinner; there was a very good Chinese restaurant where I had been dining for years. She was reticent at first and wasn't sure she wanted to go out with a total stranger. But her girlfriend urged her on, and to make matters easier and more comfortable, her friend even came with us.

We had a very nice dinner, after which I took her home to the near north side of Chicago. We talked a while, and I asked if I might call her. She said "Yes," and handed me her phone number. We started dating, and in a sense we have been dating ever since.

I think what most impressed me about her was the way she handled herself. Granted, I was a celebrity and she my girlfriend, so people, especially other women, could be very rude at times. I truly appreciated Sharon's demeanor and confidence. She always kept her composure, and instinctively she knew that she wasn't just another pretty young female on my arm.

Ours is an interracial relationship. It is also a relationship that crosses generations. When we met, I was in my fifties, and

Sharon was still in her twenties. I say that because from the start, these differences really didn't seem to matter. Of course I had been around long enough not to care what people might say or think. And Sharon had made it clear that the people who really mattered would not care if I was black and I was older. As for others, they just didn't matter. What I can say with all certainty is that from the start there was a friendship and a trust between us that is rare among two people. She has given me a serenity and a genuine caring, which I never knew before.

The following year, she asked me to visit her family in Madison, Wisconsin at Christmas. She was sure that once her family knew me, they would like me. They would know from the start that I was a gentleman, and that my intentions were the best. I cared for their daughter greatly. She was right; I was made to feel comfortable from the start. No celebrity status; not even a bit of patronizing. Everything was quite natural, and we had a very nice holiday visit. Today we still try to spend the Christmas holidays with her family.

Most relationships can thrive in good times. It's when things get tough that we best see what another person is made of. I have rarely been ill in my life; and we had been going together for about a year when I went to get a hair cut and a wash. The woman who washed my hair used a chemical that she didn't test on me. The result was a violent allergic reaction. I had welts on my head as big as half-dollars. Some were almost the size of golf balls. It was terrible.

Sharon had to take me to the emergency room at Northwestern Memorial Hospital. When I was released, she and her sister, Carol, took care of me. There was nothing very romantic about the ordeal. They had to change the bandages and the dressings on my wounds. Once during my recovery, I was scheduled to talk to a group of children in the northern part of the state. I had bandages wrapped around my head like a mummy, and a hat to cover the bandages. Sharon drove me and looked after me. She stuck by me through this awful ordeal with loyalty and caring. This brought us even closer together.

There was another time, I believe it was in 1986, when our relationship was tested. Things were not going well with her job, and she planned to go back to Wisconsin, back with her parents for a while. She was hoping that the job opportunities might be better back home. I remember saying goodbye to her in the garage before she got in her car. I wouldn't tell her what to do; I knew that was up to her. She returned to Wisconsin for about a week. I knew I would miss her, but I didn't realize just how much. It was hard for me, very hard, and I guess it was for her too, because in a week she was back in Chicago.

A year later, Sharon became pregnant. She had been ill for quite a time, very sick. I had been out of town for some time, and when I came back she was in the hospital, being fed with an I.V. She was sick, and I was frightened for her. She told me about the pregnancy, but marriage did not come up at that time. She never wanted me to marry her for that reason, but there was another factor as well. She knew about my failed first marriage and the deep pain that followed. I honestly must admit that the thought of another failed marriage just plain scared me. There was also the added complication and fear of a possible miscarriage. Again Sharon went back home to try to work things out in her mind. She did, and she returned to Chicago in the seventh month of her pregnancy. I was at her side, and have been so ever since. We began making a home together in preparation for our child.

When you fall in love, it is not for just one reason. In the end you fall in love with everything about the person. I see things in her that I have not known in anyone else. Most important we have always trusted each other. Yes, she is younger, but I'm forever young myself.

When our son, Charlie, was born on November 9, 1988, we began to build our lives together. We share each other like we have known one another for 100 years. My life has changed because I am happier now than I have ever been. We trust each other with our eyes closed. We don't give a hoot if anyone thinks about us in a wrong way, because we live together in a right and beautiful way.

After Charlie was born, we were together for about two-and- a-half years. We became more and more a family, and we started working together to make a good home. She was a big help in getting my finances together as we began saving to buy a nice house. We pulled together economically for Charlie's sake, and moved to our present home near Chicago's lakefront in June 1991. We were married on my birthday, November 29, 1991 in a Catholic Church here in Chicago. It was a small affair, with just family and a few close friends. John Wasylik was my best man, and he arranged for a limousine to drive us from the church back to our home for the reception.

We delayed our marriage for some definite reasons and some concerns we had. After my divorce, so much of my life stood still. It frightened me to think in terms of another marriage, and Sharon sensed this. Also we were both Catholic, and the question of marriage and the Church was a real concern for us. There was also the fact that I had grown children. In the long run, however, this presented no problem. My children and Sharon get along very well.

Young Charlie loves his mother dearly, and Sharon is one of the world's great mothers. Like any couple we have our misunderstandings, and we may become angry from time to time, but we never hurt each other. There is a deep bond of loyalty and fidelity between us. We both wanted to find a good person, and we are so lucky to have found each other. We started out with a friendship. We both had a good time going out, and then we ended up having love with the friendship. How very fortunate we are!

The other part of my life was still baseball, most especially my continued work with the Chicago White Sox. In 1979, Don Kessinger, former shortstop for the Chicago Cubs, succeeded Larry Doby as Sox manager. But Don couldn't get the team going and resigned in early August. He was replaced by 35 year old Tony La Russa, the same fellow who had taken over the first base coaching chores from me the year before. By 1980 it had become obvious to Bill Veeck that the expense of running a ballclub was now beyond his financial means. On the 22nd of August, Bill announced an agreement with Edward DeBartolo to sell the club and the park to him for $20 million.

However, the intimation that DeBartolo might move the team to New Orleans, coupled with his horse racing interests, did not appeal to Commissioner Bowie Kuhn. Twice the League voted against the sale. I should add, as well, that DeBartolo told me that if he bought the club, I would manage the team. That I would have liked very much, but it was not to be. On January 29, 1981, a new era in White Sox history began, when the League office approved the sale of the Chicago White Sox to Chicago real estate investor Jerry Reinsdorf and CBS sports executive Eddie

Einhorn. The new White Sox owners met while they were students together at Northwestern University.

Before Bill Veeck left the Chicago White Sox, he gave me the opportunity to become only the second man in baseball history, and the first in the 20th century, to play Major League baseball in five separate decades. Pitcher Nick Altrock, who played his first decade in the 19th century, is the only other Major League player able to claim five baseball decades. Altrock was a Washington Senator pitcher and coach, but is far better known in his capacity as one of baseball's truly great clowns.

Bill officially activated me for the final three games of the 1980 season. The big day was October 5, 1980 against the California Angels. Again, Frank Tanana was the pitcher for California. This time as I stepped to the plate to pinch hit for Greg Pryor, Tanana tipped his hat as a sign of respect to me. I took two low sliders for balls. His next pitch was a sinker around my knees. I could see the ball fine; I still had my eye, but my timing was off. I swung late and popped out to the catcher in foul territory. I had one more chance in the final game of the season, and it was a repeat. Again I popped to the catcher behind the plate.

In 1981, the White Sox tapped the free agent market and came up with catcher Carlton Fisk and slugger Greg Luzinski. In the strike-shortened 1981 season, we finished in third place 8 1/2 games behind the division-leading Oakland Athletics. In 1982 the White Sox signed outfielder Steve Kemp and first baseman Tom Paciorek. We established a team record in 1982 by starting the year with eight straight wins. We finished third again, with an improved record of 87-7, six games behind the Western Division Champion California Angels. But more significantly, we put together back to back winning seasons for the first time since 1966-67.

Of course, 1983 was the big year. The White Sox added Seattle fastballer Floyd Bannister to the pitching staff. Bannister, who led the American League with 209 strikeouts in 1982, joined LaMarr Hoyt, Richard Dotson, and Britt Burns to give the White Sox the best starting rotation in the League.

It was a strange year to say the least. We started slowly, not even reaching the .500 mark until late June. From then on, we were near unbeatable. During the second half of the season, in fact, Hoyt, Dotson, and Bannister went something like 42 - 5 between the three of them. Pundits said we looked 'ugly' winning, and 'Winning Ugly' became the 1983 team logo. We thoroughly pulled away from everyone, and just kept rolling. At season's end, we won the American League West by a record 20 games over the second-place Kansas City Royals. We were the only American League West team that year to sport a better than .500 record. Unfortunately, things did not go as well in the American League Championship Series, as the Baltimore Orioles beat us in the best of five series, 3 - 1, to capture the American League flag. Outfielder Ron Kittle with 35 homers and 100 runs batted in was the American League Rookie of the Year, and LaMarr Hoyt led the League in wins for the second straight year with a 24 -10 record. Hoyt was selected the American League Cy Young winner for 1983.

The White Sox also hosted the 1983 All Star Game at Comiskey Park, and what a sheer delight. It was here that the very first All Star Game had been played exactly 50 years earlier. I had always enjoyed playing in the All Star Game and appeared in seven myself. I am also very proud to have batted .300 in my 20 plate appearances as an American League All Star.

What made the game so special was that the greatest collection of baseball talent past and present gathered in Comiskey Park to commemorate the 50th anniversary of the All Star Game, conceived by Arch Ward of *The Chicago Tribune,* for the Chicago World's Fair of 1933. There were 88 former Major League stars participating in the festivities, including 41 Hall of Famers. Also present were 13 of the 15 living participants from the first game.

It was certainly a great day as the stars from the past and the present day stars shared the same locker rooms. It was also a time for awe. The late Mayor Harold Washington chatted attentively with White Sox Hall of Famer Luke Appling. Appling was the Mayor's favorite ballplayer when he was a boy growing up in Chicago.

At the 1982 All Star Game in Montreal, I had the honor of representing all the Cubans who ever played Major League baseball. It was the first All Star Game to be held outside the United States. The theme for this game was "Baseball—An International Game." The same year, I attended, in an official capacity, the dedication of the Negro Baseball Hall of History in Ashland, Kentucky. I was also a special guest that year at the fourth annual Negro Baseball League Players Reunion.

No story of these later years would be complete without a few words about John Wasylik. In 1988, John became my agent and my business manager. But even more rewarding, he has become my very close friend, and like a brother to me.

Our meeting was purely accidental; call it fate or destiny. We met when the two of us were walking our dogs, so it can be said quite truthfully that our dogs brought us together. John and I had lived in the same building for some time, but I had never seen him. When he was 50 years old, he gave up his business because of a severe illness. He spent much of the next three years in the hospital. John was in the importing business and did quite well as an importer, a distributor, and a designer before a tumor on his spine forced him out of work. He was an excellent businessman whose work took him around the world.

When we met, John wasn't a baseball fan, yet he knew me because of my reputation. When I saw him a second time, he was sitting across the street on a bench. I liked the jumpsuit he was wearing, and I asked where I could get one like that. He said he could order one in my size if I liked. After that we would meet more regularly. Our conversations eventually became more personal. I told him I made a lot of personal appearances, but thought that many times I was not being paid enough. These were the personal appearances not connected with my work with the White Sox.

We had a nice rapport, and I could tell intuitively that he was an honest man. So one day I asked him what he was doing with his time. He said that because of illness he had not done much for years. That's when I asked him if he would consider being my agent. He said he would like to talk the matter over with his wife, Mae. It had been Mae's love and support during his recuperative years that gave him the confidence he needed. Mae thought it would be a good idea for both of us, so John became my exclusive agent and business manager. I have not had one second of regret. We never had a written contract; we do our business with a handshake. This is the way it has always been. We have done very well together, and have had a lot of fun along the way. I paid John the ultimate compliment one man can give another, when I asked him to be my best man when Sharon and I were married. He was honored to accept.

On November 29, 1993, I turned 68 years old. Does life begin at 60? Let's just say that the past ten years have been among the happiest of my life. I have a new home now. A loving wife and a wonderful little boy who gives us both so much joy. I work for the classiest baseball organization in the world: The Chicago White Sox. If anyone thinks I am just posturing by saying this, then let him ask any other Chicago White Sox employee and I bet he will get the same answer. I am actively involved in the game of baseball, which I still love with the passion of a younger man. With all the passing years, I remain in close contact with Billy Pierce and Chico Carresquel, two teammates with whom I started my career more than 40 years ago. I have said this before, but there was never a group of ballplayers who fit together as well as the original "Go Go" Chicago White Sox. I am not being pompous or demeaning when I say that the city of Chicago has not seen the likes of us since.

I was shocked and saddened in 1990 to hear that my former wife, Edelia, passed away in San Diego. At the time I was on tour with the White Sox, and my daughter, Marilyn, tried to get in touch with me by calling the ballpark and leaving a message for me to get back to her. But each day I checked in at the hotel, rather than the park, so I didn't get the message. One morning I went to the bank on business. I asked the banker to get in touch with Edelia in San Diego to ask her for her social security number. When he reached her home, a friend answered the phone and told him that Edelia had died about twelve days earlier. When he broke the news to me it came as a total shock. How very sad I felt. I wish I had known earlier, so I could have gone to San Diego to be with my daughter and to pay my final respects.

I am a lucky man. I was able to do the one thing I loved most in the world and to make a good living doing it. How many people can say that? I have lived to see my children grow into solid and productive adults. My son, Orestes Jr., has found new meaning in life through his association with religion; and he lives in Madison, Wisconsin. My daughter, Cecilia, is happily married, and has made me the proud grandfather of Lorenzo, my 11-year-old grandson. Marilyn still lives in San Diego, and I am very proud of her. She is finishing her degree at San Diego State University and will graduate this year with a degree in marketing. Her mother's death was a terrible blow to her. Alfreda,

Edelia's mother, is over 90 years old and a total invalid, and Marilyn still looks after her. She refuses to send her grandmother to a nursing home. That's quite a young lady, if I must say so myself.

Any regrets: sure there have been some. On the whole, however, they have been relatively few. My life has taken me across countries and continents. I have had the honor to play professional baseball in both the American Negro Leagues and in the Major Leagues. I have played alongside and against many of the greatest baseball players to ever play the game. I am so fortunate to live in the United States of America, the greatest land of opportunity in the history of the world. I have paid my dues, and have lived long enough to learn a few lessons in life. I have earned the right to say some things that I think must be said. Yes, I have been a lucky man. A very lucky man indeed!

A friend of ours asked one of Minnie's friends if Minnie would give an autograph to my son David. David has leukemia and it would really be quite a treat, because he loves baseball so much. As the story came back to us, when Minnie was approached he thought about it and said "No!" It really shocked everyone because Minnie gives autographs so freely. Minnie said, "No, I don't want to give you an autographed picture. I want to meet this young man."

When Minnie came to the house, he gave David the autographed picture and sat and talked for two-and-a-half hours. Basically he stressed that while baseball was wonderful, staying in school and respecting your parents was the most important thing. When he talks about Minnie, David gets a huge grin across his face.

Minnie's willingness to come out and talk was so special. Minnie is no longer just a celebrity; we feel like he is a neighbor and a good friend. There's an exceptional quality to Minnie, his willingness to be friendly and to always stop to say hello.

Minnie escorted David onto the field when David was an honorary bat boy. Through the Make a Wish Foundation, we got four tickets for a White Sox game at which David was a batboy.

Carol Forbes

I thought it was really neat that he came to our house. At first I thought I would just get a picture. Then a couple of days later when I heard he was coming over for dinner, I was totally shocked. I thought he might be like most of the players who don't sign autographs. We asked him lots of questions, like what were the most home runs he hit in a season. He told us about all the times he got hit by a pitch. It really lifted up my spirits. He made me feel so much better. He made me feel real good just by being here.

Minnie walked me through the locker room at the White Sox game when I was a batboy and told me whose locker was whose. He showed me Bo Jackson's training pool. He showed me the weightroom and the massage room. I saw the batting cages under the seats where there was a little pitching machine. I walked down a hallway and up to the dugout where everybody was. The whole park was empty except for the people who were hovering around the dugout. My mother made arrangements for us to get there early, and the Stadium just looked beautiful. I was very happy. Minnie Minoso is a hero to me.

David Forbes

20

REFLECTIONS AND
A FEW REGRETS II

After the 1951 season, Paul Richards commented that I homered in my first game, that I homered in my last game of that season, and in between I was even better. I like to think that much of my life has been lived the same way. My readers may rightfully ask what lessons and observations I can now make as a result of my six decades in professional baseball, and my nearly seven decades of life.

Baseball is the greatest sport in the world. There is a tendency today to dismiss it, and laud the merits of other sports. There are those who say that baseball will one day be replaced as our national pastime; that in time it will succumb to the more "exciting" sports, such as football and basketball. Without taking one thing away from football and basketball, let me assure you that baseball will survive. It has gone through some changes and accommodations, but the true essence of the game and its popularity is as much intact today as ever. Just look at the record crowds. When I first came to the United States, there was a saying that "Baseball is as American as motherhood and apple pie." It certainly is. It is imprinted indelibly into the culture of all the Americas.

But the world has changed greatly in recent years. So it should not be surprising that baseball has changed as well.

After all, baseball is an integral part of the society in which we live. Much has been made of the skyrocketing salaries that players command today. I don't fault the players for making as much as they can; they are professionals and should be paid according to the level of their skills and productivity. What bothers me are the multi-year contracts. I think two years is enough on any contract. More than that cannot help but erase the incentive to play up to full capacity.

I have a great problem when these same players do not give 100 percent of themselves to the game and to the fans. For the money they make, they owe the fans 100 percent every time they step on the field. What we have we owe to the fans, and this should not be forgotten.

Players should also respect the proper way to wear a baseball uniform. Like everything else in the game, the uniform should be respected. I have never forgotten the lesson the great Cristobal Torriente taught me when I first played for Marianao in the Cuban Professional League nearly 50 years ago. That was when he told me that a ring in my shoelace was not the proper way to wear my uniform. I feel the same today about players wearing earrings, and caps turned backwards. Some may argue that I am old fashioned and I have to accommodate myself to change. I would answer by simply saying that good taste is never old fashioned.

Two other changes in the game provide fodder for controversy: the designated hitter and artificial turf. I like the designated hitter rule and think it is time for the National League to adopt it too. It allows players the opportunity to stick around the game longer. In my day, many ballplayers retired when they were still fully capable of winging a good bat. At 35 or 36, most players were considered over the hill, and it was time to call it a career. But a lot of older players can still hit a baseball. Look no further than Dave Winfield, whose great career would not have lasted this long if the D.H. rule did not apply. I know if the designated hitter rule applied in the 1960s, I could have had a longer and more productive career. Even today, I believe that I can still face big league pitching, and with enough practice to get my timing intact, I would do a decent job.

I don't like artificial turf. Baseball was meant to be played on the grass. The artificial turf is hard on a player's legs. It can feel like playing on hot concrete. The time is coming, I feel, when more and more ball parks will return to grass infields.

The story that I have presented has taken me over many roads and byways. Like everyone, I was forced to make decisions along the way. Sometimes I made a bad call, and I take full responsibility for my mistakes. Yet in life we learn by our mistakes if we are lucky. We only grow and learn to handle life by living it to the fullest. Only by facing and challenging adversity, can we develop the confidence to fully appreciate the value of what we have.

There is lots of adversity in the story of my life. Fortunately, I was able to keep it from the public eye. A real professional must do that. I faced and experienced the same discrimination and bias as others of my race and culture; these things are never easy. Yet today, I see too many people use discrimination for political ends and purposes, and that is sad. Too many athletes, I am afraid, milk this card far too much. Today everybody has to be so careful of what they say, or they will be charged with discrimination and prejudice, sometimes costing them their jobs and careers. This too, is sad.

There is a time to let go of what was, and deal constructively with what is ahead. Bad and hurtful things have happened to all of us, but what useful good is gained by perpetuating a legacy of discrimination and victimization? What good does this do our children today? Only through hard work, respect for yourself, respect for your profession, and respect for others, can anyone attain real success. This is what I tell young people today. This is what I will tell my son as soon as he is old enough to understand what I am saying.

But politics enter more than just the political area. Politics influence baseball as well. We see this all the time when it comes to a topic dear to my heart, the Hall of Fame. I am not the only former Major Leaguer who feels that Cooperstown has become far too political. I see no reason why there should be a separate Old Timers Committee. All ballplayers should be in the same pool. All should be declared eligible by the same selection committee. All should be judged on their merit and their contribution to the game.

There are many deserving baseball players who have not made it into Cooperstown. A lot of great ballplayers have been slighted. Similarly, there are others whose credentials do not measure up to those who have been selected. It is not my place to say who shouldn't be in the Hall of Fame. I am a professional and I'm not going to take shots. There are guys who never hit .300 or drove in 100 runs who somehow are in there. But someone would have to go a long way to convince me why Nellie Fox and Orlando Cepeda are not in the Hall of Fame today. Nellie just missed in his final year of eligibility with 74.6 percent of the 75 percent needed. Since then he has been ignored by the Old Timers Committee. One look at the record of Orlando Cepeda is enough to make any case stick. Orlando Cepeda belongs in the Hall of Fame, pure and simple!

Having said this, I am going to plead my own case. Through the 1940s, '50s and into the '60s, I played in the two greatest baseball leagues ever, the Negro Leagues and the Major Leagues. Some might argue that I played only 11 seasons as a regular, that this is not enough. So what! There are other players with a lesser number of productive years who are in the Hall. I would just like to lay my record out, and let the readers decide for themselves.

From 1951 through 1961, I hit over .300 eight times. I drove in more than 100 runs four times. I scored more than 100 runs four times, and more than 90 runs nine times. I led the American League in stolen bases three times, and in triples three times. I led in doubles once, in base hits once, and in total bases once. Four times I hit more than 20 home runs. I played in seven All Star Games. I won three Gold Gloves for fielding. Five different times I was among the top five hitters in the American League.

Those who saw me play, the writers, other players, and the fans all say that I was a complete baseball player. They say I could do all things well, and could beat you in many different ways. In the past, I have let others laud my credits. Now I feel that I have earned the right myself. I gave more than 100 percent at all times. I made things happen on the ballfield, both in the Majors and in the Negro Leagues. I hit for average, I drove in runs, I scored runs, I ran the bases well. I was a base stealer. I won three Gold Gloves. I did it all, and I did it well. If ever the powers that be deem me worthy of Hall of Fame honors, I will treasure my selection with the deepest pride and humility. But I have no desire to be selected posthumously. If it is going to happen I want it to happen while I am alive.

I always disciplined myself never to say "I can't!" Instead I think that I always "can." I played baseball like I tried to live my life. If I do well one day, I try better the next. I have always believed that you gain respect by giving respect. Perhaps that is why I have been so fortunate. People who know me respect me. Many times when I appeared tough on the outside, I was bleeding and crying inside. I have given baseball my whole life. This was my dream; and this is my story. In this book I hope I have been able to present a clearer insight and a deeper look into the man behind the story.

The accolades are wonderful, but even more wonderful is the love and affection I have received over the years from the fans, and especially from the kids. I am not too proud to say that I cry at times. I think if you are able to cry, there is always something to give from the heart. I don't cry when I'm scared. I cry from sentiment, and that is when it does the most good.

Today I am still a part of baseball, and how fortunate I am to have remained associated with the Chicago White Sox. This is a first-class organization run by first-class people. I am very proud that my uniform number, Number 9, has been retired by the club. I was only the third player to have his number retired. Luke Appling was first and Nellie Fox was second. Since then Luis Aparicio, Ted Lyons, Billy Pierce, and Harold Baines numbers have been retired too. That makes only seven players in the more than 90-year history of the club. That puts me in a select circle of company, I should say.

Another grand day in my life was when I officially became a United States citizen in 1976. I only regret that I hadn't done it sooner. By then it was obvious that the Communist government of Fidel Castro was so firmly entrenched, that there was little likelihood that freedom would be restored to the Cuban people. At the same time, my name, "Minnie" Minoso, became official. Today I can sign checks and other documents with both names, Orestes or Minnie.

I am continually on the go making public appearances on behalf of the ballclub. As much as possible, I try to involve myself with kids. I have never been too busy to give an autograph, nor do I ever intend to be. Working as a goodwill ambassador can be a full time job. John and I travel across the country as well as overseas. The past year has been a particularly busy one. In July I hosted the 5th Annual Minnie Minoso Golf Classic, benefiting the Cystic Fibrosis Foundation.

Later that month I had the honor of participating in the 4th Annual World Children's Baseball Fair held in San Diego. My commemorative bat was auctioned off in Japanese by Sadaharu Oh, and in English by Jim "Mudcat" Grant. Two years earlier I had the thrill of playing a benefit baseball game in Tokyo for the World Children's Baseball Fair. Finally we went to Laredo, Texas where I was inducted into The International Latin Sports Hall of Fame.

My life is richer today, and more complete, than it has ever been. So many people who have enriched my life along the way have passed from the scene. My parents, Carlos and Cecilia, my sister, Juanita, and my brother, Cirilo. Edelia, my former wife. Nellie Fox and Sherman Lollar from those great "Go Go" teams of the 1950s. Frank Lane and Paul Richards, the two gentlemen who brought me to Chicago to become a Major League star. And of course Mr. Bill Veeck, who dispatched scout Bill Killifer to the Negro League All Star Game in 1948 to look over a couple of young Cuban ballplayers named Jose Santiago and Orestes Minoso. The rest is history.

I look ahead now to the future. It is a continual dream and hope that one day the Cuban people will be free, and Cuba a democratic country. When Fidel Castro took over in 1959, I warned some baseball players of his Communist leanings. I guess I just recognized the dangers early. Yet Castro alone did not make Cuba a Communist country; he could not have done it alone.

The Cuban people supported him. Fortunately most people now realize this was a big mistake. Hopefully, some day soon the more than 30 years of Communist rule will become only a bad dream in the evolutionary process of bringing freedom and democracy to Cuba. I look to that day in anticipation and longing. Until that time, I remain steadfast in my resolve never to return. This I told my father when I left in 1961; I will not set foot in a Communist Cuba.

If the day comes when democracy and freedom arrive, I will lend whatever support is within my means. I will do my part to help rebuild the fabric of the country. However, the United States is now my home, and it has been so for almost 35 years. It is here I will live. And it is here I will finish out my life.

There is one more thing I would like to say, and I say it because it is important, especially today. I speak with and talk to lots of kids. I would urge all fathers to stay close to their children, and listen to what they tell you. Remember it is better to have two glasses of milk with your son or daughter then five glasses of beer with the boys. I have a five-year-old son myself whom I will try to guide in the right direction. Stay in school and value your education, I will tell him. Without a good education, all the cards are stacked against you.

Would I want young Charlie to be a baseball player? Sure, why not! Like his dad, he would have to give 100 percent at all times. But whatever he may choose, I just want him to have a good life, to respect himself, and to respect others, and always remain true to himself.

This is what we Minosos are all about.

EPILOGUE

When the gates of the old Comiskey Park closed for good in 1990, the doors of the oldest playing field in the Major Leagues became a part of our past. Called the "Baseball Palace of the World" when it opened its doors in 1910, Charles Comiskey's personal landmark stood tall at the corner of 35th and Shields.

There are so many wonderful memories attached to the old ballfield, too many to really recount. Many baseball players whose careers were spent, at least in part, in a Chicago White Sox uniform were on hand for the closing festivities. It was to be a special day for me, because on the last day of the season, with the gates closing for good, I would be in uniform once again, to become Major League Baseball's first and only six-decade player.

This was supposed to happen, but it didn't. When we arrived at Comiskey Park early the day before, a young man in the publicity department informed us that there was a fax that had been delivered to the public relations department. He said it concerned me.

John and I stood in front of the gentleman in charge of public relations, who proceeded to read the fax. There was no emotion in his voice. It was just matter of fact, business as usual. He informed us that the Commissioner's Office thought having me play was a travesty for baseball. I wasn't physically able and it would make the whole game appear like a circus.

When this was told to us, I held my composure, but tears were streaking down John's face. I think he knew the effect on me.

I was disillusioned and felt very badly. Soon we heared that NBC was coming to cover the story. Billy Pierce was also invited in on the interview. The lights in the park were turned on to display the organization's support for me. Later I heard that American League President Bobby Brown had also been in my corner.

Jerry Reinsdorf felt badly about this as well. He tried to shoulder some of the blame. He thought perhaps that he fed the story to the media too far in advance, and the whole thing turned into a media affair. He said he should not have made it known, that he should just have put me in and let me play without any fanfare. "Minnie," Jerry said with remorse, "I made a mistake."

I called the Commissioner's Office hoping to get an explanation. I spoke with Steve Greenberg, Deputy Commissioner to Fay Vincent. Greenberg told me that Vincent wasn't in, but that he would certainly give him the message that I called. He took my number and assured me that Fay Vincent would get back to me. That was it. No phone call ever came. Not even a courtesy call from either Vincent or Greenberg.

Did Greenberg ever give the message to Fay Vincent? There's no way of telling for sure. However, someone close to the Commissioner's Office told me that Steve Greenberg was involved in each and every decision that came out of that office.

I had a lot of respect for his father. But Hank Greenberg would never handle things this way. He would tell you everything up front. You knew where you stood. When Hank Greenberg said he would do something, you could be sure it would be done. I have known Steve since he was a little boy. Let's just say he is no chip off the old block. Hank was a straight shooter.

This is where I meant to leave the matter rest when I started writing my story. I made my statement and I would stand by it. However, while we were writing this book, another controversy ensued over the same matter. This time, however, it was not the Commissioner's Office that blocked my way to a sixth Major League decade. Because this is a recent occurrence, and because the episode attracted enough media coverage, I will allow my readers to make their own judgments, and draw their own conclusions. I will say only that it was in no way an executive or management decision on the part of the Chicago White Sox. Yet, because I had no desire to be divisive in any way to the organization, I withdrew from the controversy. But I was disappointed.

I can still swing a bat, and I can still hit big league pitching. Some people just remain determined in their beliefs that I cannot.

Disappointment is not the end of the world. Nor should it be. The game of baseball is bigger than hurt feelings. It is bigger than multi-year contracts and astronomical salaries. It's bigger than superstars, owners, agents and scouts. Baseball is a national institution, grand and glorious. It is our National Pastime. And unless I miss my bet, it will survive us all. It's here to stay. That is why I love it so much!

When I set out to write this book, I did so because I felt it was time to open my heart, and delve beneath and beyond the publicity, the media hype, the image and the perceptions that follow those of us in the public eye. There were many things I have not been able to say until now. But I could never have told my story alone. This was a collaborative effort in every way between myself, John Wasylik, my agent, and my writer Herb Fagen, who took the text of my story, organized it, and put it into words.

If my story gives our readers a chance to think, pause and reflect, if my readers better understand the real Minnie Minoso, the true story of a man and his times—his trials and travails, the dreams and the glory, the love and the heartbreak, and the great game of baseball, what it has meant to so many for so long, we will consider this book a worthy effort.

Orestes "Minnie" Minoso